BELA LUGOSI

AND THE

MONOGRAM 9

By **Gary D. Rhodes** and **Robert Guffey**

Foreword by **Larry Blamire**

Bela Lugosi as *The Ape Man* (1943), perhaps the most immediately recognizable of his Monogram Nine films.

Designed by Michael Kronenberg

Printed in the United States

Published by BearManor Media
P. O. Box 71426
Albany, Georgia 31708
books@benohmart.com

Library of Congress Cataloguing-in-Publication Data
Rhodes, Gary D.
Bela Lugosi and the Monogram Nine / Gary D. Rhodes and Robert Guffey
p.cm.
ISBN 978-1-62933-429-5 (Hardback)
ISBN 978-1-62933-428-8 (Paperback)

1. Lugosi, Bela, 1882-1956.   2. Monogram Pictures.   I. Rhodes, Gary D.
II. Guffey, Robert.   III. Title.
PN2859.H86 L838 2018

For Robert J. Kiss,
the greatest researcher I have ever known
– G.D.R.

and

To my brother,
Buddy,
who loves this Weird Stuff as much as I do
(and who gave me my first copies of *White Zombie* and *The Ape Man*)
– R.G.

Designed by George Chastain in 2018, this fantasy poster publicizes a planned, but unmade Lugosi/Monogram film.

Foreword

By Larry Blamire

When I was a kid my first ambition was to be a ballplayer, and of course the biggest underdogs at that time were the *Boston Red Sox*, the *Chicago Cubs* and the *Monogram Nine*. Especially the latter. They were dupey, scratchy, shoddy-looking and woefully underpaid. Also, they only played late at night, late at night, which I thought was odd.

Most of their batting averages were low, like *Black Dragons,* and some, like *Spooks Run Wild* and *Ghosts on the Loose,* were accused of not even trying, not taking the game seriously. The Monogram Nine did have one star though; *Invisible Ghost,* a (moving) pitcher with an impressive ERA, who had the chops to play for any of the majors, thanks in large part to the managing of Joseph Lewis.

I first became aware of Joseph H. Lewis as a kid watching episodes of the TV western series *The Rifleman,* which seemed endlessly in syndication. His name was tagged on the end of what appeared to be a huge number of episodes. As I grew older, still a fan of the show, I became quite conscious of the considerable craft involved in creating such mood, such suspense, such tight storytelling with so many interesting camera setups of rich black and white cinematography. Later still I realized how fast he had to shoot these things, and on what limited budget. Eventually—as someone driven to inhale movies like air—I discovered his acclaimed work on *Gun Crazy* and *The Big Combo,* and discovered just how respected Lewis was, not just as a director, but as an artist.

But not always. Like Anthony Mann, William Castle and many others, he started out on movies where you figure the director just wanted to get the damned thing done.

When I began making films, I quickly, and of necessity, learned that that is one's primary goal: *getting the damned thing done.* This necessity has the unfortunate effect of shoveling a lot of those good intentions to the back. Notions of craft, nuance, art—certainly even the vaguest idea of creating something seen by future generations—can become the losers. Don't get me wrong. It isn't that one doesn't try. There is still that golden apple, that mad desire to make something wonderful. But time is money and a low budget often means you have to get it done now, rather than well.

It doesn't surprise me that Mr. Lewis did not recall details fifty years later about a shoot of several days. Directors then had no concept of a poverty row gig having any life beyond some brief shelf time at the bottom of a theatrical twin bill.

But it's hard to keep a good man down. Despite just about everything in the universe to the contrary, certain things have a way of showing through. Certain innate abilities, instincts, even just good sound storytelling, as well as the happy accidents that occur more than we probably know. The creation of art can have a fleeting, wraithlike delicacy or all the subtlety of a lightning strike.

Joseph Lewis could not help being artistic. It was simply there, beginning to emerge. And so, early flashes of brilliance appear in something like *Invisible Ghost.* Like many creators, it's hard to imagine Lewis saying, *"Now I shall make art."* But sometimes when one simply sets out to craft well, that's exactly what happens, even under pressure.

Finding these diamonds in the rough is particularly satisfying to me, as it appeals to my lifelong love of underdogs (like the Red Sox, at one time). It has me championing such cinematic obscurities as Frank Wisbar's atmosphere-oozing *Strangler of the Swamp,* Mark Robson's 1949 western *Roughshod,* Tommy Atkins's speedy 1934 train thriller *The Silver Streak,* Richard Fleischer's 1949 pulp noir *Follow Me Quietly,* or (speaking of Monogram) Sidney Toler's final Chan film from 1946, *The Trap* (yes, I am a fan). When it comes to bargain basement fare, I will happily look beyond lack of budget, rough edges, indifferent acting, technical blunders, to embrace those gleaming tendrils that reach out and touch me. Like much art, it defies logic, but who ever said art needed to be logical?

Which brings us to dream logic.

As a lifelong surrealist and sometime absurdist with the invisible necktie to prove it, I am ecstatic to report that no small amount of attention is devoted by Gary and Robert to the surrealist aspects of the Monogram Nine. The first stage plays I wrote contained, to varying degrees, a stream of consciousness approach. I didn't know what I was doing of course, and that was important. Not that I *knew* it was important, because that lack of knowledge was *also* important. I'll stop here, for sanity's sake, but this is just the kind of discussion the authors have with these films. They explore the surreal aspects of these movies driven by the sheer need to *get things done and get them done fast.* With no time to really think about stuff, the filmmakers were tapping into something they may not have realized. Don't tell me Charles Griffith didn't *go with the flow* when he wrote one of my favorite films *Attack of the Crab Monsters*, opening up his mind to a carefree come-what-will frenzy that is the only possible way to explain *"Harken to all things metal, for I may be in them."*

I'll say no more on surrealism, but please don't think this is lunacy. Well, it is. But it's *good, thoughtful, fascinating* lunacy. And if this is insane, I'll take two please.

Above all, the essays contained herein are fashioned with loving care. Now I certainly don't need anyone to tell me *why* I enjoy certain movies. But man, I love when someone presents all kinds of new angles and approaches and elements I hadn't thought of, and next thing I know I'm seeing a film with new eyes, even though I've seen it numerous times.

Then we have the lynchpin of these nine rather disparate movies, Bela Lugosi. His career arc with relation to this stint at Monogram is well explored. And, happily, two loving chapters are spent on *Invisible Ghost*, which arguably gives Lugosi his only real "sympathetic monster" outside of the far less complex *Frankenstein Meets the Wolfman* (interesting to note another "sympathetic monster" in a Joseph Lewis film a few years later: Steven Geray's lead in the exceptional *So Dark the Night).*

So, it's time to trot the Monogram Nine out onto the field. Why shouldn't these nine "Rodney Dangerfields" finally get the comprehensive and analytic respect they deserve? Not to hail them as some kind of masterpieces, which they are not, but to give a fair and balanced assessment that fully takes into account their limitations, and embraces them. There is an abundance of provocative food-for-thought here.

Bela Lugosi's poor step-children are finally stepping out of the academic shadows.

Larry Blamire is the writer-director of such films as The Lost Skeleton of Cadavra *(2001),* Trail of the Screaming Forehead *(2007),* The Lost Skeleton Returns Again *(2009), and* Dark and Stormy Night *(2009).*

Portrait still of Bela Lugosi in
Return of the Ape Man (1944).
(Photo courtesy of Bill Chase)

Introduction

By Gary D. Rhodes and Robert Guffey

Since its beginnings, American cinema has felt the gravity of the film series. From Charlie Chaplin to Charlie Chan, from Happy Hooligan to James Bond, the film series has benefitted producers economically and at times critically. Much like sequels and remakes, film series return given characters and/or actors to the screen, narratively and thematically cannibalizing their forebears, all in hopes of selling movie tickets.

In June 1941, Sam Katzman's Banner Picture Corporation heralded its nascent "Bela Lugosi Series," one of two the company promoted, the other being the "East Side Kids."[1] At that point, only one of its Lugosi movies had appeared at theatres, though others were in the planning stage, including an unproduced project called *The Kiss of Death*.[2] Over the three years that followed, Katzman and his partner Jack Dietz considered various other projects for Lugosi, perhaps none more fascinating than Poe's *The Gold-Bug*.[3]

In the end, Banner completed nine films with Lugosi, all released by the Monogram Pictures Corporation in the years between 1941 and 1944: *Invisible Ghost* (1941), *Spooks Run Wild* (1941), *Black Dragons* (1942), *The Corpse Vanishes* (1942), *Bowery at Midnight* (1942), *The Ape Man* (1943), *Ghosts on the Loose* (1943), *Voodoo Man* (1944), and *Return of the Ape Man* (1944).

What Katzman called his "Bela Lugosi Series" became known in the 1990s as the "Monogram Nine," a phrase that has also attempted to name the notional grouping, and perhaps more accurately so, given that Lugosi portrayed different characters in each of the movies. Some of the nine bear similarities; others do not. The category identification

The premiere of *Invisible Ghost* in Chicago in 1941. From the time of their release, many critics have decried the Monogram Nine. We challenge that view. *(Photo courtesy John Antosiewicz)*

Bowery at Midnight (1942, pictured here) and the other entries in the Monogram Nine are not realistic; they are bizarre and strange, populated by crazy, larger-than-life characters who live in wacky, alternative worlds. *(Photo courtesy John Antosiewicz)*

is thus as apt as it is problematic.

Response to these films varied during World War II, but it's fair to say most critics were underwhelmed. In 1941, for example, *Daily Variety* wrote:

> Boogie man Bela Lugosi ... has been seen to much better advantage than in The [sic] *Invisible Ghost*. Picture tries hard to stir sufficient horror to rate the 'chiller' brand but succeeds only slightly. ... Considerable confusion results from incomplete development of the plot, partly due to writing and partly to production limitations.[4]

Those writing about the Monogram Nine during the rest of the twentieth century were often much harsher. William K. Everson described the films as "abortions."[5] Arthur Lennig deemed them "barely adequate."[6] Even Gregory William Mank has called them "tasteless," a "professional embarrassment, another sad debasement" for Lugosi.[7] As has so often been the case in horror film criticism, what one person writes becomes repeated over and over again.

That said, renewed attention to the Monogram Nine in the 1990s tended to herald the group, to the extent Mank has complained that

Given its importance in the notional grouping, we devote two chapters to *Invisible Ghost* **(1941).** *(Photo courtesy of Bill Chase)*

they have received "overpraise." Others disagree sharply. Consider Adam Mudman Bezecny, who wrote in 2017, "I had a chance to binge Lugosi and Katzman's 'Monogram Nine' and got hooked at once – they lit a fire inside me."[8]

Why the evolution? Home video formats of various kinds have made seven of the Monogram Nine readily available, with DVDs of them selling often for as little as one dollar. But their accessibility in recent decades is not in and of itself particularly revealing. After all, reissues of these films played theatres after World War II, and they also appeared regularly in late-night television screenings throughout the fifties. Most of these movies have been relatively easy to see, including long before any serious critical reevaluation began.

Perhaps it is instead distance, not from the films, but from the era in which they were made, that has made the difference. To many viewers at the time and during the decades that followed, the Monogram Nine

On the set of *The Ape Man*, Bela Lugosi (center) is flanked by producer Jack Dietz (left) and gorilla-suited Emil Van Horn (right). *(Photo courtesy John Antosiewicz)*

were overacted and underproduced, illogical and incoherent. But their increasing age has recast such condemnations into what we perceive as appropriate praise: in the 21st century, they seem so different not only from modern cinema, but also from the major studio fare of Classical Hollywood, enough so as to make the aforementioned deficits into advantages. The entries in the Monogram Nine are not realistic; they are bizarre and strange, populated by crazy, larger-than-life characters who live in wacky, alternative worlds. In nine films, the improbable chases the impossible. And their running times truly run, dashing ever more quickly towards postmodern finish lines.

Herein we participate in the effort to recover the Monogram Nine, offering not production histories, which have been undertaken in the past, most notably in Tom Weaver's book *Poverty Row Horrors!*, but instead analysis founded on historical contexts.[9] Given its importance as the first entry in the series and the notoriety of the auteur who directed it (Joseph H. Lewis), we devote two chapters to *Invisible Ghost*. From there, we present single chapters to the remaining eight films, attempting to understand them anew, particularly in light of their greater, and we believe, more appropriate critical acceptance. To be sure, some of these films are far superior to others (an issue we explore), but the entire group is worthy of (re-) investigation.

The Monogram Nine represent cinematic dissonance, but not cinematic detritus. "The folks at Monogram never forget you," Tom Weaver once wrote.[10] We offer the same sentiment in return.

Gary D. Rhodes
Belfast, Northern Ireland

Robert Guffey
Long Beach, California

(Endnotes)

1   Advertisement, *Daily Variety*, June 10, 1941, 8.
2   Advertisement, *Daily Variety*, April 4, 1941, 7.
3   "Bela Lugosi Goes Poe," *Daily Variety*, February 14, 1944.
4   "*The* [sic] *Invisible Ghost*," *Daily Variety*, April 11, 1941, 3.
5   William K. Everson, "The Last Days of Bela Lugosi," *Castle of Frankenstein* 8 (1966), 24.
6   Arthur Lennig, *The Immortal Count: The Life and Films of Bela Lugosi* (Lexington, Kentucky: University of Kentucky, 2003).
7   Gregory William Mank, *Bela Lugosi and Boris Karloff: The Expanded Story of a Haunting Collaboration* (Jefferson, North Carolina: McFarland and Company, 2009), 433.
8   Adam Mudman Bezecny, "The Monogram Monograph: Preface," February 15, 2007. Available at: http://mudmansalist.blogspot.co.uk/2017/02/the-monogram-monograph-preface.html.
9   Tom Weaver, *Poverty Row Horrors! Monogram, PRC, and Republic Horror Films of the Forties* (Jefferson, North Carolina: McFarland and Company, 1993).
10 Weaver, 104.

Bela Lugosi (left) became the first horror movie star of the sound era. Boris Karloff (right) became the second. Here they are pictured in 1939 with Jesse L. Lasky, promoting his CBS radio show *Gateway to Hollywood*.

Chapter 1

Invisible Ghost and the "House Where Anything Can Happen"

by Gary D. Rhodes

Writing in the May 1, 1941 issue of the *Hollywood Spectator*, a film critic noted his displeasure at attending the premiere of Orson Welles' *Citizen Kane* (1941). "After the first half hour, I began to wonder what the story was all about," he complained. "From there on, I was more bored than entertained." In years to come, of course, his view proved to be in the minority. The critic also confessed that he had not caught the name "Rosebud" on the burning sled at the end of the film; his wife had to point it out to him on the drive home.[1] Not only had he been incorrect in his assessment, but he had also been careless in his viewing.

Elsewhere in the very same issue of the *Spectator*, another critic spoke with even greater disdain about Joseph H. Lewis' *Invisible Ghost* (1941). "[Lugosi] is a finished actor," he wrote, "but he will be finished for good if he is obliged to continue frightening little children with such inconsequential roles as the demented murderer in *The [sic] Invisible Ghost* ... It is only mildly interesting and can please only those who are shrieker fans–for even whodunit fans will not like it because we all know from the start whodunit."[2] As with *Kane*, once again we can see the carelessness of a *Spectator* critic: *Invisible Ghost* has no definitive article in its onscreen title.

Invisible Ghost **gave Lugosi one of his most complex horror movie characters.** *(Photo courtesy of Bill Chase)*

The names Orson Welles and Joseph H. Lewis appeared under the same cover again over twenty-five years later in Andrew Sarris' book *The American Cinema: Directors and Directions, 1929-1968*. Sarris considered Welles to be a "pantheon director," and believed *Citizen Kane* had "influenced the cinema more profoundly than any American film since *Birth of a Nation*."[3] While he spoke well of such movies as *The Lady from Shanghai* (1948) and *Touch of Evil* (1958), Sarris believed *Kane* was Welles' major contribution to the cinema.

By contrast, Sarris included Joseph H. Lewis in his section "Expressive Esoterica," beginning his discussion by quoting a previous critic who saw any attempt to "awaken the world to the merits of Joseph H. Lewis" as problematic due to the perceived limitations of his early works. "Admittedly, in this direction lies madness," the critic concluded.[4] Sarris cited Lewis' *My Name Is Julia Ross* (1945) as the beginning of a consistent and personal style, and suggested *Gun Crazy* (1950) was Lewis' "one enduring masterpiece."[5] Here we get a different argument than Sarris offers for Welles: rather than starting with a masterpiece and forever after creating inferior work, Lewis honed his abilities on over twenty apparently unimportant films before directing *Julia Ross*. While he did not analyze Lewis' early work, Sarris did offer a brief rejoinder to the aforementioned critic: "madness is always preferable to smugness."[6]

Writing about Lewis a few years later, Myron Meisel specifically mentioned *Invisible Ghost*, giving him credit for exemplifying "more fluidity of style than is customary" in a Monogram movie. Nonetheless, Meisel seemed careful to avoid smugness or madness, noting:

> It is almost as easy to overrate his early, ludicrously ephemeral work as it is to underrate it. *The [sic] Invisible Ghost* (1941), *The Mad Doctor of Market Street* (1942), and *The Boss of Hangtown Mesa* (1942) are only arguably related to art, yet, given the intractable awfulness of the goings-on, Lewis manipulates his camera and scissors with startling integrity.[7]

Meisel's essay provides more depth than Sarris, but still offers only vague generalities about Lewis' early work. And he repeats the *Hollywood Spectator*'s mistake of appending a definitive article to the title of *Invisible Ghost*.

When I interviewed Lewis aboard his yacht in Marina del Rey in 1996, he spoke in vague terms about *Invisible Ghost*. Though a wonderful *bon vivant*, Lewis seemed to have even less interest in the film than either Sarris or Meisel. He admitted that he might have learned something from its star Bela Lugosi, but could not identify what it might have been. Lewis then emphasized the fact that many of his B-movies were made in *days*, rather than weeks; his comment seemed both an excuse for his limited memory of *Invisible Ghost*'s production, as well as perhaps its individual merits as he saw them.

But *Invisible Ghost* deserves more individual attention than Sarris, Meisel, or Lewis cared to give it. Certainly it gained some renewed appeal based upon the fact that the cult of its star Bela Lugosi grew much larger and more vocal during the 1990s. However, such attention might force us yet again to consider that *Invisible Ghost* bears no definitive article in its title. More than just reflecting carelessness on the part of previous authors, that fact should remind us that there might be many *Invisible Ghosts*, ranging from the one viewed so dismissively by those writing on Lewis in the past to the one viewed by Lugosi fans in the 1990s, who very much rechristened it as a Lugosi film.

I recommend another approach to the film, reclaiming it as a Joseph H. Lewis film, but one that desperately needs to be considered on its own merits, something that has not occurred in the past. In the same way that Welles inherited the "great man" biopic and reinvented that genre in *Citizen Kane* (1941), Lewis attempted a similar kind of reinvention with *Invisible Ghost*. He begins with the premise that he must grapple with and overcome Bela Lugosi's image and the expectations of a typical Lugosi horror film. To consolidate his control over the film, Lewis then exerts authorial intent by use of a roving camera synthesized with a complex handling of editing and sound. Those elements result in a horror film that is in many respects ahead of its time, and one that deserves the respect it has not previously received.

Directing Bela Lugosi

By the time he starred in *Invisible Ghost*, Bela Lugosi had been working professionally as an actor in four different countries over the span of four decades. He had appeared in over seventy films since 1917 and had collaborated with such important directors as Michael Curtiz, F.W. Murnau, Victor Fleming, Tod Browning, Raoul Walsh, Robert Florey, William Dieterle, and Edgar G. Ulmer. Ten years had passed between his Hollywood breakthrough in Universal's *Dracula* (1931) and the production of *Invisible Ghost*. In that span of time, Lugosi had lived the life of an American film star.

Immediately after *Dracula*, he was arguably one the hottest properties in Hollywood, but a combination of problems rapidly changed his fortunes. He mishandled his finances, going bankrupt in 1932. In an apparent effort to avoid typecasting, he did not star in *Frankenstein* (1931), which created another horror film star in Boris Karloff. Lugosi soon began appearing in low-budget fare such as Monogram's *Mysterious Mr. Wong* (1935), which hardly bolstered his image as a major actor. Then Hollywood stopped producing horror films in late 1936, due in large measure to a British ban on horror films.[8] Once again, Lugosi faced financial doom, tied to a genre that disappeared from the cinematic landscape until Universal made *Son of Frankenstein* in 1939, a move that followed the successful reissue of *Dracula* and *Frankenstein* in 1938. The new film meant the comeback of horror, and of Bela Lugosi.

However, Lugosi – perhaps acting once again out of necessity – repeated his earlier career move of intermingling low-budget films at lesser studios with his work at the majors; it was a problem amplified by ratio, as his work on "Poverty Row" increasingly outnumbered his work at major studios. This resulted in a slow, inexorable decline in the overall quality of his films from the dawn of the forties to his infamous work with Edward D. Wood, Jr. on *Glen or Glenda* (1953) and *Bride of the Monster* (1955). Indeed, the world of low-budget filmmaking cast a shadow over Lugosi even after his death in 1956 with the posthumous release of Wood's *Plan 9 From Outer Space* (1958), a movie that featured brief shots of Lugosi, as well as of a stand-in wearing a cape.[9]

Aside from the trio of Ed Wood films, Lugosi's most famous and beloved grouping of low-budget movies would be those that have affectionately become known as the "Monogram Nine," a reference to that same number of films he made during the early 1940s for the Monogram Pictures Corporation, one of the more prominent and venerable production companies that constituted Hollywood's Poverty Row.[10] In some respects, the grouping is logical: Lugosi made all nine of the films at the same company during a four-year period, and – at least to a degree – they featured repetition of cast and crew and even library music.[11] Most notably, of course, they all starred Lugosi, with the term "Monogram Nine" emphasizing stardom (and company affiliation) over, for example, directorial control as a determinant factor in how they should be viewed or discussed.

Under scrutiny, however, the notional grouping suffers; the foundation of the category cracks from the fissures of difference. One of the nine films, *Bowery at Midnight* (1942), is more of a crime thriller than a horror movie, whereas *Voodoo Man* (1944) is the only one of the group in which the supernatural is an explicit factor.[12] Two others – *Spooks Run Wild* (1941) and *Ghosts on the Loose* (1943) – are comedies featuring the East Side Kids, neither of which involves supernatural content despite their titles. Four more – *Black Dragons* (1942), *The Corpse Vanishes* (1942), *The Ape Man* (1943), and *Return of the Ape Man* (1944) – are essentially mad scientist films, though *Black Dragons* places more emphasis on a Japanese spy organization in the US than it does on the (non-"mad") plastic surgery used to make the spies appear less Asian. And overall, these three-to-four mad scientist films bear greater similarity to some of Lugosi's non-Monogram movies – particularly *The Devil Bat* (1940), made at PRC and featuring both a notable actor (Dave O'Brien) and canned library music that would return in his Monogram films – than they do to other entries in the "Nine."

That includes *Invisible Ghost* (1941). More than any other entry in the "Monogram Nine," it is a film that needs to be wrested from that category. It was the first of the nine films, so of course it was not affected in any way by its successors. As will be shown, it does not bear narrative similarities to any other Lugosi film, let alone others in the "Nine"; the same could be said of the character that Lugosi portrays. And it was the only film in the "Monogram Nine" – or indeed, the whole of Lugosi's filmography – to be directed by Joseph H. Lewis.

Much as we might now attempt to remove *Invisible Ghost* from the Monogram Nine (and by extension, from Lugosi's filmography, at least to the extent the film might be seen as a "Joseph H. Lewis film" rather than, or certainly, in addition to, being seen as a "Bela Lugosi film"), Joseph H. Lewis had to contend with the same dilemma in directing the film. How does a young director – a director hoping to create a unique film in order to further his career, but one that would also remain safely within the parameters of what a B-movie needed to be so that he could continue to find work – contend with the weight and breadth of Lugosi's experience as an actor, as well as the sheer power of his image, which was so consolidated by 1941?

The answer to that question came in part thanks to *Invisible Ghost's* script, written by Al and Helen Martin, and the character Lugosi would portray, "Mr. Charles Kessler." A few previous filmmakers had grappled with Lugosi's image by casting him in roles that would defy audience expectations, at least to a degree. Edgar G. Ulmer's *The Black Cat* (1934) featured Lugosi as Dr. Vitus Werdegast, a man who takes revenge on Boris Karloff's villainous Dr. Hjalmar Poelzig by literally skinning him alive, but who is at the same time the film's nominal hero. More surprising still was Sol Lesser's tactic of casting Lugosi as Chandu the Magician in the twelve-part serial *The Return of Chandu* (1934). In it, Lugosi was a hero without the baggage carried by Vitus Werdegast. Lesser's decision was even more fascinating when considering that Lugosi earlier had starred as the villain Roxor in the feature film *Chandu the Magician* (1932).

But *Invisible Ghost* gave Lugosi a more complex character than either *The Black Cat* or *Return of Chandu*. Charles Kessler would not be a hero, which was a rather simple inversion of Lugosi's villainous persona. Plagued by his wife's infidelity as well as her disappearance from his life, Kessler is nearly driven to tears at her memory. He has also developed the annual habit of celebrating their wedding anniversary with a dinner for two, pretending that she is with him even while her seat is empty. His problems are amplified by the occasional appearance of his wife (Betty Compson) at the window of his home, an event that sends him into a trance. Kessler is neither a hero nor a villain, but a cuckolded

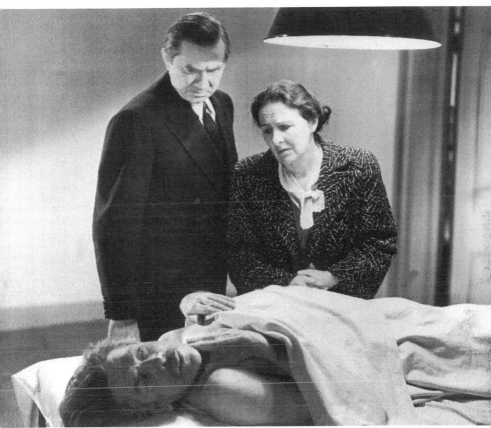

***Invisible Ghost* features a sophisticated use of dark humor.** *(Photo courtesy of Bill Chase)*

husband who unknowingly, unwittingly becomes a murderer. He is a victim of tragic proportions.

But at times, Kessler becomes something more complicated still. In two scenes, Lewis has Lugosi subtly parody his association with the horror genre. After his visit to the morgue and discovery that Jules the gardener (Ernie Adams) is not actually dead, Kessler informs his daughter, "It was ghastly." Later, after Kessler discovers his wife's portrait has been ripped, he judges it to be "the work of a madman." Both moments represent rich dark humor, informed not only by the audience awareness that Kessler is actually the murderer (something which Kessler does not yet know), but also the fact that the horror film star Bela Lugosi is reciting such unlikely dialogue.

To be sure, parodies of horrifying movies and actors associated with them had a history in America that dated to the 1920s. *The Hollywood*

Revue of 1929 (1929) featured the comical song *Lon Chaney's Gonna Get You If You Don't Watch Out,* for example, and the cartoon *King Klunk* (1933) offered a comic takeoff on *King Kong* (1933). Bela Lugosi had certainly participated in such parodies, time and again. In the short subject *Intimate Interviews* (1932), he played a rather staged version of himself, "scaring" interviewer Dorothy West at the end of their brief encounter. The following year, he portrayed a wax figure of "Bela Lugosi as Dracula" come-to-life in a 1933 *Hollywood on Parade* short subject in which he bites an actress portraying Betty Boop; the following year, he played a comical game of chess with Boris Karloff in a 1934 short subject that parodied a scene from *The Black Cat.* Those were in addition to his acting in such feature-length horror comedies as *The Gorilla* (1939) and *You'll Find Out* (1940).

However, Lewis achieved something different in *Invisible Ghost,* different even than what the Broadway play (1941) and film version of *Arsenic and Old Lace* (1944) would do with Boris Karloff's image. This is true specifically because neither the overall film *Invisible Ghost* nor the overall character of Charles Kessler is a parody of either the horror movie or of Bela Lugosi. Rather, Lewis inserts two brief moments that offer a sophisticated intermingling of postmodernist humor within a film that otherwise proceeds as an insular and generally serious plotline. Such an approach was distinctive, as it would remain until such later films as Peter Bogdanovich's *Targets* (1968), Douglas Hickox's *Theatre of Blood* (1973), and – by substituting genre conventions for star identification – Wes Craven's *Scream* (1996).

Controlling the Space

Connected to the question of how to contend with Bela Lugosi was the issue of aesthetic design. For Lewis, that meant determining what kind of visual landscape he could create within the confines of his low budget and – as he underscored in my interview with him – his limited production schedule. His decision became an effort to impose control over the storyline, the other actors, and the set just as he had attempted to do with Lugosi. This meant an emphasis on carefully planned scenes that are shot in such a way as to maximize their effect in editing, as well as an emphasis on moving camera that not only allows Lewis to control the space, but to comment thematically upon characters who exist within it.

To be sure, *Invisible Ghost* includes some limitations in its visual design of the sort we might expect in a B-movie of the 1940s. For example, full-screen newspaper headlines quickly and cheaply convey important narrative information, ranging from the fact that Ralph Dickson (John McGuire) will be put on trial for the murder of Cecile Mannix (Terry Walker) to the announcements of Dickson's conviction and pending execution. The courtroom itself is tiny, with the judge surrounded by darkness, thus preventing the need for a fully dressed set. And when Kessler and his daughter Virginia (Polly Ann Young) visit the governor to plea for a stay of execution, we do not see the governor's face, thus eliminating the need for anything more than an extra's shoulders.

That is all in addition to an expected use of post-production effects. To expedite the movement of the story, for example, wipe transitions separate the courtroom testimony of Mr. Kessler, Ralph's one-time landlady (actress unknown), Jules (Ernie Adams), and Evans (Clarence Muse), allowing Lewis to show them all in a rapid succession of closeups and medium shots. Similarly, wipes also help expedite the movement of characters; the gardener Jules steals food in the kitchen for Mrs. Kessler (Betty Compson), then a wipe transports him outside of the Kessler home. In this instance, the wipe not only condenses narrative time, but it also conceals what otherwise would have been an awkward edit.

Despite the limitations he faced, however, Lewis succeeds in providing an array of more sophisticated images that would not generally be associated with B-movies of the period. For example, on a trio of occasions, Kessler is pictured in his home with flames of a fireplace crackling in the foreground, a shot often seen in A-budget Hollywood films of the period, but illustrating a kind of added attention that would not mark the average Monogram film. Consider also the shot in which the camera focuses on a Holy Bible as Kessler recites Psalm 23: 6. The camera then tilts up to Virginia, then moves back to show an over-the-shoulder of Kessler just before the phone rings. "Yes? [pause] I see," Kessler says before hanging up the phone and telling Virginia, "It's all over." Here Lewis transforms the budgetary need to limit camera set-ups into a well-timed and carefully executed single shot that contains the whole of the Kesslers' reaction to Ralph's execution.

More strikingly, when suspicion for the murders falls upon Evans, Lewis illustrates his skill at shooting with a specific eye towards editing, which by extension allows him to maintain some control over the post-production process. We see a closeup of Evans, then the camera tilts upward to show a closeup of Mr. Kessler. The film cuts to a closeup of Paul Dickson (John McGuire), which then tilts down to a closeup of the psychiatrist (Lloyd Ingraham). The result offers an uncomfortable series of closeups, one after the

Shot A	Shot B
Shot C	Shot D
Shot E	Shot F

other, edited with straight cuts, resulting in a sequence that is somewhat outside of the norms of the classical Hollywood style. In terms of its aesthetic design and thematic purpose, it reminds one very much of a similar sequence in Huston's *The Maltese Falcon* (1941), in which Wilmer (Elisha Cook, Jr.) regains consciousness to see that the others in the room have decided he will be the fall guy for the film's murders. But here Lewis has bested Huston, at least in terms of chronology, as *Invisible Ghost* was released nearly six months before *The Maltese Falcon*.

Nowhere does Lewis show his ability to shoot a scene with plans towards editing and pacing (and, in this case, the use of post-production sound) more successfully than when Kessler murders Cecile. In a trancelike state, he

Shot G

Shot H

Shot I

Shot J

Shot K

approaches and enters her bedroom door in Shot A, the camera panning from screen left to right as he opens it. We hear dance music, though do not yet understand its origin or purpose. As he enters the room in the same shot, Cecile – who is lying in bed under a blanket – speaks his name with surprise. After he shuts the door, Shot B shows Kessler approaching Cecile's bed; he immediately takes off his robe. The setup, shot with the camera adjacent to her bed, has every indication of a sexual crime in the making.

Then a match-on-action cut to Shot C shows Kessler holding his robe with both hands. Lugosi's eyes stare directly into the camera lens, violating the classical Hollywood taboo against doing so. Given the rarity of such an image, we are immediately led to remember a similar shot in *Dracula* (1931), in which Lugosi stares directly into the camera lens at no one in particular, and – since Lewis has placed his camera in Cecile's approximate position – we might even more clearly consider *White*

Zombie (1932), which includes shots of Lugosi staring into the camera lens with his gaze connected to victims like Beaumont (Robert Frazer). But here Lewis will go beyond both films, which had used the effect to suggest the characters' hypnotic power over others. *Invisible Ghost*, by contrast, has him leering lustily at the audience, which has been forced into Cecile's point of view. Rather than hypnosis or mesmerism, Kessler appears to have very physical plans.

Shot D is a medium shot of a frightened Cecile grasping at her blanket, while Shot E offers a closeup of a radio. Only now do we understand that the dance music we have heard since Shot A is music that the characters hear. Then Shot F, a medium closeup, returns us to Lugosi, staring into the camera with a devilish grin on his face. More than any prior shot, his hands are holding the robe in such a way as to suggest a pending strangulation. After he walks closer to the camera, Lewis cuts to Shot G, which again shows Cecile cowering in her bed. Shot H then repeats Shot E, but only for the space of one second, as the increasing tempo of editing underscores Kessler's increasing proximity to Cecile and her increasing fear. Shot I then shows Kessler's staring face in a closeup, and Shot J shows Cecile one last time; each shot is approximately one second long. Then Shot K returns us to Kessler's staring face in what has become an extreme closeup, which itself recalls extreme closeups of Lugosi in *White Zombie*. He now raises his robe in such a way that it causes the screen to go black. We hear Cecile scream, then Kessler lowers the robe slightly to reveal only part of his face. A quiet groan from Cecile suggests she is still alive, causing Kessler to raise the robe once more, covering the camera (and Cecile's) view of Kessler and ending the scene (and Cecile's life). The blackness of the robe has removed the need for a optically-printed fade-to-black.

While it's important to focus on significant scenes or images in *Invisible Ghost*, we should also recognize that the film is more than just a poverty row horror film punctuated by occasional moments of visual sophistication and power. Specifically, we should consider Lewis' ongoing reliance on moving camera throughout the film. Here he controls the space by synthesizing it, much as Kubrick will later do with the Overlook Hotel in *The Shining* (1980). At times this heightens the fact that we the viewers are, at least for the bulk of the film, trapped inside the Kessler home along with the characters. The camera moves behind the Kessler dinner table early in the film; it moves when Cecile enters the kitchen to speak to Evans, and it tracks behind Kessler when Virginia tells him she loves Ralph. The camera follows Evans as he approaches Cecile's bedroom, it tracks behind Police Lieutenant Williams (George Pembroke) as he investigates Cecile's murder, and it moves through a candelabra to follow Virginia as she goes to bed. Indeed, the camera follows all of the key characters in the film, imbuing it with the occasional look of a higher budget film, while also simultaneously and ironically exploring the movements of persons who cannot escape the Kessler home.

In larger terms, the moving camera also reinforces the fact that Lewis alone controls the space. It is he that allows or does not allow visual access, as his cinematography can choose to reveal or conceal, depending on the scene. For example, at times his camera, by way of passing in front of the set, appears to penetrate through walls as it moves from room to room without need of a door or other passageway. By contrast, while Lewis uses moving camera to show Evans approach Cecile's bedroom the morning after her murder, he does not allow the camera to move inside her room. We are only allowed to see her dead body from the hallway, pictured at a distance as framed through her bedroom door.

His moving camera can also proceed methodically. After stylishly showing and simultaneously not showing Jules' apparent murder by letting it play out as shadows on the wall, Lewis forces us to observe Jules' corpse (or a body we presume to be dead, as he later reawakens in the morgue) with a close and lingering scrutiny, building up the event with a very slow camera move downward from a table to the floor. Lewis then reveals Jules' body in a carefully planned and executed move, rather than a cut or even a tripod-bound tilt. Here again we see Lewis working against a tight schedule for a shot that was unnecessary to complete the project, but wholly necessary to his planned regimen of moving camera.

Lewis's moving camera also reveals important narrative and thematic information as well, as when it accentuates the curious link between Mr. Kessler and Mrs. Kessler. Her reappearances provoke his murderous trances, and at the climax of the film, Kessler's awareness of that fact seems to cause Mrs. Kessler's death. The two are psychically linked in a manner that is reminiscent of Dracula and Mina in Tod Browning's *Dracula* (1931), Svengali and Trilby in Archie L. Mayo's *Svengali* (1931) and Legendre and Madeline in *White Zombie*. Visually we understand the Kesslers' bond from the very first shot in *Invisible Ghost* when the camera shows a painting of Mrs. Kessler in the entrance hallway of their home before moving backwards and to screen right to reveal Mr. Kessler descending the stairs and approaching the painting.

At the end of the film, that opening shot is repeated, but reversed as if it is a mirror opposite. It begins by showing Kessler (and his police escorts) descending the stairs. The camera pans to screen left to follow Kessler to the painting. Lewis cuts to a closeup, the edit allowing us to see Kessler by himself, apart from the police. He looks up at the painting and speaks to it as if it really is his wife. The camera then tilts upward to show her likeness. Lewis depicts her portrait in a closeup that echoes how he has just pictured Kessler. Even after her death, the two remain linked, as Kessler's closing dialogue confirms.

In addition to connecting the Kesslers by use of camera movement, Lewis also visually emphasizes their shared mental problems. For example, in the film's first scene, he shows Kessler seated at a table as reflected in a mirror, after which, thanks to a camera pan, we again see the painting of Mrs. Kessler hanging in the hallway. And then there is our introduction to Mrs. Kessler, during which she recounts her traumatic car crash to Jules. When she finishes her story, the camera pans to a nearby mirror to show her bemoaning the fact that she cannot go home. But nowhere are their problematic mental states more clear than when they appear in the frame together. On four occasions, Kessler and his wife examine each other through window glass just as if they are looking into mirrors, the result of which triggers his murderous trances.

Kessler's visual transformations from kind businessman to unwitting murderer are themselves notable. He undergoes the transition five times, the first four of which rely on the camera lens racking out and then back into focus. During that time, Lugosi changes his expression into an intent but controlled rage. The first two transformations also feature a shift in lighting from high key to low key that coincides with the shift in focus. Here we see the reliance on a camera trick to create a character's onscreen transformation into a monster. Mamoulian's *Dr. Jekyll and Mr. Hyde* (1932) had previously done the same in a more sophisticated manner; it employed the use of makeup as well as a shift in the actor's expression. Walker's *Werewolf of London* (1935) is another example. However, the camera-based transformation was relatively rare until Waggner's *The Wolf Man* (1941) and subsequent appearances of the same character throughout the forties. Once again, Lewis was somewhat ahead of the game, as *Invisible Ghost* appeared in theatres nearly seven months before *The Wolf Man*.

Moving from Past to the Future

With *Invisible Ghost*, Lewis directed a film that in many ways was ahead of its time. The use of the camera to visualize Kessler's transformation is but one example, and it may well be the least interesting. While in some respects *Invisible Ghost* is in a dialogue with the horror movie's past, Lewis uses its tone, setting, and characters to infuse the genre with what would become new codes and conventions years or even decades later.

For instance, the aforementioned use of humor surrounding Lugosi's identification with the horror genre is not the only way in which Lewis brings a comic sensibility to the film. At times, he draws on the same kind of comic relief that pervaded the horror film of the 1920s and 1930s; that is to say, brief humorous interludes to relieve the horror inspired by other scenes. Immediately we might think of Martin (Charles Gerrard) in *Dracula*, for example, or Albert Conti and Henry Armetta as the police sergeants in *The Black Cat*. Within *Invisible Ghost*, that means some unfortunate and decidedly unfunny dialogue given to African-American actor Clarence Muse, whose character Evans asks Jules if he "look[s] pale" after the arrival of Ralph's brother Paul. It also means Detective Ryan (Fred Kelsey) cornering Evans and demanding to know where he was on the night of January the Thirteenth, a date that has no meaning to the story; instead of answering, Evans offers him coffee, which Ryan gladly accepts. Their interplay is little more than the reworking of a similar joke from *The Laurel-Hardy Murder Case* (1930), which featured Fred Kelsey as a detective interrogating Stan Laurel.

Rather than depend solely on comic relief as used in previous horror films, Lewis also includes moments of some rather sophisticated dark comedy. Certainly James Whale had previously explored dark comedy within the horror genre, particularly in such films as *The Old Dark House* (1932), *The Invisible Man* (1933) and *Bride of Frankenstein* (1935). Lewis does the same with the unexpected reawakening of Jules' "lifeless" body at the morgue, which prompts his wife to shout, "Get him out of here! He isn't dead!" The dialogue is rife with comedy embedded in an otherwise horrific moment; it is of the type that one can imagine having appeared in one of Whale's movies, screamed perhaps by Una O'Connor, or appearing decades later in the cinema of Sam Raimi.

But Lewis also offers an even darker form of comedy with the discovery of Cecile's corpse. Evans attempts to rouse Cecile by knocking on her door as he hears her radio playing, as it apparently has been all night long. A workout program is being broadcast. The announcer's voice prepares his listeners with instructions, and then has them begin exercising; he is relentless in his rhythmic enunciation of "One-Two-Three-Four, One-Two-Three-Four." Evans opens the door to find Cecile lying stiffly; he touches her and realizes that she is dead. The oblivi-

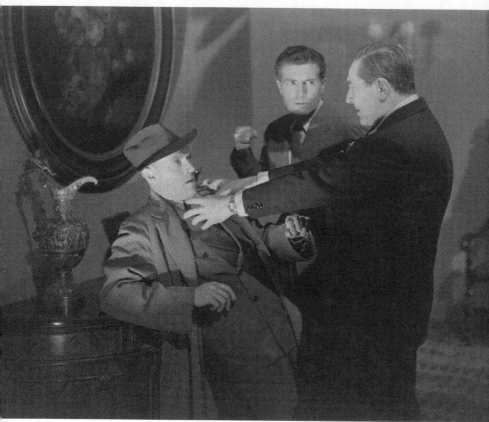

The characters of *Invisible Ghost* are trapped in their geography. *(Photo courtesy of Bill Chase)*

ous radio announcer continues, his directions to the exercising listeners providing a marked contrast to Cecile's lifeless body. Here the black comedy is arguably more unsettling and more subtle than anything ever constructed by Whale. Indeed, it seems decidedly out of place in 1941, smacking more of the hotel bathroom scene in Jean-Luc Godard's *Alphaville, une étrange aventure de Lemmy Caution* (1965) or the *Singin' in the Rain* rape sequence in Stanley Kubrick's *A Clockwork Orange* (1971), both of which would also play sound against onscreen action to achieve uncomfortably dark humor.

As Cecile's murder suggests, *Invisible Ghost* presents a house under siege, the killer's identity unknown to the other characters who are trapped within its four walls. Certainly that places the film into the "old dark house" tradition, bringing to mind such films as Leni's *The Cat and the Canary* (1927) and Whale's *The Old Dark House*. *Invisible Ghost* even includes the requisite stormy night and shots of a lightning bolt striking in the night sky.

And yet *Invisible Ghost* appropriates those few elements from the old dark house films and transforms them into something quite different. After all, the crimes at the Kessler home take place over a much longer period of time than those in a typical old dark house film. Early in the narrative, Cecile inquires about the murders and notes that there had been "a lot of them." An undetermined number of deaths over an unknown period of time, all of which occur before the film's running time has started; the murders we do witness proceed to take place over the series of many days, if not longer. In other words, it is not as if the characters are forced to stay in the Kessler home for only one single night due to the reading of a will (*The Cat and the Canary*) or a terrible storm (*The Old Dark House*).

Instead, characters are trapped in the Kessler home without an end in sight, due either to family obligation (Virginia) or to employment (Evans, Jules, Cecile, and Marie). We learn that a court has tried to shut the house down, but that Mr. Kessler, who "carries a lot of weight around here," has not allowed them to do so. "Sentimental reasons" and the hope of his wife's return anchor him to the property. With few exceptions – specifically Ralph's trial and execution, the Kesslers' visit to the governor, and Jules' recovery at the morgue – the majority of the film's running time traps the audience at the Kessler home as well.

Here again *Invisible Ghost* seems to point the way to the future as much as it does to the past. Horror film landscapes of a later era – sleep-away camps, small towns under threat, and houses without bad storms or washed-out bridges – will smack similar to the Kessler home in that the pending victims can easily leave: they just choose not to do so, even as murders occur. And, much like the horror movies of the 1970s and 1980s, Lewis places emphasis on the depiction of those murders, as well as on the discoveries of the corpses. That means taking great pains to stage each one of them differently.

Not only are the characters trapped in their geography, but two of them, Mr. and Mrs. Kessler, are trapped in the past, though it is a past that Lewis largely conceals from us. We understand that Mrs. Kessler has cheated on him and that she was in a bad car crash, but we learn no concrete information. Locked somewhere in the recesses of Mr. Kessler's mind, and in the shadows within the Kessler home, are hidden details about the affair and Mr. Kessler's reaction to it. However, Lewis gives us only a negative narrative space of the sort that Val Lewton would employ in such films as *The Seventh Victim* (1943), and that film noir would exploit in the post-war period. The result means the audience must supply the film's most lurid, debased content on its own.

And then there is the lovely young couple. As in so many horror films of the thirties, ranging from *Dracula* and *White Zombie* to *The Black Cat* and *The Raven* (1935), we have a young hero and heroine that are thrown into a dangerous and horrifying situation. Certainly Virginia Kessler seems innocent, but, in marked contrast to prior films in the genre, that is hardly the case with Ralph Dickson. Even when we first meet Ralph, he is easy to dislike. Because it is her father's wedding anniversary, Virginia intentionally asks Ralph not to come by the Kessler home, but he ignores her wishes. Admitting him into the home, Virginia invites him into a sitting room, but Ralph again ignores her wishes, lingering at the dining room door to spy on Mr. Kessler, a husband speaking to a wife who isn't there.

But being rude and insensitive is not Ralph's major crime. Instead, it is that he represents a breed of young horror film victims that would proliferate in the splatter film era of the 1970s and 1980s. What we learn soon after his arrival at the Kessler home is that he and Cecile know one another. Later, when Ralph begins to walk home, Cecile confronts him, threatening that Virginia will have to learn "sooner or later" about their prior relationship. Though he implores her to remember that he "never said he loved [her]," Cecile argues that she would make Ralph a good wife. Later in the film, Ralph recounts their sexual liaison in coded language: "I knew Cecile a couple of years. She offered me the companionship I needed." Ralph's onetime landlady also underscores the sexual side of the relationship by noting to the court that she "thought they were married." The court's verdict seals Ralph's fate. He must die in the electric chair.

Invisible Ghost cannot allow the standard horror film plotline of the thirties and forties to proceed. Of course the governor cannot prevent Ralph's execution, because Virginia cannot reunite with Ralph, as, say, Mina and Harker do at the conclusion of *Dracula*. Officially Ralph is put to death for a murder that Kessler committed, but that is incidental rather than central. Ralph dies for the same reason that Cecile dies: their sexual promiscuity dictates it. After all, the same is true for Mrs. Kessler; the fact she has had an affair with another man leads to her eventual demise. It is in their deaths that *Invisible Ghost* most clearly leads the way to the future of horror films, to the 1970s and 1980s when premarital sex or adultery leads to punishment meted out by torture and then death.

Conclusion

During his investigation, Police Lieutenant Williams quite rightly refers to the Kessler home as a "house where anything can happen and usually does." Lewis' emphasis on the speed at which he made films like *Invisible Ghost* was also a well-founded observation, as *Invisible Ghost* is hardly perfect. For example, a careful viewer cannot help but notice that when Detective Ryan's stiff body falls forward, actor Fred Kelsey's open eyes shut midway to the floor. The moment hardly inspires the seriousness or the shock that Lewis intended.

Nor does *Invisible Ghost* overall show the maturity and consistency of vision of later Lewis films like *Gun Crazy*, *The Big Combo* (1955), or *Terror in a Texas Town* (1958). It would be in fact easy to argue that it suffers by comparison to such Lewis films as *My Name Is Julia Ross* and *So Dark the Night* (1946). And yet such comparisons are finally unproductive; *Invisible Ghost* can and should stand on its own merits.

The May 1, 1941 issue of the *Hollywood Spectator* was indeed lacking judgment in its observations about *Citizen Kane*, as the passage of time has shown. But – even if its review of *Invisible Ghost* represents a much lesser affront to our sensibilities – the *Spectator* review of that movie needs revision as well. Much the same might now be said of Sarris and Meisel, both of whom offered more nuanced views of Lewis than the *Spectator*, but both of whom remained overly skeptical of his early films. Investigating *Invisible Ghost* in the 21st century reveals a unique film worthy of being removed from simplistic categories of Lewis' "ephemeral" work, as well as from the Lugosi "Monogram Nine." While we should of course remain open to many interpretations of *Invisible Ghost*, if a definitive article must be forced in front of its title, it should be in singular recognition that [The] *Invisible Ghost* is one of Lewis' important achievements, as at its best it possesses a sophisticated visual style and a prescient artistic vision that deserves ongoing inquiry, even more so than Lewis himself believed.

(Endnotes)

1   W. B., "Comments on Current Pictures: *Citizen Kane*," *Hollywood Spectator* May 1, 1941, 6-7.
2   Comments on Current Pictures: *The* [sic] *Invisible Ghost*," *Hollywood Spectator* May 1, 1941, 14.
3   Andrew Sarris, *The American Cinema: Directors and Directions, 1929-1968* (New York: Dutton, 1968), 78.
4   *Ibid.*, p. 133.
5   *Ibid.*, p. 133.
6   *Ibid.*, p. 133.
7   Myron Meisel, "Joseph H. Lewis: Tourist in the Asylum." in *Kings of the Bs*, edited by Todd McCarthy and Charles Flynn (New York: Dutton, 1975), 81-103.

8   For more information on the British ban, see Tom Johnson, *Censored Screams: The British Ban on Hollywood Horror in the Thirties* (Jefferson, NC: McFarland, 1997).

9   For more information on the life and career of Bela Lugosi, see Gary D. Rhodes, *Lugosi* (Jefferson, NC: McFarland, 1997); Gary D. Rhodes, *Bela Lugosi, Dreams and Nightmares* (Narberth, PA: Collectables, 2007). Regarding the 1958 date for *Plan 9 from Outer Space*, it is worth underscoring that the film was released to theatres that year. Repeated use of the date 1959 by prior authors is incorrect.

10   For more information on the "Monogram Nine" and other low-budget horror movies of the forties, see Tom Weaver, *Poverty Row Horrors! Monogram, PRC, and Republic Horror Movies of the Forties* (Jefferson, NC: McFarland, 1993).

11   For example, actor Vince Barnett appeared in *The Corpse Vanishes* (1942) and *Bowery at Midnight* (1942), John Carradine appeared in *Voodoo Man* (1944) and *Return of the Ape Man* (1944); Louise Currie appeared in *The Ape Man* (1943) and *Voodoo Man*; J. Farrell MacDonald appeared in *Bowery at Midnight* and *The Ape Man* (1943); Wanda McKay appeared in *Bowery at Midnight* and *Voodoo Man*; Wheeler Oakman appeared in *Bowery at Midnight*, *The Ape Man*, and *Ghosts on the Loose* (1943); Dave O'Brien appeared in *Spooks Run Wild* (1941) and *Bowery at Midnight*; George Pembroke appeared in *Invisible Ghost* and *Black Dragons* (1942); Angelo Rossitto appeared in *Spooks Run Wild* and *The Corpse Vanishes*; Minerva Urecal appeared in *The Corpse Vanishes* and *The Ape Man*; and Terry Walker appeared in *Invisible Ghost* and *Voodoo Man*.

     In addition, William Beaudine directed *The Ape Man*, *Ghosts on the Loose*, and *Voodoo Man*; Wallace Fox directed *The Corpse Vanishes* and *Bowery at Midnight*; and Phil Rosen directed *Spooks Run Wild* and *Return of the Ape Man*. Gerald Schnitzer contributed to the story for *The Corpse Vanishes* and wrote the screenplay for *Bowery at Midnight*; Marcel Le Picard shot *Invisible Ghost* (along with Harvey Gould), *Spooks Run Wild*, *Voodoo Man*, and *Return of the Ape Man*; and Carl Pierson edited *Bowery at Midnight*, *The Ape Man*, *Ghosts on the Loose*, *Voodoo Man*, and *Return of the Ape Man*.

12   While I believe *The Corpse Vanishes* draws upon notions of supernatural vampires, I do not believe the supernatural is explicitly at work in its narrative.

Photo portrait of André Breton, the founder of the surrealist movement.

Chapter 2

Invisible Ghosts: The Films of Bela Lugosi as Borderline Surrealism

by Robert Guffey

1.

"Write quickly, without any preconceived subject, fast enough so that you will not remember what you're writing and be tempted to reread what you have written."

—André Breton, "Manifesto of Surrealism," 1924

The above advice was offered by André Breton, the founder of surrealism, to budding artists who wished to practice surrealism themselves. But this mode of artistic creation was not the sole property of avant-garde surrealists. It was also, by necessity, the working method of a whole generation of screenwriters pounding out storylines for the masses throughout the 1930s, '40s, and '50s. This surrealist methodology applies not just to the writing of screenplays, but to the actual act of committing these stories to film. B-films were often written within three or four days and sometimes shot in an equal amount of time. No one involved in the production had much time to prepare—not the actors, not the director, and least of all the screenwriters.

A young Ray Bradbury once hung a sign on his typewriter that read,

"DON'T THINK." Before his death, the poet Charles Bukowski requested that the following two words be etched into his tombstone: "DON'T TRY." The beauty of not thinking, of not trying, when creating any kind of art is that mysterious and wondrous ideas sometimes erupt from the sleeping brain and sneak out into the real world while one's consciousness isn't paying attention. The early surrealists in France wished to evoke this mysterious phenomenon, on purpose, via the method of automatic writing—simply putting pen to paper and allowing the words to flow with neither rhyme nor reason. Purely on accident, half a world away, a whole community of writers were also practicing automatic writing. But most of them knew nothing about surrealism, and few of them were interested in making "Art." They were little "a" artists who were interested in grinding out a product in order to make money. In Hollywood, particularly during the 1930s and '40s, strict deadlines necessitated that the most productive writers were those who *didn't think* about what they were writing and *didn't try* to produce anything of any social value whatsoever. It just so happened that these were also the goals of committed European revolutionaries who called themselves surrealists. The screenwriters under discussion in this essay called themselves "hacks" and were probably proud of it. Breton, a committed Marxist to the day of his death in 1966, would be appalled at the very notion that the basic tenets of capitalism could actually be the unwitting accomplice of surrealism. Breton believed that surrealism and revolutionary Marxism were inextricably linked; without one, the other could not exist. Breton was wrong.

But he's not the only genius who was ever wrong about something.

Breton believed that surrealism could be a medium with which to introduce revolutionary ideas into the minds of the masses, to shock them out of their somnambulism with beautifully disordered nonsense. Breton was *right* about this. What he didn't realize is that he and his colleagues would not be the ones to introduce surrealism to the masses. Breton and his colleagues were avant-garde artists who held the common man in contempt. They published their works in obscure literary magazines in Europe that would never be seen by the "besotted underclass." The very "sheeple" Breton wished to liberate from the shackles of reality would never waste precious time in between work shifts at the local steel factory by reading nonsensical poetry jotted down by effete Frenchmen. But what these average people *did* like to do was see movies.

Without knowing it, thousands of filmgoers in the 1920s, '30, '40s, and '50s were introduced to surrealist techniques and philosophies in

John McGuire (left), Polly Ann Young (center), and Bela Lugosi (right) discover an unseen murder victim in a publicity still for *Invisible Ghost*. *(Photo courtesy of Bill Chase)*

the form of cheapjack B-films. Even more poetically, the filmmakers themselves—for the most part—did not know they were making surrealist movies. This is the perfect surrealist conspiracy, for neither the conspirators nor the victims of the conspiracy were aware it was happening. One might consider this to be the ultimate exercise in automatic writing and telepathy, conducted on a mass scale by unwitting vessels of the surrealist spirit itself, a strange behavioral experiment that could only be comprehended in full several decades after the conspiracy had long been completed.

The very process of making B-movies, a process that remained in place in Hollywood until the early 1960s, encouraged and necessitated surrealist methodologies. A few filmmakers, the cutting-edge ones who understood their place in the Hollywood hierarchy and used it to their advantage, might very well have been aware of this, but most were not. The basic method of churning out these little celluloid dreams and nightmares enabled industrious filmmakers the ability to write, direct, edit, and distribute their films within a very short space of time—within a matter of months, or even weeks, sometimes. Very often the small-minded businessmen who ran the movie studios didn't care what was actually *in* the films just as long as they generated money. This process was a veritable breeding ground for all manner of surrealist techniques and obsessions: automatic writing (as mentioned before), synchronicity, chance, happenstance, coincidence, telepathy, etc. It's a breeding ground that no longer exists in modern day Hollywood. There's too much at stake now, economically, to allow chance or happenstance to have anything at all to do with producing a finished film. Every detail is planned out well in advance. Modern Hollywood has so many safety measures in place that art can't even happen by accident.

In the Golden Age of Hollywood, however, art almost never happened *except* by accident, and that was never more true than in the case of the B-films.

2.

"[E]ver since I have had a great desire to show forbearance to scientific musing, however unbecoming, in the final analysis, from every point of view. Radios? Fine. Syphilis? If you like. Photography? I don't see any reason why not. The cinema? Three cheers for darkened rooms."

–André Breton, "Manifesto of Surrealism," 1924

Bela Lugosi has often been referred to as the "King of the B-films." After briefly enjoying mainstream success via his successful turn as Bram Stoker's Count Dracula, as well as in other starring roles in major studio productions such *The Black Cat* (1934) and *The Raven* (1935), the bottom fell out of the horror market in 1936 due to a ban on such gruesome fare in England. Since England was one of the major markets for such films, Hollywood initiated its own unofficial ban on horror films that lasted about two years. When this ban was finally lifted late in 1938, Lugosi found himself appearing in the occasional "A-film" such as *Son of Frankenstein* and *Ninotchka*, but for the most part the rest of his career would be spent starring in B-films.

Word spreads fast around Hollywood, and always has, even back during its Golden Age. Everyone in town knew that Lugosi was in financial troubles. His name had marquee value and you could get him pretty cheap. Perfect. As Lugosi was quoted as saying in 1939, signifying his grudging surrender to the dark gods of Hollywood, "Lugosi. Horror. Box office. Fine. And I am horror."[1] As a result, Lugosi (perhaps more than any other actor) starred in the vast majority of these films that could be categorized as works of "accidental surrealism." One might say that Lugosi represents the spirit of accidental surrealism, or perhaps "surrealism for the masses." His association with such films predate his financial troubles in Hollywood. Even during his heyday, while basking in the glory of his post-*Dracula* successes on stage as well as on screen, he chose to star in Poverty Row films that owe more to surrealism and hermetic esotericism than to traditional American popcorn fare. These strange bastard children of sensationalism and expressionism permeated the nightmares of a generation lost in the crippling financial troubles of a Great Depression. These celluloid dark fantasies in which Lugosi was often the main attraction were, for the most part, surrealist at their core.

The titles of these films, some of them cinematic masterpieces and most of them nonsensical dross, unreel in one's mind like a nomenclature of the absurd: *The Thirteenth Chair* (1929), *Dracula* (1931), *The Black Camel* (1931), *Murders in the Rue Morgue* (1932), *White Zombie* (1932), *Chandu the Magician* (1932), *Island of Lost Souls* (1933), *Night of Terror* (1933), *International House* (1933), *The Whispering Shadow* (1933), *The Black Cat* (1934), *Return of Chandu* (1934), *The Mysterious Mr. Wong* (1935), *Mark of the Vampire* (1935), *The Raven* (1935), *Murder By Television* (1935), *Shadow of Chinatown* (1936), *The Invisible Ray* (1936), *Son of Frankenstein* (1939), *The Dark Eyes of London* (1939), *The Phantom Creeps* (1939), *Black Friday* (1940), *You'll Find Out* (1940), *The Devil Bat* (1941), *Spooks Run Wild* (1941), *The Wolf Man* (1941), *Black Dragons* (1942), *The Ghost of Frankenstein* (1942), *The Corpse Vanishes* (1942), *Night Monster* (1942), *Bowery at Midnight* (1942), *Frankenstein Meets the Wolf Man* (1943), *The Ape Man* (1943), *Ghosts on the Loose* (1943), *Return of the Vampire* (1944), *Voodoo Man* (1944), *Return of the Ape Man* (1944), *The Body Snatcher* (1945), *Zombies on Broadway* (1945), *Scared to Death* (1947), *Abbott and Costello Meet Frankenstein* (1948), *Mother Riley Meets the Vampire* (1952), *Bela Lugosi Meets a Brooklyn Gorilla* (1952), *Glen or Glenda* (1953), *Bride of the Monster* (1955), *Plan 9 from Outer Space* (1958).

But perhaps none of them are more absurd than Joseph Lewis' *Invisible Ghost* (1941).

3.

"This world is only very relatively in tune with thought, and incidents of this kind are only the most obvious episodes of a war in which I am proud to be participating. Surrealism is the 'invisible ray' which will one day enable us to win out over our opponents. 'You are no longer trembling, carcass.' This summer the roses are blue; the wood is of glass. The earth, draped in its verdant cloak, makes as little impression upon me as a ghost. It is living and ceasing to live that are imaginary solutions. Existence is elsewhere."

—André Breton, "Manifesto of Surrealism," 1924

Ernie Adams (left) is about to receive some unwanted attention from Bela Lugosi unless John McGuire (right) does something about it... quick! *(Photo courtesy of Bill Chase)*

The shadow of an ape?
The portrait of a beautiful woman.
Good evening.
Dinner's served.
Good evening to an invisible woman?
Is this guy nuts?
Clarence Muse serves the ghost.
Mirror image.
Daughter. Virginia.
"They're" having dinner.
Ralph enters.
What's all the mystery about?
After dinner, we're taking a long walk.
It must seem weird to someone who's never seen
it before.
Never forgets.
I guess he's not the only one who resorts to
make believe.
An uncanny feeling.
Cecilia?
I think this is a crazy house.
Jules.
I'll show you where we keep our linens.
Little mousy man stealing food?
Mrs. Kessler. In the basement?
I want to go home.
I can't go home now... can I?
More mirrors.
Late again, Jules.
All these horrible murders....
Amnesia.
Virginia's been cheated on, just like her dad?
Hello, Casanova.
Have you gone crazy?
The servants see all.
The maid's a stalker?
I promise I'll make you a good wife, Ralph, I
promise I will.
Love? He's a fine boy.
Thank you for the dinner.

The dirty secret emerges.
A psychic link?
Cut in half by a window.
Somnambulism.
Hypnotism?
A trance.
Automatic killer.
A lateral shot through the wall.
Sleepwalking fiend.
What's that music playing?
1940s popular music.
The beautiful maid.
Kessler comes undone.
Radio.
Creeps toward the camera.
Has he always been insane, or has his wife made him so?
Exercise lessons on radio.
Dead body in bed.
Contrast.
Lateral shot through wall.
I tried to wake the new maid....
The chauffeur.
How many murders have there been?
I'm practically engaged to a Ralph.
Ralph Dickson.
He never loved her.
Engineer.
I thought they were married.
Dickson sentenced to die.
Slanting, diagonal shadows in a prison.
Ralph Dickson takes the final walk—
—juxtaposed with Lugosi reading from the Bible.
Ralph is executed.
It's all over.
Overhead shot.
Ralph returns from the dead.
My name is Dickson.
It can't be.
Apparently your brother never told you about me.
Sorry to have startled you.

Do I look pale? I feel pale.

Fire in the foreground.

Secret emerges from the basement again.

Paul Dickson.

There's the wife again.

(How much more effective these scenes would be without a musical score.)

Grabs heart.

Back into the trance.

Uh-oh.

Pulling off robe.

Going to kill the butler.

Changes his mind.

Wants to kill wife.

Kills others instead?

Shadows in the kitchen.

Gardener gets it.

Early serial killer movie?

Gardener died on the linoleum floor.

The butler discovers the body again.

Calls police. The body has not been touched.

Murdered?

Strangled. Well, here we go again.

You're wanted in the kitchen.

Am I seeing things?

He's the image of 'im.

Jan the 13th.

Have you had your coffee yet?

What does he mean by "the others"?

We can't leave.

If you want the truth, always talk to the servant.

There's been quite a lot of them.

He's waitin' for his wife to come back.

Well, this isn't a very pleasant way to entertain a guest.

She has eyes like Virginia.

She'll be back someday.

Coroner's Office.

Mr. Kirby.

The gardener's wife.

Another lateral shot.

Coroner leaves her alone with the body.
Mr. Mason.
He's alive!
He's not dead.
Jules Mason.
Did you recognize the man who tried to kill you?
It was ghastly.
Just a few moments longer....
Talking about murder over dessert.
The new cook.
Burning the roast.
I want to stay.
Ever read the newspapers?
What you don't know....
Lightning and chess.
It's getting late.
Such an elegant dinner.
Roast beef.
Wait until you taste my apple pie, Mr. Kessler.
Oh, he's a wonderful man.
What did I do wrong?
Slowly I turn.
The face at the window....
Cut in half by the window.
Almost kills Dickson... backs away....
Belt on the bathrobe.
Kill his daughter?
Lightning flash... breaks him out of trance....
Chance... coincidence....
Mr. Kessler?
Are you ill?
Hello, Paul.
I must have walked in my sleep.
The face at the window.
Fists grasping air.
The torn portrait.
"I wonder if anyone was hurt."
Ryan.
A dead cop behind the curtain.
Disappearing food.

The thread in the portrait.

All we want to know is if he's crazy.

That's easy.

Is it possible for someone to be normal and then go crazy only for an hour or two?

Lights go out!

We want to talk to you.

The secret enters the house.

Okay, sister, it's yours.

I'm going home... have to see my husband and my daughter.

I'm dead.

I know that woman. She's wicked. She can't go home. Mrs. Kessler....

I'm dead, Charles. Do you hear me? I'm dead.

I'm afraid to come home.

The secret dies.

She's dead.

What happened here?

We've got the murderer.

I knew you'd come back.

Kessler dies.

The invisible ghost ends.

4.

"The simplest Surrealist act consists of dashing down into the street, pistol in hand, and firing blindly, as fast as you can pull the trigger, into the crowd. Anyone who, at least once in his life, has not dreamed of thus putting an end to the petty system of debasement and cretinization in effect has a well-defined place in that crowd, with his belly at barrel level."

–André Breton, "Second Manifesto of Surrealism," 1930

In his 1993 book, *Poverty Row Horrors!: Monogram, PRC and Republic Horror Films of the Forties*, Tom Weaver describes *Invisible Ghost* as "almost *surreal*," but I would go just a tad further and say that it *is* surreal—or at least as close as a Hollywood film could get to being surreal in the early 1940s.[2] The same could be said of many of Lugosi's 1940s "poverty row" films, particularly the nine that he made for Monogram Studios between the years 1941 and 1944, but here we will focus on only one, the very first: Joseph Lewis' *Invisible Ghost*.

In *Invisible Ghost*, Lugosi plays Dr. Charles Kessler, a far more psychologically complex character than was typical for 1940s poverty row films. Indeed, Kessler's not typical of *any* American film of the 1940s, including those made by the major studios. On the surface Kessler appears to be a kindly old man who loves his daughter, and yet at the same time appears to be utterly insane. Once a year, on his wedding anniversary, Kessler hosts an elaborate dinner for his absent wife who, years before, ran off with his best friend and never returned. He even makes sure there's a place for her at the table, and talks to her as if she's actually sitting there. It seems odd for a man to go crazy only once a year, and yet he appears to do just that.

His loving daughter, as well as his servants, grudgingly humor the sad old man's eccentricities. The fact that he continues to long for a woman who betrayed him in a heartless manner seems to suggest a masochistic streak in Kessler's personality. But perhaps this streak is more than just a streak, and perhaps it's far more than merely masochistic.

It will become clear that Kessler, the gentle old doctor, wishes to kill his wife for what she has done to him. Because he can't face this ugly truth about himself, he suppresses this transgressive impulse. And by suppressing the impulse, it emerges only when Kessler's asleep.

André Breton, and the surrealists in general, believed a great deal in the power of dreams and sleep and self-induced

Little seen artwork from a Yugoslavian poster for *Invisible Ghost* in which Bela Lugosi's character is reimagined as a weird hybrid of a young Peter Lorre and Mickey Dolenz from The Monkees. *(Photo courtesy of Kristin Dewey)*

hypnotic trances. They believed everyday waking life was an illusion, the dream life infinitely more tangible and meaningful. Therefore, what was revealed in one's dreams said far more about one's "true" personality than anything one had ever thought or done in the "real" world.

Kessler suffers from somnambulism. He walks in his sleeps. And while walking and dreaming simultaneously, he also pursues another odd pastime. He kills.

Breton, a champion of using self-induced hypnosis to conjure forth surrealist works of art, once said—no doubt rhetorically, of course—that mass murder was the "simplest Surrealist act."[3] Kessler combines several surrealist tendencies into one. He's a hypnotist, a hypnotic subject, and a serial murderer all at the same time.

Charles Kessler is an unwitting surrealist.

But then again, Breton believed *everyone* was an unwitting surrealist, at least when they were asleep, and they could even be so when they were awake just as long as they were willing to drop their everyday, shallow façades and penetrate to the core of what was genuinely "real" about themselves—or rather "surreal," those secrets that lay hidden deep beneath the surface of their dream lives. The mysteries tucked away in the basements of their brains.

Sigmund Freud was an immense influence on Breton and the surrealists. They felt that Freud offered humanity the tools by which to remove themselves from the shackles placed upon them by organized religion and penetrate the previously unexplored depths of the human mind. Breton's positive attitude toward Freud never wavered, though by the end of his life he did believe that Freud's knowledge had been perverted into yet another trap for human beings rather than a means of liberation. *Invisible Ghost* is dripping with Freudian symbolism, most of it no doubt unintentional. The coauthor of the screenplay, Al Martin, was hardly known for his subtlety and layered subtext. He was a reliable craftsman who cranked out scores of scripts, for both film and television, throughout his forty-year-plus career, including the cult classics *Invasion of the Saucer Men* (1957) and *The Eye Creatures* (1965), neither of which are notable for their use of complex symbolism. Nonetheless, such symbolism exists throughout *Invisible Ghost* and could only be the product of the screenwriters (Helen Martin is credited as the screenplay's co-author) or perhaps the director, Joseph Lewis.

This latter possibility is not unlikely. Joseph Lewis was a groundbreaking director who honed his craft on Poverty Row before graduating to the big studios like Columbia where he directed such Gothic/noir hybrids as *My Name Is Julia Ross* (1945). Lewis' masterpiece, however, is *Gun Crazy* (1950). Many film critics claim that *Gun Crazy* is the best film noir ever made, and I would be hard pressed to disagree with that assessment. Throughout Lewis' oeuvre, we see him committing to film abstract representations of reality in order to tell darkly psychological stories about damaged people who transgress against the traditional social strictures of the day. This certainly describes *Gun Crazy*. Despite the fact that the film is a gritty, realistic tale of two murderous outlaws, I suspect Breton would have held some sympathy for the film and its two main characters. As Breton wrote in his very first Surrealist Manifesto in 1924:

> The mind of the man who dreams is fully satisfied by what happens to him. The agonizing question of possibility is no longer pertinent. Kill, fly faster, love to your heart's content. And if you should die, are you not certain of reawaking among the dead? Let yourself be carried along, events will not tolerate your interference. You are nameless. The ease of everything is priceless [...].
>
> I believe in the future resolution of these two states, dream and reality, which are seemingly so contradictory, into a kind of absolute reality, a *surreality*, if one may so speak.[4]

One can almost imagine one of the two main characters of *Gun Crazy* uttering these same words. Listen to this exchange between the two protagonists, Barton Tare (John Dall) and Annie Laurie Starr (Peggy Cummins), after they've successfully avoided being arrested for armed robbery and murder:

> Barton: Everything's going so fast. It's all in such high gear that sometimes it doesn't feel like me. If that makes sense.
> Annie: When do you think all this?
> Barton: Oh, at nights. I wake up sometimes. It's as if none of it really happened. As if *nothing* were real anymore.
> Annie: Next time you wake, Bart, look over at me lying there beside you. I'm yours. And *I'm* real.
> Barton: Yes. But you're the only thing that is, Laurie. The rest is a nightmare.

Of course, these words were written by the screenwriter of *Gun Crazy*, Dalton Trumbo, not Lewis. Nonetheless, it's certainly fascinating to note the repetition of a specific theme from one director's film to an-

Is Béla Lugosi reading André Breton's *Manifestoes of Surrealism* in this *Invisible Ghost* publicity still? One can only hope.... *(Photo courtesy of Bill Chase)*

other, as it might very well be an indication of that director's attraction to a particular type of subject matter, in this case the fine line between reality and *surreality* in the transgressive mind.

Bart's words could easily have slipped out of the mouth of Charles Kessler... or André Breton.

5.

"Under the pretense of civilization and progress, we have managed to banish from the mind everything that may rightly or wrongly be termed superstition, or fancy; forbidden is any kind of search which is not in conformance with accepted practices. It was, apparently, by pure chance that a part of our mental world which we pretended not to be concerned with any longer—and, in my opinion by far the most important part—has been brought back to light. For this we must give thanks to the discoveries of Sigmund Freud. On the basis of these discoveries a current of opinion is finally forming by means of which the human explorer will be able to carry his investigations much further, authorized as he will henceforth be not to confine himself solely to the most summary realities. The imagination is perhaps on the point of reasserting itself, of reclaiming its rights."

—André Breton, "Manifesto of Surrealism," 1924

The Freudian implications of Kessler's obsession results in a series of brutal murders. Kessler can't get back at his wife for leaving him, and yet he still loves her. Eros and Thanatos entwined. These polar impulses pull his brain in two. No sane mind could handle such stress. And so Kessler's mind snaps, and while asleep he projects his hatred for his absent wife on the only females who are present in his home and easily accessible to him. It's telling that Kessler never kills outside his own home. Some critics have lambasted the film for this plot point. After all, why don't the police have this house under twenty-four-hour surveillance if so many people have been brutally murdered there? This would be a fair question if this were a realistic story set in a realistic world. But it's not. It's the story about a man's mind slipping into a psychotic dream world, and the house is the physical manifestation of his disordered brain. The police in the film are symbols only, impotent phantoms that prevent none of the violence from occurring because that's not their job. Their job is simply to reveal Kessler's murderous side to himself when the doctor's sleeping brain deems it necessary, when the time is right. The house, and the people that seem to populate it, are nothing more than ghosts that haunt Kessler's troubled dreams. Most critics believe that the seemingly nonsensical title refers to Kessler's wife, since it is her recurrent appearances outside Kessler's bedroom window that seem to trigger his murderous rages. But no. The ghost in the title is everyone other than Kessler. This is Kessler's dream, and his sleeping mind is the only thing that's real. The invisible ghost is the world itself.

We learn seven minutes into the film that Kessler's wife never actually left Kessler. She tried to, but fate intervened. As she and her lover were driving away, they got into a car accident that killed the lover and left Mrs. Kessler an amnesiac, brain-damaged wreck. Somehow she made her way back to the estate where the gardener, Jules, found her wandering around in a daze. Instead of taking her to a hospital, as most people would do in the real world, Jules stuffed her away in the basement beneath the garden house. What he's doing with her down there is anybody's guess. According to Jules, he keeps her down there because he feels that Mr. Kessler would be unable to handle the sight of his wife in such a condition.

As in most neo-Gothic horror films of this type, very often there's a dirty secret hidden inside the basement or some similar underground grotto. In *The Phantom of the Opera* (1925), the Phantom makes his lair in the elaborate sewers beneath the Paris opera house. In *The Most Dan-*

gerous Game (1932), Zaroff, a psychotic game hunter, displays his human trophies only in the darkness of his basement. In *House of Dracula* (1945), the undead Count hides his coffin in the basement of the physician from whom he's ostensibly seeking a cure for vampirism (not only is Dracula not cured by the end of the picture, but the good doctor turns into a vampire too). In *Psycho* (1960), Norman Bates keeps the corpse of his beloved mother in the basement. In such films, houses—and architecture in general—are transformed into metaphors for the human brain. And the basement, or the underground, become stand-ins for the unconscious itself from which the typical "rational" human mind has become so thoroughly alienated that it does not comprehend its own motivations.

Like Charles Kessler.

6.

"I have always been amazed at the way an ordinary observer lends so much more credence and attaches so much more importance to waking events than to those occurring in dreams [...]. I have no choice but to consider [the waking state] a phenomenon of interference. Not only does the mind display, in this state, a strange tendency to lose its bearings (as evidenced by the slips and mistakes the secrets of which are just beginning to be revealed to us), but, what is more, it does not appear that, when the mind is functioning normally, it really responds to anything but the suggestions which come to it from the depths of that dark night to which I commend it."

–André Breton, "Manifesto of Surrealism," 1924

The tropes of Gothic fiction fascinated Breton and the surrealists. Despite the fact that Breton considered all fiction to be an "inferior" art form, as storytelling in general required a linear logic that precluded the beautiful non-rationality of surrealism, he granted one exception to the Gothic horror story, and in particular championed M. G. Lewis' 1796 novel, *The Monk*, generally considered to be one of the earliest and most influential Gothic novels. H.P. Lovecraft, in his book-length essay "Supernatural Horror in Literature," deemed *The Monk* "a masterpiece of active nightmare."[5] Breton, too, felt it was a masterpiece, though a masterpiece of proto-surrealism:

In the realm of literature, only the marvelous is capable of fecundating works which belong to an inferior category such as the novel, and generally speaking, anything that involves storytelling.

Lewis' *The Monk* is an admirable proof of this. It is infused throughout with the presence of the marvelous. Long before the author has freed his main characters from all temporal constraints, one feels them ready to act with an unprecedented pride. This passion for eternity with which they are constantly stirred lends an unforgettable intensity to their torments, and to mine. I mean that this book, from beginning to end, and in the purest way imaginable, exercises an exalting effect only upon that part of the mind which aspires to leave the earth and that, stripped of an insignificant part of its plot, which belongs to the period in which it was written, it constitutes a paragon of precision and innocent grandeur.

Breton caps off his analysis with the following footnote: "What is admirable about the fantastic is that there is no longer anything fantastic: there is only the real."[6]

Only the real. Breton deconstructs everyday reality by flipping the binary opposites of reality and the fantastic, or *surreality*. In Breton's world, dreams and nightmares represent reality and reality is the insignificant shadow of the fantastic that lurks in the secrets lairs beneath our waking life. This exact deconstruction occurs in Lugosi's best films, *Dracula, Murders in the Rue Morgue, White Zombie, Island of Lost Souls,* and *The Black Cat* (the 1934 version) foremost among them. It's not difficult to imagine Breton and his colleagues being sympathetic to these neo-Gothic films, particularly *The Black Cat.* In 1924, in his very first surrealist manifesto, Breton identified Edgar Allan Poe as a surrealist. (Breton would later change his mind about this, claiming that Poe's obsession with rationality, per his proto-detective stories about C. Auguste Dupin, overshadows his otherwise surrealist tendencies). Not only is *The Black Cat* ostensibly based on the Poe story of the same name, not only does it benefit from Edgar Ulmer's German Expressionist interpretation of reality, but it also boasts a screenplay (co-written by Ulmer) that manages to pack in almost every single transgressive "perversity" of which the Marquis de Sade (also identified by Breton as a progenitor of surrealism) himself would have approved. Film critic David Kalat once said of *The Black Cat* that it "was one of the most gorgeous movies ever to come out of Universal in the 1930s. It looked like the Dadaist art of the Bauhaus school had literally come to life, and Ulmer coaxed from Lugosi his most human and endearing performance ever."[7]

If there's any doubt that Breton and his intellectual colleagues would have been attracted to this type of Americanized surrealism as mani-

Clarence Muse (far left), who delivers one of the film's best performances, is about to be blamed for a series of murders he didn't commit. *(Photo courtesy of Bill Chase)*

fested in the form of commercial horror fiction, consider the following excerpt from an article written by Franklin Rosemont, the co-founder of the Chicago Surrealist Group:

> The Second World War, and the Nazi occupation of France, forced André Breton and other surrealists to seek refuge in the U.S. Regrouping in New York, they began a fruitful search for "surrealist evidence" in the New World. Among their greatest discoveries was Howard Phillips Lovecraft and the "Lovecraft circle," including Clark Ashton Smith, August Derleth, Donald Wandrei and Frank Belknap Long.
>
> In the works of these authors the surrealists found confirmations and extensions of their own quest. Appearing in *Weird Tales* and other "pulp" magazines, these works seemed to them more

truly poetic than the stuff in *Poetry* or other official organs of High Culture. Lovecraft and his friends reached beyond mere "literature" into the volatile shadows of a new mythology [...].

For surrealists today, the works of the Lovecraft Circle remain a *central source*.[8]

Not all of Lugosi's collaborators were unconscious of the surrealist movement and its potential to be a subversive force in society. Two of Lugosi's best directors, Edgar Ulmer and Robert Florey, sympathized with the surrealist movement and no doubt wished to make such groundbreaking films in America, the kind that Salvador Dali and Luis Bunuel were becoming famous for in Europe. In an interview included on the 2005 DVD release of Ulmer's 1957 horror film, *The Daughter of Dr. Jekyll*, Ulmer's daughter (and sometimes collaborator), Arianne, mentions that her father not only knew Salvador Dali, but was "very close" friends with him.[9] Clearly, therefore, it's natural to assume that Ulmer was intimately aware of surrealist techniques. Cinematographer Paul Ivano, with whom Robert Florey worked on the ill-fated screen test for *Frankenstein* (which Florey was assigned to direct before being switched by the studio executives to *Murders in the Rue Morgue*), once commented on Florey's love of surrealism. Ivano insisted that the test reel for *Frankenstein*, despite the less-than-positive reactions of the studio heads, was expertly realized. Ivano claimed that the use of shadows in the scenes was "very artistic yet nightmarish. Robert loved this for he was very adept in the Germanic style of cinematography, like *The Cabinet of Dr. Caligari*. Even his own experimental films had the same atmosphere: Surrealistic."[10]

But in the early 1930s what studio executive in America would subsidize a surrealist film? Of course, not one of them would ever do so—not knowingly, at least. The trick, therefore, was to slip surrealism in under the radar of the executives. The only way to do this would be to mask a surrealist film under the guise of a popular genre. Would a romantic musical lend itself to surrealism? Not likely. A shoot-'em-up western? Until Alejandro Jodorowsky's 1970 film *El Topo* (in which Jesus returns to Earth as a gunslinger in the Old West), the answer would be a definite "no." A gangster flick? A swashbuckling pirate adventure in the South Seas? Not likely.

Clearly, the nascent horror film (made possible, and popular, only because of the success of Lugosi's portrayal as Dracula) was the perfect vehicle in which to explore all the surrealist and expressionist techniques being employed by the most groundbreaking filmmakers in France (e.g., Dali and Bunuel's *Andalusian Dog*) and Germany (e.g., *The Cabinet of Dr.*

Caligari). Ulmer and Florey, in particular, no doubt saw the potential of the horror film being the perfect vehicle by which to surreptitiously assault dull American minds with their surrealist time bombs. And Lugosi, now firmly established as a horror star as a result of his indelible interpretation of Bram Stoker's most famous creation, was the perfect actor to star in these films.

The only reason Ulmer was able to make *The Black Cat* was because the head of Universal Studios, Carl Laemmle, Sr., happened to be out of the country at the time and wasn't around to disapprove. By the time he returned, this strange little nightmare had already been committed to film. Despite Laemmle's skepticism about the finished product, it went on to become the biggest grossing Universal film of that year. Yes, dull American minds *could* indeed handle a surrealist film—as long as they didn't realize that that's what they were watching. Surrealism, like so many other dirty little secrets in America, had to be hidden away in the basement and called by a somewhat more proper name so as not to disturb the neighbors.

Everything worthwhile in America invariably ends up in the basement, if it wasn't born there in the first place.

7.

"Nothing, in fact, can any longer prevent this country from being largely conquered. The hordes of words which, whatever one may say, Dada and Surrealism set about to let loose as though opening a Pandora's box, are not of a kind to withdraw again for no good purpose [...]. [C]onsider how far a handful of completely modern works, about which the very least one can say is that a particularly unhealthy atmosphere pervades them, has already wormed their way, admirably and perversely, into the public consciousness [...]."

—André Breton, "Second Manifesto of Surrealism," 1930

Periodically, the gardener's dirty little secret will sneak out of the basement and wander around the grounds of Mrs. Kessler's former home. On the night of her wedding anniversary, she looks up at the window and whispers, "I'm afraid to come home. He'd kill me. You'd kill *any*body." What does this mean? Is she predicting the future? Is she making this happen? (A self-fulfilling prophecy?) Or does she understand something about her husband's personality of which Kessler himself is not even aware?

The sight of his missing wife seems to stun and bewilder Kessler. He slips into a sort of self-induced trance and wanders into the maid's room. Here Lewis makes the most of his environment to stage a scene of mounting terror. The use of popular music emerging from the maid's radio in the background serves as an innocuous counterpoint to the grim reality of the murder unfolding before our eyes. It's a disturbing (and, in a way, darkly humorous) technique that has been used often since. Two examples leap immediately to mind: Stanley Kubrick's use of the song "Singin' in the Rain" during a brutal rape scene in *A Clockwork Orange* (1972) and Martin Scorsese's use of Donovan's 1960s folk song "Atlantis" during an equally violent scene in *Goodfellas* (1990).

In this first murder scene Lewis also makes use of very effective close-ups and subjective shots to put the audience in the place of the victim while the murder is occurring, a disturbing technique since exploited multiple times in far less stylish serial killer films produced throughout the 1970s, '80s, and beyond. The fact that Lewis' use of this technique remains effective to this day, due primarily to Lewis' subtlety and timing, indicates that this B-film may actually have been slightly ahead of its time rather than several steps behind it, as was suggested in many contemporary reviews. *The New York Daily News*, for example, called Lewis' direction "inadequate" and *The New York Daily Mirror* called it "terrible." Ironically, Lewis' direction is the one element in the film least vulnerable to criticism.

As the maid, Cecile (Terry Walker), shudders in fear and confusion, Kessler slips off his bathrobe slowly and deliberately: a perverse strip-tease. An expression of both sexual desire and anger flares in Kessler's eyes, then the kindly old philanthropist proceeds to strangle the woman to death. This is the most effective scene in the film, the showstopper that remains in one's mind even if one is indifferent (or even hostile) to the rest of the film.

The next morning, when the maid's body is discovered, Kessler has no memory of having committed the crime and is as baffled as everyone else, including the police. Ralph Dickson (John McGuire), the boyfriend of Virginia Kessler (Polly Ann Young), Charles Kessler's daughter, is accused of the crime by the authorities due to the fact that Ralph had been Virginia's lover, was being blackmailed by her, and lacks a strong alibi. Despite the fact that Charles Kessler does everything he can to save the young man (he even appeals to the Governor), Ralph is executed for the crime committed by Charles Kessler.

The Freudian cues couldn't be more obvious, nor could they be overlooked by any true surrealist. Not only is the young maid a stand-in for Kessler's missing, adulterous wife, but by killing the woman Kessler has also eliminated the only rival for his daughter's affections, Ralph.

Clarence Muse (left) and Bela Lugosi (right), who previously worked together in 1932's *White Zombie*, display excellent chemistry in *Invisible Ghost*. *(Photo courtesy of Bill Chase)*

Kessler's intense love/hatred for his wife will soon extend over to his daughter as well.

After Ralph is murdered by the state, who should appear on Kessler's doorstep? Ralph's doppelganger, his "ghost," a twin brother belatedly seeking answers to his brother's death. Paul Dickson (also played by John McGuire) wants nothing more than to uncover the real murderer of Cecile. The night of his arrival, Paul almost becomes Kessler's next victim.

Once again Kessler spots his wife through the window, nearly kills Paul, but instead decides to strangle Jules the gardener while the man is in the kitchen retrieving some food for Mrs. Kessler. Lewis effectively stages the murder by employing shadows thrown on the walls of the kitchen.

Kessler has managed to merge the waking and dream states into one and lives out fully his nightmares (dreams? secret desires?) without the messiness and inconvenience of having to remember what he's done in the morning. He doesn't even remember not *wanting* to remember. He can be the well-liked philanthropist the town very much wants him to be ("He's an important man around here," a police detective admits at one point, no doubt the main reason none of the policemen accuse him of the murders) while also fulfilling his dream life without any guilt whatsoever. He's gone beyond Dr. Jekyll and Mr. Hyde. Jekyll at least takes the initiative and brings about his bifurcation willingly. Kessler isn't even aware that he *wants* to be bifurcated. His disassociation is perfect and complete.

In the 1920s Salvador Dali began experimenting with what he called "paranoic" double visions, a perfect melding of two distinct images. His 1929 surrealist painting *Invisible Man*, in which two fluid landscapes overlap and appear to form a single scene, is a prime example. Perhaps the screenwriters, or even Joseph Lewis himself, were thinking of this painting when they chose the final title for the film (the working title throughout production was *The Phantom Killer*), for Charles Kessler is very clearly a "paranoic" double vision given human form.

This double vision, having easily skirted the law once the body of the gardener is found in his kitchen, imposes itself on the world around him one last time when he sees his wife's face only inches outside his window one rainy night. Lewis' use of noir lighting enlivens this scene considerably. It prefigures his masterful use of lighting in his future noir masterpieces such as *Gun Crazy* and *The Big Combo* (1955). In fact, *Invisible Ghost*, while also being borderline surrealism, could be considered borderline noir as well. Not only does Lewis' involvement with this film underscore this connection, but so does the presence of actor John McGuire, who gave such an effective star performance in what many film critics believe to be the first genuine film noir: Boris Ingster's *The Stranger on the Third Floor* (1940) co-starring McGuire and Peter Lorre. Surrealism? Noir? Horror? Drama? Theatre of the Absurd? The film is a mixture of all of these elements, like a dream that meanders from one disjointed scenario to another, or a nightmare that defies convenient analysis. To some extent, *Invisible Ghost* defies any convenient label, including such shallow descriptions as "good" or "bad."

Charles Kessler defies such descriptions as well. He's neither "good" nor "bad" because he never intends on creating any harm. It's clear from his third confrontation with his wife's "phantom" that Kessler is frustrated by his inability to resolve his lingering, psychic connections to his missing wife. At one point, after his wife's spectral visage has vanished into the rain and the darkness, Kessler impotently strokes and claws at the glass, as if wanting to caress and choke his wife at the same time. But he can do neither. So he simply balls his fists in frustration. The scene fades out, and resumes the next morning. It's not until later that we learn Kessler has—in the middle of the night—destroyed his wife's portrait, one that he has doted over constantly throughout the film. The second he sees the vandalized painting, Kessler whispers, "I wonder if anyone was hurt," as if he's subconsciously aware of the "paranoic" double vision that he has become. A few minutes later we learn that Kessler has strangled a police officer in the night (one of the very same detectives posted in the house in order to prevent another murder) and has, rather puckishly (and most improbably), arranged the body so that it appears to be standing behind the curtains in the living room. The second the curtains are parted, the corpse goes tumbling facedown onto the floor.

Though Kessler is surprised by this development, he's far more distressed by the vandalized portrait in the hallway. Paul Dickson finds a thread attached to the painting. The thread matches Kessler's bathrobe. So, naturally (per 1941 American logic), the police suspect Kessler's black butler, Evans (Clarence Muse), of both the vandalism and the murder. In *Invisible Ghost* Muse manages to turn in a sober and serious performance in what might otherwise have been a clichéd "Step-n-fetch-it" type of role. Despite the rambling script, Muse remains the anchor amidst the dream-like proceedings, the only character who responds sensibly to the strange events swirling around him. Against tremendous odds, Muse succeeds in bringing a great deal of dignity to a minor role. (It should be noted that Muse appeared in a previous film with Lugosi, the Halperin Brothers' low budget masterpiece, *White Zombie*.)

Near the end of the film, Evans is being interrogated by two police detectives, a psychiatrist, Paul Dickson, and Charles Kessler. Except for Kessler, they all seem to suspect Evans of the murder. The look on Muse's face is both amusing and realistic. One can hear the thoughts in his mind simply by reading his expressions: *Well, I knew this had to happen sooner or later.* When it comes down to accusing the wealthy white philanthropist or the black butler of murder, the butler's always going to lose.

In this film, however, the black butler does *not* lose. Fortunately for Evans, Mrs. Kessler must sneak into the house more and more frequently to scrounge for food due to the fact that her husband has strangled the one person on the grounds who knew Mrs. Kessler was still alive. Thus, with the gardener dead, there's no one around to bring her sustenance anymore. A pair of police detectives find Mrs. Kessler in the kitchen gnawing on a chicken leg. Due to her rambling, the officers immediately recognize that she's crazy and drag her upstairs. The second Kessler sees her, he slips into another trance and tries to strangle the lead detective. The only person in the room noticeably relieved by this development is Evans.

While Kessler is strangling the detective, Lewis intercuts two scenes of Mrs. Kessler dying in another room. Why she's dying now is a mystery that's never explained. There's no reason for it at all. Except....

Except perhaps she's dying because Kessler has no need for her anymore. The secret in the basement of his mind has now been revealed before witnesses. His "paranoic" double vision has been exposed to others, and therefore to himself. Perhaps Mrs. Kessler never survived that car crash at all. She even tells her husband in this final scene that she's "dead." Perhaps she *is* a ghost, in a way. Perhaps she's what the Tibetans call a "tulpa," a physical being manifested in three dimensions by the power of the mind—in this case, Kessler's mind. He desperately wanted to see his wife, and he desperately did *not* want to see his wife. He desperately wanted his wife to return to him so he could love her again. He desperately wanted his wife to return to him so he could strangle her to death. This bifurcation in his psyche resolved itself by conjuring up her "ghost." Once that bifurcation was revealed to others, and therefore—by extension—himself, he no longer had any need for her. So she died.

And once the tulpa dies, Kessler is released from her spell—a spell he put on himself by conjuring her in the first place.

The two Kesslers are the perfect melding of two distinct images, as in Dali's *Invisible Man*. Mr. Kessler is Mrs. Kessler (the fact that she has no first name in the script is certainly suggestive of her lack of individual identity), and Mrs. Kessler is Mr. Kessler. Both one and the same. Both invisible and visible at the same time. Both entwined on a psychic plane far beyond matrimony. Bonded by pain more than love. Products of the same consciousness. Till death do they part.

And part they do. Mrs. Kessler dies (disappears?), and Mr. Kessler is led away by the police past the torn portrait in the hall. Kessler stops in front of it for a moment and says, "I knew you'd come back to me." Of course he did. In a way, he'd summoned her in the first place. He'd made her live and breathe again with nothing more than convulsive desire.

8.

"Beauty will be CONVULSIVE, or will not be at all."

—André Breton, *Nadja*, 1928

If you're still not convinced that *Invisible Ghost* is an example of borderline cinematic surrealism par excellence, then consider this recent development. In 2002 Martin Arnold, the Austrian avant-garde artist, created a conceptual piece titled *Deanimated: The Invisible Ghost.*

Worldscinema, a website devoted to archiving experimental films from around the globe, describes *Deanimated* as:

> [...] an installation piece for projection as a 60-minute loop in gallery spaces. *Deanimated* is literally displaced from the theater environment typical of film spectatorship, slightly blurring the boundaries between the spaces of projection and reception.
>
> *Deanimated: The Invisible Ghost* is based on the 1941 horror film *The Invisible Ghost* with the lead actors Bela Lugosi, Polly Ann Young, and John McGuire. In *Deanimated* the actors are gradually eliminated [via digital manipulation] and thus the narrative loses it coherence. What remains are backgrounds, erratic camera movements that seem to move without focus throughout the room, capturing ghostly changes in light and shadows. In this project, Arnold asks fundamental philosophical questions about human existence and presence in absence. Although the actors are missing, they leave behind traces (such as [...] dust stirring up...) and are experienced precisely in their absence as a ghostly, unreal present.[11]

Deanimated can only be seen as an installation piece, separating it even further from the world of cinema. If one wishes to see it, one can't be a passive spectator. One has to actively seek it out. In *Deanimated* one sees Lewis' camera wandering through empty corridors and basements and dimly lit bedrooms, creating a disconcerting experience. If one has never seen the original film upon which it is based, one is left with a sense of having taken a trip through an alien, haunted world. If one *has* seen the film before, one is left with the feeling of having revisited a familiar world with an altered consciousness, like returning to a childhood home after having been away for many years. The architecture is the same, but all the people you once knew are gone. A sense of deep loss permeates *Deanimated*, and one walks away from the installation imbued with the same sense of desolation and psychic bifurcation that Charles Kessler himself must have felt as the police led him down his own haunted corridor and past the mutilated portrait of his dead wife one final time. *Deanimated* strips the architecture of Kessler's mind down to its bare essentials, revealing what the original film only hints at: Everyone in the film is an invisible ghost, a projection of a disordered consciousness. Kessler's home certainly is haunted; it's haunted by Kessler himself, and his inability to let go of the wholly illusory image of his less-than-perfect wife to which he stubbornly grasps. To let go of the past.

Arnold had previously created a similar installation based on the

Andy Hardy comedies of the 1930s, '40s, and '50s starring Mickey Rooney. In *Alone. Life Wastes Andy Hardy* (1998) Arnold digitally manipulates the original images to reveal the subversive subtext hiding just beneath the surface: transgressive messages of forbidden Oedipal desires and all manner of sexual frustrations that lie festering at the core of any repressed and puritanical society. *Deanimated* is even more successful in peeling away the seemingly shallow veneer of a pop cultural artifact and unmasking the strange face that—like Mrs. Kessler herself huddled in fear and confusion beneath the garden shack—lies hidden away just under the surface, waiting for its chance to escape.

Deanimated reifies, in artistic form, what I myself had always thought about the film: that it was far more than what it appeared to be. With digital manipulation, Arnold was able to reveal the truth behind the film: at its core, it's a surreal journey through a fractured man's mind. That surreality, implicit in Joseph Lewis' original, is made explicit by Arnold's manipulation. This is one of those rare cases in which digital manipulation is not being used to distort reality, but instead is revealing the reality underneath.

Arnold's *Deanimated* accomplishes the seemingly impossible. It manages to champion the surrealistic spirit of Lewis' *Invisible Ghost* while also placing the film—including all its many flaws and virtues—in its proper historical and sociological context.

It's the ultimate proof that *Invisible Ghost* is, at heart, a work of surrealism.

9.

"The approval of the public is to be avoided like the plague. It is absolutely essential to keep the public from entering if one wishes to avoid confusion. I must add that the public must be kept panting in expectation at the gate by a system of challenges and provocations."
–André Breton, "Second Manifesto of Surrealism," 1930

"[W]e have never ceased to maintain, with Lautrémont, that *poetry must be created by everyone* [...]."
–André Breton, "Surrealist Situation of the Object," 1935

There are so many surreal images in the films of Bela Lugosi that it would be difficult to name all of them here. Half-remembered images often come floating to the forefront of my brain, almost unbidden. In the middle of the night, teetering on the border of wake-

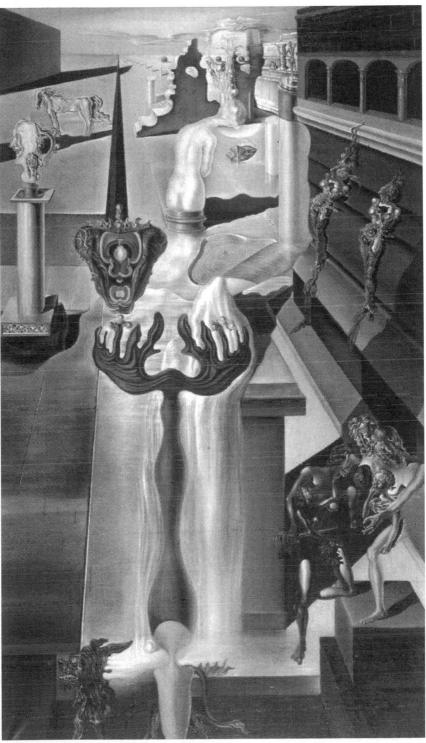
Salvador Dali's 1929 painting, *The Invisible Man.*

fulness and sleep, these images haunt my mind like invisible ghosts, brief flashes of visual poetry laced with silver nitrate, strange memories cast in monochromatic black and white: Murder Legendre holding up a white handkerchief in the air—the handkerchief is so white it almost glows—as a horde of half-alive men come shambling toward him out of the Haitian hills; the bestial Sayer of the Law stalking toward the camera, edging into an extreme close-up, while Max-Ernst-like animal-men creep behind him, howling angrily at their flawed creator; a bat-winged woman dressed in a pale white gown descending slowly, dream-like, toward the ruins of a castle; Dr. Mirakle genuflecting before the exquisite corpse of a crucified prostitute, as if in deep and respectful prayer; General Petronovich bellowing in a jealous rage while a pistol bends and melts like silly putty in his fist; Vitus Werdegast staring up in sadness and wonder at the preserved carcass of his long-lost wife while surrounded by a stylish art deco hallway decorated with deceased women, all beautiful, all frozen in time; an elegant ballerina—half-woman, half-raven—performing double pirouettes in honor of a tuxedoed man whose eyes are haunted by lust and torture; a Eurasian scientist named Poten tries to burn a man's brain with a fishbowl; amidst expressionist shadows, a broken-necked hunchback with gnarled teeth lovingly strokes the furry chest of a storybook giant, whispering/boasting that the sleeping beast "does things" for him; Dr. Paul Carruthers, dripping in perfume, runs in fear from a kite that looks like a giant devil bat; Nardo the Magician gestures proudly toward a cemetery, intoning the words, "The city of the dead. Do they, too, hear the howling of the frightened dogs?" while his dwarf assistant shrugs uncaringly; Dr. James Brewster, looking more like a cross between an ape and a penguin than a human being, getting whipped brutally by a stunning blonde in stiletto heels; the face of Armand Tesla melting into wax amidst the smoking ruins of a bombed-out cathedral; Professor Dexter walking down a darkened street with a blowtorch in his hand, searching for an ape who has just emerged from an ice cube; Joseph's crippled and pathetic shadow being strangled by a man named Gray; an undead monkey shambling along with its little arms outstretched before it, as if under a hypnotic spell; a snarling half-man/half-wolf creature wearing a pressed shirt and tattered pants embraces/strangles a bat while launching itself off a cliff side balcony toward a beach of crashing waves and sharp rocks thousands of feet below; a human being who thinks he's a vampire commands a robot to kill a septuagenarian transvestite; an unnamed spirit intoning the mantra "Beware of the big green dragon that sits on your doorstep.

He eats little boys... puppy dog tails, and big, fat snails. Beware, take care... beware!" is superimposed over a horde of stampeding buffalo; Dr. Eric Vornoff, wearing platform shoes from the 1970s, wrestles with an impotent octopus in a muddy lake in the 1950s; a grieving old gentleman takes a moment to sniff a beautiful flower before shuffling off to his death, the man's shadow still visible in the frozen frame as he cries out in agony, rising from his flimsy tomb only minutes later with an ivory-faced, obsidian-haired phantasm for a wife.

I could go on and on, but these are the enigmatic images that stand out most in my mind: cinematic riddles, low budget zen koans, two a.m. revelations, quasi-religious litanies for a postmodern generation weaned on nightmarish and non-rational images that came dripping out of a glass teat well past midnight, long past one's bedtime, long after all the adults had retreated into sleep. Even in an age where hundreds of different channels haunt the airwaves, long after the tradition of obligatory late-night spook shows have become an artifact of a fading past in which only a handful of channels were once available for the potential viewer, still programmers fill the night air with images of UFOs and ancient aliens and angry poltergeist, though more often than not these days such images will appear in the context of half-convincing documentaries that attempt to prove to the viewer that the non-rational is, in fact, rational. That the surreal is real and, therefore, unworthy of our fear, unworthy of our worship. In between these new and colorful images shot on video, however, one still sees the occasional throwback to a golden age of accidental surrealism.

As Nancy Joyce Peters wrote in the book *Surrealism and Its Popular Accomplices*:

> After the legitimation comedies and the frauds passed off as "news" have left the air, that is, *late at night and in the dark*, we are likely to find roving our television screens ubiquitous and disquieting figures—vampires, werewolves, mummies, zombies, abortive creations of diabolical doctors, and other masked and mutant beings. Monsters and magical practitioners have always been inseparable from the human imagination, a fact confirmed in ancient civilizations, rites and myths of tribal peoples, folk tales of peasant societies, the fantasies of childhood and the dreams of "civilized" adults. Only the means of expression changes [...].
>
> In poetry, content, especially latent content, is always sovereign over form. Sometimes the maker of a film is quite unaware of the

resonances of the marvelous it emanates. Dream figures of animals appear as regularly as they once did in legends told around fires on starry nights in the past, and their sense of enchantment is not limited to the dialogues concerning radioactive mutation. Transformation into cat, wolf, ape, spider, cobra, alligator, plant, owl, bat, vulture, wasp: an uncannily familiar scenario expressing universal impulses to live outside social regulations prescribed by human law and to recognize deeply felt bonds with earth's other creatures. Here is a potential meeting ground, in film, with the wisdom of non-Western cultures, a hint of a future myth for all humanity which might break the chains of habitual conventions [...].

Under the surface, horror films deal with *essentials*: the exaltation of desire, wishes for the excessive possibility, the truth inhering in the non-rational, and the absolute necessity for transmuting and surpassing present reality. The protagonists are on a quest as authentic as that of a medieval knight or a historic revolutionary. The dreamers are not satisfied. And although the passages of transformation are dangerous, dreamers will change the world [...]. Deprived of love, living a living death, disoriented among the electric rays of the 19th century's magneto apparatus and 20th century weaponry, the monster destroys an alienating world. Portraying in fantasy the images of defiance, negation and revolt, the horror film grants a powerful assent to freedom.[12]

And the films starring Bela Lugosi in particular, perhaps above all others, are overripe with such surrealistic representations of freedom from the knowable and the mundane.

10.

"As has been proved to me after the fact, the definition of Surrealism given in the first Manifesto merely 'retouches' a great traditional saying concerning the necessity of 'breaking through the drumhead of reasoning reason and looking at the hole,' a procedure which will lead to the clarification of symbols that were once mysterious."

–André Breton, "On Surrealism in Its Living Works," 1953

No matter what any critic in 1941 said about *Invisible Ghost*, and no matter whether the film is considered by viewers to be "good" or "bad" today, the fact is that the film is unquestionably unique. That Joseph H. Lewis and Bela Lugosi crossed paths for this one project (one artist on his way up in Hollywood, the other on his tumultuous way down) is fortuitous, as it gave Lugosi the chance to demonstrate that he could pull off a sensitive, sympathetic, nuanced performance even while portraying a serial murderer, and it gave Lewis the chance to demonstrate that he was capable of constructing an effective thriller with his own distinctive *noir* touches even within the confines of a screenplay that makes sense only in the context of dream-logic. Both artists benefited greatly from this too-brief collaboration, and it's unfortunate the two men never worked together again.

> "It is common knowledge that Surrealism saw in it the means of obtaining, most often under conditions of complete relaxation of the mind rather than complete concentration, certain incandescent flashes linking two elements of reality belonging to categories that are so far removed from each other that reason would fail to connect them and that require a momentary suspension of the critical attitude in order for them to be brought together."
>
> –André Breton, "On Surrealism in Its Living Works," 1953

(Endnotes)

1   Gary D. Rhodes, *Lugosi* (Jefferson, North Carolina: McFarland, 1997), xv.
2   Tom Weaver, *Poverty Row Horrors!: Monogram, PRC and Republic Horror Films of the Forties* (Jefferson, North Carolina: McFarland, 1993), 31.
3   André Breton, *Manifestoes of Surrealism* (Ann Arbor: The University of Michigan Press, 1969), 125.
4   Ibid. 13-14.
5   H.P. Lovecraft, *Supernatural Horror in Literature* (New York: Dover, 1973 [1927]), 30.
6   Breton, *Manifestoes of Surrealism*, 15.
7   David Kalat, "Audio Commentary" (prod. David Kalat), *The Strange Woman* (DVD, All Day Entertainment, 2005).
8   Franklin Rosemont, "Lovecraft, Surrealism & Revolution," in Franklin Rosemont (ed.), *Surrealism & Its Popular Accomplices* (San Francisco: City Lights, 1980), 17.
9   "Daughter of Edgar Ulmer" (prod. David Kalat), *The Daughter of Dr. Jekyll* (DVD, All Day Entertainment, 2005).
10 Pierre Fournier, "Dare You See It?," *Monsterpalooza*, No. 1, 2011, 58.
11 "Deanimated: The Invisible Ghost," *Cinema of the World*, Worldscinema.org (accessed June 25, 2012).
12 Nancy Joyce Peters, "Backyard Bombs and Invisible Rays: Horror Movies on Television," in Franklin Rosemont (ed.), *Surrealism & Its Popular Accomplices* (San Francisco: City Lights, 1980), 39-42.

Lugosi the red herring of *Spooks Run Wild*, one of the most enduring of his character types. *(Photo courtesy John Antosiewicz)*

Chapter 3

Spooks Run Wild, Herrings Turn Red, and Magic Beats Monsters

by Gary D. Rhodes

Once Tod Browning's *Dracula* (1931) transformed Bela Lugosi into a star, Hollywood studios typecast him in six roles. He appeared as many different characters in many different films, but still played just six basic roles, over and over again, for the space of a quarter of a century, until his death in 1956.

Lugosi's most famous role, without question, was the supernatural vampire. One can certainly debate about how many times he played the part onscreen. *Dracula* (1931), *The Return of the Vampire* (1944), and *Abbott and Costello Meet Frankenstein* (1948) immediately come to mind. He portrayed an actor *pretending* to be a vampire named Count Mora in *Mark of the Vampire* (1935), and he also portrayed "Bela Lugosi as Dracula," a wax figure come-to-life in the short subject *Hollywood on Parade* (1933). But more important than the number of films was the iconic vampire status Lugosi held during his lifetime, and in the decades that followed.

Secondly, there was Lugosi the Foreigner, who arguably appeared in all of his Hollywood movies, but that category definitely included the roles he played in *Women of All Nations* (1931), *Broadminded* (1931), and *International House* (1933).[1] American audiences had little difficulty accepting him as Middle Eastern or Russian or almost any other kind of

"Other." On a few occasions, Lugosi the Foreigner could be sympathetic or even heroic; *The Black Cat* (1934), *The Return of Chandu* (1934), *The Mystery of the Mary Celeste* (1935, aka *Phantom Ship*), and *The Invisible Ray* (1936) serve as examples. Or he could be cold and distant, as in *Ninotchka* (1939), or even horrifying, as in *Island of Lost Souls* (1933), with his accent being so foreign as to make him spokesperson for Dr. Moreau's man-beasts. Or he could exemplify all of these traditions in a single film, as in his role of Bela the Gypsy in *The Wolf Man* (1941).

Lugosi the Criminal stole, killed, and sometimes pillaged. Here was the scofflaw side of Lugosi the Foreigner, with his roles not only including everyday rogues and criminal masterminds, but also Asian heavies and Nazi fifth columnists. Murder, mail fraud, and various other high crimes and misdemeanors are committed in: *The Best Man Wins* (1935), *Mysterious Mr. Wong* (1935), *Postal Inspector* (1936), *SOS Coast Guard* (1937), *The Dark Eyes of London* (1939, aka *The Human Monster*), *Black Friday* (1940), *The Saint's Double Trouble* (1940), *You'll Find Out* (1940), *Black Dragons* (1942), *Bowery at Midnight* (1942), *Ghosts on the Loose* (1943), and *Genius at Work* (1946).

And then there was Lugosi the Mad Scientist, trying to create new life, sustain old life, take another life over, or just introduce general chaos, domestically or globally. Here are the doctors of *Murders in the Rue Morgue* (1932), *The Raven* (1935), *The Phantom Creeps* (1939), *The Devil Bat* (1940), *The Corpse Vanishes* (1942), *The Ape Man* (1943), *Return of the Ape Man* (1944), *Voodoo Man* (1944), *Zombies on Broadway* (1945), *Mother Riley Meets the Vampire* (1952, aka *Vampire Over London*), *Bela Lugosi Meets a Brooklyn Gorilla* (1952), and *Bride of the Monster* (1955).

Much as Lon Chaney, Jr. portrayed variations of his famous role Lennie from *Of Mice and Men* (1939), Lugosi would at times repeat his characterization of Ygor, the fifth of the six categories. Inaugurating the role in *Son of Frankenstein* (1939), he played Ygor again in *The Ghost of Frankenstein* (1942) and – in terms of the shooting script, insofar as Ygor's brain being inside the Monster's body – in *Frankenstein Meets the Wolf Man* (1943). A few other Lugosi roles invoked Ygor to greater or lesser degrees, particularly those in *The Black Cat* (1941), *The Body Snatcher* (1945), and *The Black Sleep* (1956).

The sixth and final role that Lugosi played was that of the Red Herring, his popular association with the horror genre making him automatically suspicious in all of his post-*Dracula* films. Guilty until proven innocent: that was Lugosi in a number of movies, beginning with Tarneverro in *The Black Camel* (1931), a Charlie Chan mystery. In it, one character admits to being "afraid" of Lugosi's turban wearing "mystic," who seems culpable until the film's climax. Even Chan's boss is convinced that Tarneverro is the right answer to the question of whodunit.

In *The Death Kiss* (1932), Lugosi played film studio executive Joseph Steiner, the prime suspect in the murder of a famous actor. After the mystery is solved, amateur sleuth Franklyn Drew (David Manners) confesses to him, "At first I could have sworn it was you." The following year, in *Night of Terror* (1933), accusations of wrongdoing fall on Lugosi's Degar, yet another turban wearing mystic. "That man has murder in his eyes," one character claims, incorrectly as it happens. Like Tarneverro and Steiner, Degar is innocent, even if the film's plotline and Lugosi's screen past suggest otherwise. The same was true of Lugosi's characters in the serial *The Whispering Shadow* (1933) and in the feature *The Gorilla* (1939). To be Lugosi the Hollywood Star was to forever reside under the shadow of suspicion.

It was no surprise, then, that Lugosi would portray a red herring at Monogram, or that it would also draw upon the aforementioned roles he had portrayed in Hollywood, elements that helped make the red herring seem guilty. Under its original title *Ghosts in the Night*, Phil Rosen directed Lugosi's second Monogram film in early August 1941.[2] By the middle of that month, the project was rechristened *Spooks Run Wild*.[3]

To the extent that *Spooks Run Wild* has spurred much comment, it's usually because the film became the first of two that paired Lugosi with the East Side Kids, the team of Leo Gorcey, Huntz Hall, Bobby Jordan, and others, who were at various times also known as the Dead End Kids and the Bowery Boys. *Spooks Run Wild* has also drawn a minor amount of attention because it utilized one of Carl Foreman's first screenplays (co-written with Charles R. Marion), an early work in a career that would later include *High Noon* (1952) and *The Bridge on the River Kwai* (1957).

And yet, much more can and should be said of *Spooks Run Wild*, a film too often dismissed in Lugosi's canon. Along with comical scenes and malaprop dialogue for the East Side Kids, the film surprisingly gave Lugosi the most developed red herring role of his career, one that operates amid such longstanding generic conventions as fake haunted houses and somnambulism. Here was the essence of American horror entertainment, one that dates to the colonial period: the supernatural is exposed as a fraud.

In *Spooks Run Wild*, supernatural horror functions as a *trompe l'oeil*, a type of cinematic ruse, as the film's real villain is not Lugosi's character, but instead an all-too-human monster, a rapist and a murderer. He is

Nardo (Lugosi) seems to go out of his way to be mistaken for Dracula. *(Photo courtesy John Antosiewicz)*

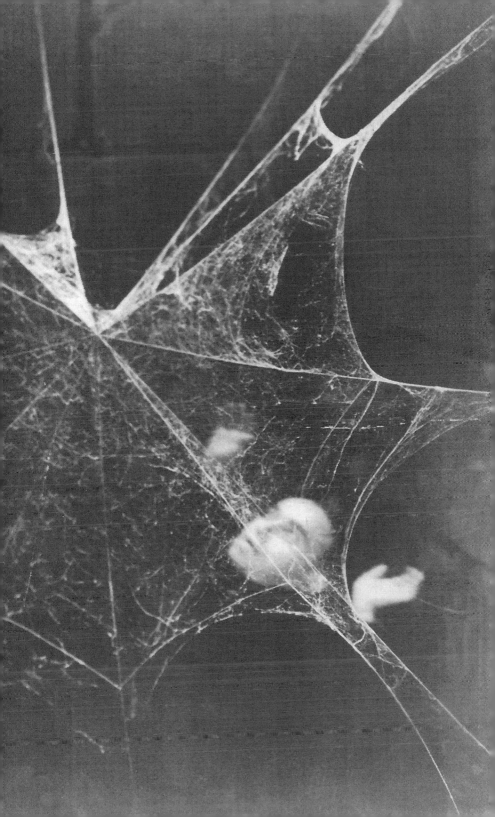

a "maniac," one of the most frightening of the era, in large measure because his crimes are similar to those that appeared with awful regularity in newspapers across America during the 1930s. Given that it was ostensibly a comedy, *Spooks Run Wild* creates an uncomfortable mood, one more troubling and complex than many of Lugosi's other films, including those that featured him as red herrings.

Red Herrings

There is much debate as to why red herrings are called "red herrings." Their narrative purpose is very clear: they intentionally distract us from important issues at hand. But why that specific terminology gained common currency is difficult to determine. After all, no herrings are red. Perhaps the term results from the historical use of kippers to throw hunting dogs off the scent they are pursuing. Or perhaps it dates to a different practice; a text published in 1697 referred to herrings being used to train horses.[4] Whatever its origin, the red herring character had become a popular literary device by the twentieth century, already a longstanding cliché by the time Lugosi starred in *Spooks Run Wild*.

His character Nardo is mistaken for the film's "Monster" primarily because he bears resemblance to screen vampires like Dracula. A store attendant (P.J. Kelly, credited onscreen as "P.J. Kelley") reads a book on the subject authored by Dr. Von Grosch (Dennis Moore), which claims the Monster thirsts "for the flow of bright red blood." Later, Muggs (Leo Gorcey) recites from a different copy of the same book: "In the night he prowls about seeking new victims, and in the daytime he sleeps in a coffin." And then there are other descriptions of the Monster. After meeting Nardo, the store attendant recalls his "glaring eyes and red lips," his "coffins," and his dwarf Luigi (Angelo Rossitto), who looks "like a little black spider." Von Grosch informs us the Monster is "strong" at night. Danny (Bobby Jordan) describes him as a "ghoul" that "sucks the blood out of you." And Muggs explains that it takes "silver bullets" or "blessed iron" to destroy him.

Fulfilling the needs of a red herring, Nardo seems to go out of his way to liken himself to Dracula. He wears evening clothes and a cape; Luigi wears a cape as well. Nardo travels with three crates; one of them is clearly marked a "coffin." At a cemetery gate, he asks in the dark of night: "The City of the Dead... Do they too hear the howling of the frightened dogs," dialogue that recalls Dracula's "The children of the night! What music they make!" Later, he glares down at the unconscious and bedridden Peewee (David Gorcey), an image not dissimilar to the vampire's

Spooky suits of armor appear in many films produced before *Spooks Run Wild*, including in *The Ghost of the White Lady* (Great Northern, 1914).

nighttime visits to Lucy (Frances Dade) and Mina (Helen Chandler) in Tod Browning's *Dracula*. And at one point, he advances on Skinny (Donald Haines) and Scruno (Ernest "Sunshine Sammy" Morrison) in an extremely menacing fashion, accentuated by lighting that makes him seem all the more, well, monstrous.

Nardo seems content to act like the Monster in other scenes as well. With a guilty look on his face, he reads a newspaper headline about the Monster's kill-spree. Once he discovers the East Side Kids have been reading Von Grosch's book, he angrily throws it aside, declaring to his assistant, "Luigi, our guests must not leave the house!" He tries to convince Muggs that he "sees not things as they are," but rather as his "imagination paints them." He sneaks up on Scruno and smiles, rather than attempting to reassure him that he means no harm. This is all in addition to Nardo's inexplicable "knowledge of medicine," to the extent that he has a "mild sedative" on hand ready to inject into Peewee.

But *Spooks Run Wild* features more red herrings than just Nardo, including the long-vacant and cobweb-filled Billings estate. "This is a very old house," Nardo tells the East Side Kids, "and in some respects a very strange one." Billings was murdered at home, with Danny and Muggs

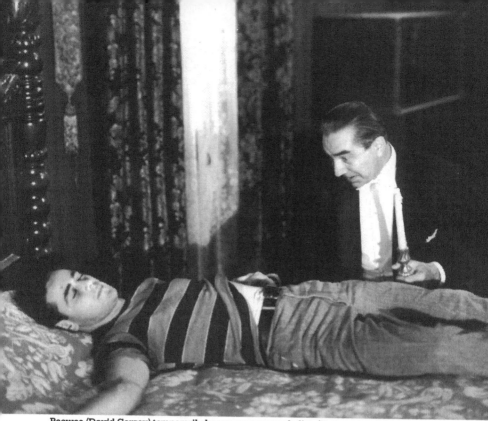

Peewee (David Gorcey) temporarily becomes a somnambulist. *(Photo courtesy John Antosiewicz)*

sharing the bedroom where the crime occurred. The door to another bedroom mysteriously locks and unlocks itself. And a secret underground passage contains a human skeleton for no apparent reason.

Even individual members of the East Side Kids end up providing the potential for scares. The Billings home contains no less than four suits of armor, with Muggs getting inside one of them.[5] Holding a candelabra, Muggs-in-armor approaches Skinny and Scruno without identifying himself. The two are clearly afraid, with Scruno dubbing the ghostly automaton "Mr. Tin Man." After Muggs finally reveals himself, Scruno admits, "You liked to scared us to death." While Muggs is still in costume, a second animated suit of armor appears. This time it's Glimpy (Huntz Hall), who temporarily withholds his identity as well.

Haunted suits of armor are one of the oldest tropes in horror entertainment, dating to Matthew Gregory Lewis' stage play *The Castle Spectre*, first performed in London in 1797 and then staged repeatedly in America during the early nineteenth century.[6] Jeffrey N. Cox has called it the "quintessential Gothic drama."[7] In its narrative, the servants are "fully persuaded" that the ghost of a deceased Earl "wanders every night through the long galleries, and parades the old towers and dreary halls which abound" at the "melancholy mansion."

Scene I of Act II takes place in the Armory, with suits of armor "arranged on both sides upon Pedestals, with the Names of their Possessors written under each." The character Motley convinces Percy to dress in the Earl's "complete armour [sic]," in order to eavesdrop on other characters "unobserved." Motley takes down the armor and says, "Here's the helmet – the gauntlets – the shield. So now, take the truncheon in your hand, and there we have you armed cap-a-pee." After encountering the ghostly (but still very much human) suit of armor, one character confesses, "To be frightened out of my wits by night, and thumped and bumped about by day, is not likely to put one in the best humor."

Over a century later, Paul Dickey and Charles W. Goddard's play *The Ghost Breaker* opened on Broadway in 1913. Its lead American character (played by H.B. Warner) proves there is no real ghost in an old European castle, only a villain pretending to be supernatural.[8] Critic Burns Mantle wrote, "Here the shadows are long and dark, the ghosts weird and mysteriously articulate. In the corners stand numerous shades in full suits of armor."[9] One of them, "apparently inanimate, comes to life, lays about with a broad sword, receives the discharge from the hero's pistol without serious inconvenience, but ultimately takes a quick plunge to a cold and watery death through a swinging trap [door] arranged for innocent intruders."[10]

In 1914, H.B. Warner reprised his role for Lasky's five-reel film adaptation of *The Ghost Breaker*. Together with his African-American servant Rusty (J.W. Burton), Jarvis reveals the castle ghosts are fakes, led by a Duke who tries to scare away interlopers so that he can secretly search for a hidden treasure.[11] Along with the film's villain, Rusty "is made to disguise himself in a suit of ancient armor." *Variety* complained, "The 'bit' has no purpose in the film story, introduced in a vain effort to inject comedy."[12] When *The Ghost Breaker* was remade with Wallace Reid in 1922, the suit of armor returned.[13] The animated prop appeared in subsequent films as well, including *Get that Girl* (1932), *Mark of the Vampire* and *The Ghost Breakers* (1940).

Allusions to Dracula and mysterious suits of armor are not the only horror traditions cited in *Spooks Run Wild*. Consider the character Peewee: though wounded and sedated, he opens his eyes and begins sleepwalking, leaving Scruno to believe he has become a "zombie." For much of the film, the somnambulistic Peewee perambulates throughout the home, eventually returning safely to his bed. Here the plot invokes a lengthy tradition of literary sleep-walkers. As Eric G. Wilson has noted, "During the Romantic period, writers on both sides of the Atlantic explored the sleepwalker as a merger of holi-ness and horror."[14]

One of the earliest to do so was Charles Brockden Brown. Born in Philadelphia in 1771, Brown became America's first great novelist.[15] The title character of his *Edgar Huntly* (1799) suffers from sleepwalking. Dis-cussing the novel, Justine S. Murison observed that:

> somnambulism has a way of up-setting common beliefs that the mind controlled the body: the waking self could be completely absent or histrionically present in the behavior of the sleepwalker, neither of which attests to the presence of mind.[16]

Brown returned to the topic in his 1805 short story *Somnambulism*, in which the narrator believes he may have committed the grisly murder of his lover and her father while in a dreamlike state. Later tales of this type included Henry Cockton's *Sylvester Sound, the Somnambulist*, se-rialized in *Magazine for the Millions* in 1844. Its phantasmal "spirit" is revealed to be a sleepwalker. Esther

Lugosi's Nardo is actually one of the best magicians in America, so famous the East Side Kids don't recognize him. *(Photo courtesy John Antosiewicz)*

Serle Kenneth used a similar plot device in her short story *The Haunted Chamber* (1879).[17]

Nineteenth-century newspapers commonly reported on the activities of real somnambulists. One rode a bicycle in her sleep; another awoke in an undertaker's coffin with no memory of having gotten inside it.[18] In 1882, a jailed murderer allegedly recreated his "dreadful crime" each night while asleep in his cell.[19] Seven years later, a man used sleepwalking as his excuse for having attempted to "outrage" a fifteen-year old girl in her own bedroom.[20] And, in an echo of fictional literature, a "ghost" in Illinois in 1894 was exposed as a harmless somnambulist.[21]

The most famous nineteenth-century sleepwalker was Jane C. Rider, the "Springfield Somnambulist." While slumbering, she would get up and sew in the dark. She also prepared dinners. When members of the household encouraged her to return to bed, she insisted – with her eyes still closed – that it was daytime. At times, she sleepwalked with her eyes wide open, as Peewee does in *Spooks Run Wild*. And once Rider was awake, like Peewee, she had no memory of her nighttime activities. The press reported on her "paroxysms" at length in 1834, judging them to be as authentic as they were extraordinary.[22]

Robert Wiene's *The Cabinet of Dr. Caligari/Das Cabinet des Dr Caligari* (1920) remains the most famous example of a screen somnambulist. However, many earlier moving pictures had depicted sleepwalkers, ranging from Essanay's *The Somnambulist* (1908) to Thanhouser's *The Somnambulist* (1914). A number of these films drew upon nonfiction accounts. For example, both Lubin and American Mutoscope and Biograph distributed the British-made film *The Somnambulist* (1904), which Lubin retitled *The Sleepwalker's Dream*. It featured a woman who rises out of her bed and begins walking "as though in a trance." She makes her way over adjacent rooftops until, "missing her footing, she is violently thrown to the ground, fifty feet below." A police officer discovers her "extinct" body, the story recalling many deaths and injuries sustained by somnambulists in the nineteenth century.[23] But then, an edit returns her to her boudoir, where she is still asleep. The events have only been "a dream, a hideous nightmare."[24] The film's story was a trick.

Magic

Though mistaken for the Monster, Nardo is actually one of the best magicians in America, so famous, in fact, that none of the characters recognize him. He and Luigi have traveled to the Billings estate in order to "practice some new routines." At the end of *Spooks Run Wild*, Nardo offers an impromptu performance, including his "famous disappearing cabinet." That the East Side Kids initially took him for a villain makes sense, not only because of his similarity to Dracula, but also because magicians had long been involved in a fascinating interplay with the supernatural.

During the late nineteenth century, the celebrity magician became a "wizard arrayed against wizardry, an exposer of 'supernatural humbugs,'" as Leigh Eric Schmidt has written.[25] For example, Harry Kellar (originally Keller) became a magician after having travelled with the Davenport Brothers, who promoted themselves as genuine mediums. In 1885, Kellar announced, "It is the mediumistic tricks I am bent on exposing."[26] He did so onstage, in the press, and even at court.[27] In 1893, Herrmann the Great, who by that time had performed in America for three decades, informed a journalist, "I have never seen a spiritualistic manifestation that I could not reproduce through perfectly natural means."[28] In the early twentieth century, Harry Houdini famously pursued the same cause.

Magicians not only exposed spiritualists, but also performed some of their tricks. Simone Natale has written:

> The audience expected to find in these shows phenomena similar to those observed at a spiritualist séance, but within a different interpretative framework: in contrast to mediums, in fact, magicians openly admitted that their feats were the result of illusion and trickery, rather than of supernatural agency."[29]

During the 1860s, for example, the "Great Wizard" Robert Heller promised illusions that surpassed any performed by "legitimate conjurors or illegitimate spiritualists."[30] His wife gave "second-sight" performances onstage, but Heller made clear that the couple possessed no supernatural powers, adding, "What I do is solely by the aid of sleight of hand and scientific appliances ... There is no such thing as a real ghost."[31]

Somewhat paradoxically, though, illusionists embraced publicity that depicted the supernatural. As Fred Nadis has observed, "Magicians wished to offer 'shows of wonder' that fulfilled the audience's nostalgia while yet assuring audiences that miracles, ultimately, had no place in the modern world."[32] Audiences knew that Herrmann the Great was a professional magician, but he still found himself compared to Satan.[33] Kellar's posters regularly featured images of devils and ghosts. The same was true of his successor Howard Thurston. A circa 1899 poster for Helman the Great (aka H. Morgan Robinson) pictured him in a graveyard with devils and bats; its text pronounced him the "Napoleon of Necromancy."[34] And even with his reputation for being "The Handcuff King," Houdini was occasionally described as a "necromancer" and "wizard."[35]

Much the same is true of Nardo. Just before his career is exposed, Nardo draws upon the intersecting traditions of horror and magic, presenting the illusion of Muggs' severed head on a platter inside a darkened room. The grisly image dates to Salome's evil request for John the Baptist's head; it gained renewed currency due to the invention of the guillotine. From the time of the American Civil War, illusionists regularly staged decapitations to thrill and chill their audiences.[36] As early as 1864, for example, a magician named Simmons presented a "feat of decapitation" in which his "own head [was] removed and conveniently carried under his arm."[37] Other magicians made heads float in the air after being cut off, as Muggs' head seems to do in *Spooks Run Wild*.[38] Others displayed these heads on platters, as Nardo also does with Muggs'.[39]

Severed heads onscreen date to the earliest days of cinema, including in the very first horror-themed film ever made. In August of 1895, Alfred Clark and William Heise made *Execution of Mary, Queen of Scots*, which used "stop-motion substitution" to show the decapitation of its title character by the blow of an axe.[40] Without moving the camera, the filmmakers replaced the actor portraying Mary with a dummy before shooting the decapitation. The two images were thus spliced together, making the execution appear to take place in a single, continuous shot.[41] Here was the first special effect in the history of the cinema: the same cut altered the film and Mary's body.

Cinematic tricks and special effects became a new kind of magic, of course, famously explored by early filmmakers like Georges Méliès and Segundo de Chomón. Tod Browning became a key exponent of screen trickery in Hollywood, including in *Mark of the Vampire*. As already mentioned, Lugosi's character in that film is not a vampire, nor is the character Luna (Carroll Borland): both are actors hired to help catch a murderer. However, some of their actions definitely seem to be supernatural, including when no other characters are watching them. They walk through a spider web without disturbing it, for example. Count Mora twice transforms from bat to human form. Luna's vampiric displays are even more impressive: she flies down to the castle floor with enormous wings, as if existing in a transitional state between bat and human. Here are tricks meant to fool the audience, to make Count Mora and Luna convincing red herrings.

Given his career as a magician, some of Nardo's actions are logical. He escapes from a locked room, as well as from bound ropes; presumably he has talents similar to Houdini. But other aspects of Nardo's behavior are almost as inexplicable as those of Count Mora and Luna, including (as already noted) his menacing advances on the East Side Kids. He claims that Mariana Billings was "beautiful" when he sees her grave, but later admits he was "never in this house until tonight." Whether Mariana Billings ever existed is in question, as her "grave" is a fake; underneath its headstone is an entrance to a secret passageway. And when the cemetery caretaker fires at Nardo and Luigi, they vanish into thin air. The trick might be one they perform successfully onstage, but how they do it without advance preparation during the middle of the night in a graveyard is difficult to justify.

Stranger still are numerous tricks that occur even when Nardo isn't nearby. A white spider – the "ghost of the black widow" – descends near Scruno. Muggs sees a skull inside a tobacco canister, but it disappears before the other East Side Kids see it. The same canister later moves of its own accord across a table, frightening Scruno when the others aren't present. The basic trick has deep roots, appearing onscreen at least as early as Georges Méliès' *Le Revenant* (1903), distributed in America in 1903 under the title *The Apparition, or Mr. Jones' Comical Experience with a Ghost*.[42] One of the most charming ghost films of the period, it features a character disturbed by a candle that moves back-and-forth across a table without human assistance.[43] The same trick reappeared in later films like *Hold That Ghost* (1941) with Abbott and Costello. Released over two months before *Spooks Run Wild*, the film might have inspired Carl Foreman and Charles R. Marion, whose tricks and red herrings converged with an interest in real monsters.

Human Monsters

Spooks Run Wild's twist ending divulges its biggest trick: the Monster is actually Dr. Von Grosch, who arrives in town just after Nardo.[44] His name and attire echo Professor Van Helsing (Edward Van Sloan) in Browning's *Dracula*, the reference being all the more pronounced given Nardo's similarities to Dracula. But that's another deception. Von Grosch is a human monster, a "dangerous maniac." He not only kills his victims, but also commits "inhuman" sex crimes as well. As the worried Mayor (Jack Carr) asks the Constable (Guy Wilkerson), "What kind of proof do you want... some little girl murdered out in the woods?"

Human monsters are plentiful in films prior to *Spooks Run Wild*, of

This is not the human monster you are looking for. *(Photo courtesy of Bill Chase)*

course. In fact, before Lugosi ever starred in the Monogram Nine, the company issued his British-made film *The Dark Eyes of London* (1939) in America under the title *The Human Monster* (1940). In it, Lugosi plays a vicious character that murders innocent victims in order to collect on their life insurance policies. Non-Lugosi horror movies also relied on such characters, time and again, among them the insane husbands in *Almost Married* (1932) and *Murders in the Zoo* (1932).

Lust drives many of these characters. Count Zaroff (Leslie Banks) in *The Most Dangerous Game* (1932) opines, "Hunt first the enemy, then the woman … Kill, then love. When you know that, you will have known ecstasy." The Moon Killer (Preston Foster) in *Doctor X* (1932) seems to be a cannibalistic madman who murders to satisfy his "desires" (though the film's conclusion reveals his real intent to be otherwise)[45] Most explicit of all is Buckley (Ted Edwards) in *Maniac* (1934, aka *Sex Maniac*), who goes insane after being injected with an experimental formula. In what was probably the most graphic onscreen assault of the period, he gropes a partially nude woman. And yet, none of these screen villains are sex-crazed serial killers.

By contrast, the American press of the 1930s is replete with examples of the type that likely inspired *Spooks Run Wild*.[46] In the spring of 1937, the *Chicago Tribune* reported on an "unusual wave of sex crimes" that "terrorized law-abiding citizenry and [gave] anxiety to law enforcement authority" in New York, Brooklyn, Buffalo, Detroit, West Chester, and Cincinnati.[47] To describe the assailants, journalists used terminology that would later be heard in *Spooks Run Wild*, specifically "maniac."[48] Language in these articles also painted them as monsters that were human, but just barely. In 1938, authorities in Washington, D.C., for example, attempted to find a "sex maniac" with "long ape-like arms."[49]

Some of these sex maniacs were responsible for crime sprees. In 1935, Chicago police undertook a "frantic hunt" for a "man sought in a series of sadistic attacks on several women."[50] Two years later, the bodies of three small girls were found near Inglewood, California. Two of them had been raped. All three had been strangled to death.[51] Then, in 1941, the press reported on the "sex killings of a score of women that baffled officers in Washington and New York for several months." Convicted murderer Jarvis T.R. Catoe admitted, "I don't know how many gals I done in," adding, "Maybe it was eight... nine... or ten. But I recollect I done 'em, because I got a burning desire. It was a sort of like a spell come all over me." He confessed that he "raped them and strangled them."[52]

In some respects, Dr. Von Grosch's crimes are reminiscent of Catoe's, whose murders began in 1938, but in other ways they are quite different. Unlike Catoe, Von Grosch is apparently well educated. He is the author of the book on the Monster, having created a fictitious, supernatural character to pursue as a fiendishly clever cover for his crimes and as an alibi for being in the same vicinity when they happen. Von Grosch trades on his name – well known enough that a rural store attendant has heard of him – to commit "outrages" (another term common in the period) on woman after woman. He is, in other words, a sex fiend *and* a serial killer.

During the film's climax, Von Grosch's urges do come over him "sort of like a spell." Even though he knows that several characters are at the Billings home, he lures Linda (Dorothy Short) to that very location, asking that she follow his "orders to the letter." Once there, he locks the door to their room, takes off his glasses, and advances on her. Closeups of their faces in partial darkness underscore the revelation that he is the

The final gag in *Spooks Run Wild* relies on Muggs (Leo Gorcey) and Nardo (Lugosi).
(Photo courtesy John Antosiewicz)

film's real villain. Linda begins screaming as he grabs her. When Von Grosch hears the East Side Kids pounding on the door, he repeatedly fires at it with his gun, but makes no effort to escape. After he's out of bullets, he resumes groping Linda, more interested in her body than anything else. Muggs breaks into the room and saves the day, finally putting an end to Von Grosch's reign of terror.

Conclusion

Following a preview in early October 1941, Monogram released *Spooks Run Wild* near the end of the same month, just in time for Halloween.[53] Critical reviews varied. *Daily Variety:* "Monogram has a neat little program picture, with plenty of action and plenty of laughs."[54] *Film Daily:* "Horror and comedy neatly mixed in pic that should find favor as supporting film fare."[55] *Motion Picture Daily:* "The basic idea was a sound one, but the story runs wild too. ... The preview audience was in commotion most of the time, laughing both at and with the picture."[56] *Motion Picture Herald:* "*Spooks Run Wild* turns out to be a burlesque on horror pictures. It wasn't meant to be. ... There is jerky direction by Phil Rosen of poorly presented script material."[57]

It is the latter, negative view that became entrenched in the ensuing decades. But whatever the film's limitations, it weaves a tapestry of earlier horror and comedy conventions, some dating back nearly 150 years, others of a more recent vintage. For example, as the film ends, Muggs enters Nardo's disappearing cabinet, hoping to reappear with a beautiful woman in his arms. When the curtain reopens, he is unknowingly kissing Scruno, a variation on a racist scene that appeared in the cinema as early as Edwin S. Porter's *What Happened in the Tunnel* (1903).

And then there is the fact that *Spooks Run Wild* was in one respect prescient, presenting Lugosi as a magician, a role he would play again in the film *Scared to Death* (1946), as well as onstage at repeated live appearances in the post-war period. These performances culminated in the "Bela Lugosi Horror and Magic Show" in 1950-1951, as well as on the *You Asked for It* television program in 1953.[58] The former featured a trick called "Lugosi and the Bloody Guillotine"; the latter presented a cabinet illusion in which a woman disappeared.

But however much *Spooks Run Wild* connects to Lugosi's career and the history of horror, it was unique in its ominous portrayal of a sex-crazed killer, one as intelligent as he is dangerous. And one that was starkly different than any of the six roles Lugosi repeatedly played. It would take Hollywood many years to produce another quite like him. The reason to appreciate *Spooks Run Wild* might well not be Lugosi or the East Side Kids, but rather Von Grosch, a character made all the more disturbing because he appears not in a drama, but in a comedy.

(Endnotes)

1 From his first appearance on the American stage, Bela Lugosi became the exotic foreigner, his dark features and thick accent transforming him into the Other. Though the stories and roles would vary, Lugosi the Foreigner appeared before audiences repeatedly, including in such plays as *The Red Poppy* (1922), *Arabesque* (1925), *Open House* (1925), and *The Devil in the Cheese* (1926). The same was true of such silent films as *The Silent Command* (1923), *The Rejected Woman* (1924), and *Daughters Who Pay* (1926). The dawn of the talkie even more strongly positioned Lugosi as the Foreigner. He could be vaguely coded as Indian (*The Thirteenth Chair* of 1929), Arabic (*Renegades* in 1930), or Italian (*Oh, for a Man* in 1930).

2 "13 New Pictures Start in Hollywood Studios," *Film Daily*, August 5, 1941, 11.

3 "Title Changes," *Daily Variety*, August 15, 1941, 6.

4 Robert Scott Ross, "Popularization of 'redherring' by English political agitator William Cobbett," *Comments on Etymology*, vol. 38, no. 1-2, (Oct./Nov. 2008), 62-69.

5 The previous year, Muggs had pretended to be a ghost in the film *Boys of the City* (1940).

6 M. Susan Anthony, *Gothic Plays and American Society, 1794-1830* (Jefferson, NC: McFarland, 2008), 6.

7 Jeffrey N. Cox, "Introduction," in *Seven Gothic Dramas, 1789-1825*, edited by Jeffrey N. Cox (Athens, Ohio: Ohio University Press, 1992), 40.

8 "H. B. Warner in *The Ghost Breaker*," *The Billboard*, March 15, 1913, 4.

9   Burns Mantle, "*The Ghost Breaker*, a Medley of Oo-oo! Hist! Zip! Bang!", *Chicago Tribune*, March 9, 1913, B1.

10   "*The Ghost Breaker* at Lyceum Theatre," *New York Times* March 5, 1913, 17.

11   "*The Ghost Breaker*," *New York Dramatic Mirror*, December 9, 1914, 38.

12   "*The Ghost Breaker*," *Variety*, December 12, 1914, 28.

13   "*The Man on the Balcony* Opens at Garrick; Gertrude Hoffmann Dances at the Belasco," *Washington Post*, October 30, 1922, 5.

14   Wilson, 329.

15   Punter, 166.

16   Justine S. Murison, "The Tyranny of Sleep: Somnambulism, Moral Citizenship, and Charles Brockden Brown's *Edgar Huntly*," *Early American Literature*, Vol. 44, No. 2 (2009), 247.

17   Esther Serle Kenneth, "The Haunted Chamber," *Ballou's Monthly Magazine*, August 1879, 140.

18   "Rode Bicycle in Sleep," *New York Times*, October 22, 1904, 1; "Somnambulist Asleep in Coffin," *New York Times*, November 7, 1905, 6.

19   "Murder Will Out," *The National Police Gazette*, November 25, 1882, 3.

20   "A Fiend's Shocking Act," *Washington Post*, August 13, 1889, 1.

21   "Evanston's Ghost Is Identified," *Chicago Tribune*, November 24, 1894, 6.

22   See, for example: "The Springfield Somnambulist," *Spirit of the Age and Journal of Humanity*, March 13, 1834, 1; L.W. Belden, "An Account of Jane C. Rider, the Springfield Somnambulist," *The Boston Medical and Surgical Journal*, September 10, 1834, 1.

23   Examples include "Fatal Case of Somnambulism," *Wheeling Register* (Wheeling, West Virginia), December 19, 1878, 1; "A Somnambulist's Fall," *New York Times*, July 16, 1883, 12; "A Somnambulist's Fall," *New York Times*, October 31, 1885, 4; "A Somnambulist's Fatal Fall," *New York Times*, October 28, 1889, 9; "A Somnambulist's Fall," *New York Times*, March 17, 1890, 1; "A Somnambulist's Fall from a Roof," *New York Times*, October 24, 1895, 9; "Somnambulist Kills Himself," *New York Times*, July 8, 1896, 5; "Somnambulist's Fall Proves Fatal," *Washington Post*, June 25, 1897, 10; "Fall of Three Stories Wakens a Somnambulist," *Chicago Tribune*, May 13, 1901, 1; "Somnambulist Badly Hurt," *Washington Post*, August 9, 1904.

24   *Lubin's Films* (Philadelphia: Lubin, May 1905), 10. Available in *A Guide to Motion Picture Catalogs by American Producers and Distributors, 1894-1908: A Microfilm Edition* (New Brunswick: Rutgers University Press, 1985), Reel 3.

25   Leigh Eric Schmidt, "From Demon Possession to Magic Show: Ventriloquism, Religion, and the Enlightenment," *Church History*, Vol. 67, No. 2 (June 1998), 275.

26   "The Tricks of Mediums," *Chicago Tribune*, April 24, 1885, 10.

27   "Kellar Knew It All," *New York Times*, June 25, 1888, 2; "The Tricks of Mediums," *Chicago Tribune*, April 24, 1885, 10; "Exposing the Medium," *Chicago Tribune*, February 26, 1890, 3.

28   A. Herrmann, "The Tricks of Indian Jugglers and of Spiritualists," *Current Literature*, January-April, 1893, 83.

29   Simone Natale, "Specters of the Mind: Ghosts, Illusion, and Exposure in Paul Leni's *The Cat and the Canary*," in *Cinematic Ghosts: Haunting and Spectrality from Silent Cinema to the Digital Era*, edited by Murray Leeder (New York: Bloomsbury Academic, 2015), 64.

30   Advertisement, *New York Clipper*, November 5, 1864. For more information on Robert Heller, see "Our Dramatic Portrait Gallery," *New York Clipper*, October 22, 1864, 220.

31   "Heller and the Devil," *Washington Post*, November 16, 1878, 1.

32   Nadis, 115. For more information on Helman the Great, see *The Daily Republican* (Monongahela, Pennsylvania), April 8, 1896, 1.

33   "The First Night of M. Hermann [*sic*]," *Chicago Tribune*, April 1, 1862, 04.

34   Noel Daniel, editor, *Magic, 1400s-1950s* (Cologne, Germany: Taschen, 2009), 242.

35   See "No Sweat-Box in His," *Los Angeles Times*, August 15, 1899, 13.

36   See, for example: "City Summary," *New York Clipper*, May 11, 1878, 54; Advertisement, *New York Clipper*, November 19, 1881, 578; "Illinois," *New York Clipper*, December 14, 1889, 669; "Pennsylvania," *New York Clipper*, November 9, 1895, 567; "Illinois," *New York Clipper*, March 24, 1900, 86; "Pennsylvania," *New York Clipper*, January 23, 1904,

1142.

37   "Miscellaneous," *New York Clipper*, March 5, 1864, 374.

38   See, for example: Advertisement, *New York Clipper*, April 27, 1867, 22; "Circuses," *New York Clipper*, August 15, 1874, 159.

39   "Reminiscences of Jeppe and Fanny Delano," *New York Clipper*, December 25,1915, 8.

40   *The Execution of Mary, Queen of Scots* is available on the DVD boxed set *Edison: The Invention of the Movies* (New York: Kino, 2005).

41   Charles Musser, *The Emergence of Cinema: The American Screen to 1907* (Berkeley, University of California), 86-87.

42   *Supplement No. 6, Geo. Méliès of Paris* (New York: Star Films, 1903). Available in *A Guide to Motion Picture Catalogs by American Producers and Distributors, 1894-1908: A Microfilm Edition*, Reel 4.

43   A copy of *The Apparition, or Mr. Jones' Comical Experience with a Ghost* appears under the title *Le Revenant* on the DVD boxed set *Georges Méliès: First Wizard of Cinema* (Los Angeles: Flicker Alley, 2008).

44   One could argue that Dr. Von Grosch is not the film's only villain. The cemetery care taker shoots at Nardo without even giving him a chance to answer the question, "What are you doing here?" Later he "takes a pot shot" at the East Side Kids immediately after yelling "Stop!" His flimsy excuse, which the Constable accepts without question: "Can't have anyone prowling around in the dead of night, you know." Though he is only shooting buckshot, the caretaker seems dangerously trigger-happy.

45   The conclusion of *Doctor X* reveals the Moon Killer's true motivation: he needs human skin for his experiments on "synthetic flesh."

46   See, for example: "Girl-Killer Described," *Los Angeles Times*, December 1, 1935, "Ex-Convicts Rounded Up In Brickbat Murders Here," *Los Angeles Times*, April 7, 1937, A2: 1; "Pennsylvania Sex Killer Is Sentenced to Chair," *Washington Post*, April 13, 1937, 4; "4 year Old Girl Raped and Slain New N. Y. Beach," *Chicago Tribune*, August 14, 1937, 5; "All Park Loiterers Rounded Up in Search for Slasher of Coed," *Washington Post*, October 18, 1937, 1; "Sift Mass of Clews for Sex Killer," *Chicago Tribune*, May 28, 1938, 1; "Sex Maniac Confesses Killing Girl, 8," *Washington Post*, September 12, 1938, X22; "Louisiana Mob of 1,000 Lynches Boy as Sex Killer," *Washington Post*, October 14, 1938, X1; "Lures Man to Home and Sets Him Afire: Suspected Sex Maniac Causes Death of Jersey Plumber," *New York Times*, January 28, 1939, 3; "$7,500 Bounty on Killer," *New York Times*, May 9, 1940, 19.

47   "Victims of a Sex-Crime Wave," *Chicago Tribune*, May 2, 1937, G7.

48   See, for example: "Girl, 16, Feared Slain, Hidden by Sex Maniac," *Washington Post*, February 13, 1937, 3; "Victim Outwits Moron Posing in Woman's Dress," *Chicago Tribune*, April 3, 1937, 15; "Hunt Maniac In Double Slaying at Los Angeles," *Chicago Tribune*, April 6, 1937, 7; "Sex-Crazed Maniac Accused of 2 Attacks," *Atlanta World*, July 20, 1937, 1; "Man Resembling Assailant of Coed Attacks 2nd Girl," *Washington Post*, October 26, 1937, 1; "Maniac Hunted as Sex Slayer of Young Co-Ed," *Chicago Tribune*, March 29, 1940, 3.

49   "Police Hunting 'Ape-Man' Here as Sex Maniac," *Washington Post*, December 10, 1938, X1.

50   "Suspect Held as Sex Maniac Freed on Alibi," *Washington Post*, September 22, 1935, 3.

51   "Crime," *Chicago Tribune*, July 4, 1937, 8.

52   "D.C. Sex-Killer Describes Early Murder Tendencies," *Chicago Defender*, September 6, 1941, 1.

53   "*Spooks* Previewing," *Daily Variety*, October 2, 1941, 1.

54   "*Spooks Run Wild*," *Daily Variety*, October 6, 1941, 3.

55   "*Spooks Run Wild*," *Film Daily*, October 9, 1941, 8.

56   Vance King, "*Spooks Run Wild*," *Motion Picture Daily*, October 7, 1941, 6.

57   "*Spooks Run Wild*," *Motion Picture Herald*, October 11, 1941, 306.

58   For more information, see Gary D. Rhodes and Bill Kaffenberger, *No Traveler Returns: The Lost Years of Bela Lugosi* (Duncan, OK: BearManor Media, 2012), 286-305.

Bela Lugosi plans his typical deviltry in this publicity still from *Black Dragons*, a political thriller designed to tap into primal fears magnified by the recent bombing of Pearl Harbor. *(Photo courtesy of Bill Chase)*

Chapter 4

Black Dragons: Postmodern Paranoia, Wartime Racism, Celluloid Propaganda, and the Evolution of the Cinema of Hysteria

by Robert Guffey

ALIEN JAP IN STOCKTON SLAIN
Murder Similar To Previous Slaying

STOCKTON, Feb. 20. (AP)—Shigemasa (Frank) Yoshioka, 43, an alien Japanese, was shot to death today in the rooming house he operated.

Roomers said they heard the bell at the street door ring several times before dawn. Yoshioka responded to the ring and could be heard leading the caller to a vacant room.

Then two shots were fired, and the roomers heard someone running down the hall and stairway to the street.

Police Captain James C. Dewey said there was no witness to the slaying, which followed the pattern a gunman used in killing J. Kino, Japanese alien, Jan. 26.

In neither case, Capt. Dewey said, was there any indication of robbery, nor could burglary have been a motive.

Mrs. Yoshioka said she knew of no enemies her husband might have had.

—1942 newspaper article, reprinted in *Wartime Hysteria:*
The Role of the Press in the Removal of 110,000 Persons of Japanese
Ancestry During World War II, a collection of actual newspaper and magazines
articles compiled by the Japanese American Curriculum Project (1973)

In the early 1990s the experimental Los Angeles novelist Steve Erickson began writing about a hitherto unknown genre of cinema he calls "the Cinema of Hysteria." I think the first time I came across the phrase was in Erickson's *L.A. Weekly* review of David Lynch's 1992 film *Twin Peaks: Fire Walk with Me*. The review seemed (and this is true of a lot of Erickson's nonfiction, particularly his movie reviews) bifurcated. He hated the movie. He loved the movie. Love? Hate? Neither of these terms matter when it comes to the Cinema of Hysteria.

I can't explain exactly why, but the second I saw the phrase in print I somehow knew what Erickson meant without having it defined for me. (I don't believe Erickson ever got around to actually defining the term in that review.) I next saw the phrase in Erickson's 1996 novel *Amnesiascope*. At one point the main character, Erickson himself, lists various examples of the Cinema of Hysteria without, again, offering a concrete definition: *In a Lonely Place, The Shanghai Gesture, Bride of Frankenstein, A Place in the Sun, Gilda, Gun Crazy, Vertigo, One-Eyed Jacks, Splendor in the Grass, The Fountainhead, The Manchurian Candidate*, and *Pinocchio*.

If I *thought* I knew what the phrase meant before, the second I saw this eclectic list I was now certain I was on Erickson's wavelength. But who can know for sure? I don't know the man.

The truth is, I'm just going to hijack the phrase and employ it for my own purposes.

This was the first time I had felt outright hostility from a Caucasian. Looking back, it is easy enough to explain. Public attitudes toward the Japanese in California were shifting rapidly. In the first few months of the Pacific war, America was on the run. Tolerance had turned to distrust and irrational fear. The hundred-year-old tradition of anti-Orientalism on the west coast soon resurfaced, more vicious than ever. Its results became clear about a month later, when we were told to make our third and final move…
—Jeanne Wakatsuki Houston & James D. Houston,
from Chapter 2 of *Farewell to Manzinar*, 1973[1]

Imagine you're living in the United States of America in the early morning hours of December 7th, 1941. There are rumblings of war on

Bela Lugosi murders one of his numerous victims (Japanese saboteurs disguised as Caucasian Americans) in this bizarre—and purposely befuddling—mélange of science fiction, horror and espionage tropes. *(Photo courtesy of Bill Chase)*

the horizon, but you pay no attention to them. War is not a popular notion in the States. No real American would ever stand for it. After all, why should we send our sons and brothers and husbands to die in a European war in which the U.S. has no personal stakes?

The question becomes moot when, at precisely 7:48 A.M. Pacific Standard time, 353 Japanese aircraft attack the United States naval base at Pearl Harbor, Hawaii, resulting in the deaths of over 2,300 Americans, including dozens of civilians.

Suddenly, the unthinkable war is now not only thinkable, it's desirable. Formerly blasé Americans are now volunteering to join the military. Some of them are in the streets, hunting for blood and vengeance.

And one of them approaches his producer at Monogram Studios located at 4376 Sunset Drive and says, "Sam, have I got an idea for ya… it'll be a real money maker… trust me…."

From "Dancing in the Dark," Steve Erickson's review of Darren Aronofsky's film, *Black Swan* (2010), a cinematic tone poem that appropriates the familiar tropes of a horror film—lycanthropy, self-mutilation, murder, madness, suicide—to tell the tale of an obsessed (and repressed) dancer torn asunder by the unbearable duality of her own mind:

> *Black Swan* is the most prominent candidate in a long time for American film's most clandestine canon, the Cinema of Hysteria. These are movies that work on a level beyond rationality, in the realm of obsessive reverie, making no sense literally or logically and yet we understand them completely. They go back at least as far as 1935's *The Bride of Frankenstein*, a horror picture by designation but in fact far more peculiar, up through the doomed romance *A Place in the Sun*, the id-racked western *Johnny Guitar*, and the frenzied *Written on the Wind* in the postnuclear late '40s and '50s. More or less skipping the '60s and '70s when strangeness was usurped by psychedelia, the Cinema of Hysteria reasserted itself during the '80s and '90s in the masochistic epiphanies of Scorsese's *The Last Temptation of Christ*, Kubrick's nocturnal plunge into the libido in *Eyes Wide Shut*, and the perverse fantasias of David Lynch.[2]

The producer in question, Sam Katzman, must have said yes immediately, and the resultant screenplay written within a matters of days, for the entire film was in production by the end of January of 1942 and released in theatres nationwide by March 6th. The film is the first to respond to the events of Pearl Harbor in the form of pop culture. And what an odd response it is. To my knowledge, no World War II scholar has ever analyzed this film. No scholar of the detention centers built in the wake of Pearl Harbor has ever mentioned the film either. And yet it's the clearest, and most confusing, record of the American zeitgeist at that time. It's a cinematic cave painting, the Chauvet of World War II America. And the principal Paleolithic individuals responsible for its creation are Sam Katzman and Jack Dietz (producers), Barney A. Sarecky (associate producer), William Nigh (director), Harvey Gates (screenwriter), Bela Lugosi (star), and Joan Barclay (co-star).

The stories, the murmurs, the headlines of the last few months had imprinted in my mind the word HATE. I had heard my sisters say, "Why do they hate us?" I had heard Mama say with lonesome resignation, "I don't understand all this hate in the world." It was a bleak and awful-sounding word, yet I had no idea at all what shape it might take if ever I confronted it. I saw it as a dark, amorphous cloud that would descend from above and enclose us forever. As we entered Los Angeles, I sat huddled in the back seat, fearing any word I uttered might bring it to life.

–Jeanne Wakatsuki Houston & James D. Houston,
from Chapter 19 of *Farewell to Manzinar*, 1973[3]

Credits role over an Asian serpent wrapping itself around a planet crowned by a rising sun.

FBI agent Clayton Moore (left), the future Lone Ranger, looks on with Joan Barclay at his side as yet another murder victim is uncovered by J. Edgar Hoover's finest. *(Photo courtesy of Bill Chase)*

Bela Lugosi works his sinister magic on yet another victim of his complicated revenge scheme, which shares many similarities with the basic plot of Alexandre Dumas' *The Count of Monte Cristo*, a novel emulated by countless Hollywood thrillers. *(Photo courtesy of Bill Chase)*

Bridges explode. Buildings fall. Signs of sabotage all across this great nation of ours.

A group of old white men in a mansion, alone.

A mysterious man named Monsieur Colomb, a very sick man.

Weird sort of fellow.

An hypnotic injection.

Not far from 4736 Sunset Drive, Monsieur Colomb disappears from the back of a taxi cab driven by a dwarf.

A ceremonial Japanese dagger is found clutched in the hands of a dead white man. The body lays sprawled on the steps of a Japanese embassy.

An industrialist from Detroit. A small white card arrives in the mail.

PLASTIC SURGERY. RESULTS GUARANTEED.

Room 213. Don't go in there.

Another Japanese dagger. More corpses.

Colomb magically vanishes and reappears throughout the house of a man only hours dead.

"...Mister Ryder.... *thank* you."

A corpse lies face down on a table. Colomb hovers over him, forcing him to speak to his niece (or is she?) through a closed door. Does Colomb use ventriloquism, or is he somehow in control of the dead man's spirit?

Ventriloquism and the dead. Necrotriloquism?

More bodies dumped on the embassy steps. (They should place some guards there to prevent that from happening.)

"Jap daggers!"

The butler disappears. So many white men are disappearing in this movie.

"The others are expecting you... before midnight."

"Alice, will you marry me?" "What for?" "So I can beat you up!"

"Who knows... in this crazy world?"

Colomb again disappears from the back of a taxi cab. How is he doing it? He's Bela Lugosi. He needs no explanation. The supernatural abilities are implied by the name of the actor.

Even a banker can be a slave.

Unions are no damn good.

"Feminine emotions."

The niece refers to her own uncle by his last name. Why? At first this seems to be a mistake on the part of the screenwriter. It's not.

The butler is in the basement, bound and gagged.

The niece is really an Operator!

Someone's posing as the fake niece's uncle. Yes, a fake niece has been sent to spy on a fake uncle.

A man in a black hood.

An awkwardly placed flashback.

Heil Hitler!

Black Dragons. Wily Asians. Yellow sons of bitches, prepared to serve the Empire until death.

Death masks!

Two Lugosis in an underground prison cell. One of 'em's a pissed-off Nazi. The other just looks sick. One of 'em's got a pack of knives on him. The other doesn't.

The black hood is removed. Something hideous beneath. Why?

I don't know.

All is right in the world... but nothing is what it seems.

The capital building in Washington, D.C.

Buy war bonds, you fools, or you'll all die, and your beautiful daughters will be raped by microcephalic Japs who have been transformed into white men. Why, I'd rather have that sinister Hungarian, Lugosi, get his hands on her pre-pubescent body than those dirty little yellow freaks. The End.

Confusion.

Mama picked up the kitchenware and some silver she had stored with neighbors in Boyle Heights. But the warehouse where she'd stored the rest had been unaccountably "robbed"—of furniture, appliances, and most of those silver anniversary gifts. Papa already knew the car he'd put money on before Pearl Harbor had been repossessed. And, as he suspected, no record of his fishing boats remained. This put him right back where he'd been in 1904, arriving in a new land and starting over from economic zero.

It was another snip of the castrator's scissors, and he never really recovered from this, either financially or spiritually. Yet neither did he entirely give up. One of the amazing things about America is the way it can both undermine you and keep you believing in your own possibilities, pumping you with hope.

–Jeanne Wakatsuki Houston & James D. Houston,
from Chapter 19 of *Farewell to Manzinar*, 1973[4]

Let's sort through the confusion, shall we? In his 1993 book, *Poverty Row Horrors!: Monogram, PRC and Republic Horror Films of the Forties*, Tom Weaver calls this film, "a minor landmark in the history of incoherent cinema."[5] Indeed, the film is incoherent to the extreme. The first time watching it (for most sane people, there would never be a second time... or a *first*, for that matter), it's almost impossible to know what the hell's supposed to be happening.

We are introduced to six rich industrialists at a chi-chi party. Young, beautiful women are fawning over these old men who seem to be discussing important matters of state. After the party is over, however, and

The hypnotic powers displayed by other famous Bela Lugosi characters, such as Count Dracula, Murder Legendre in *White Zombie* (1932), and Chandu the Magician in *The Return of Chandu* (1934), are on full display in this film as well. *(Photo courtesy of Bill Chase)*

the six old men are alone together, we see a different side to their ostensibly one-dimensional personalities. They seem to be involved in some kind of sabotage against the United States, but we have no idea why. Who are they working for? They don't seem to be German. They're certainly not Japanese. Are they traitors?

We won't know the answer to this question for about an hour later, and the film's only sixty-one minutes long. This makes everything that happens from the first scene onward completely confusing. What's remarkable is the fact that the screenwriter (and the director) clearly *intended* it to be confusing. Films in the 1940s, for the most part, did not wish to disorientate or disturb their audiences. The few films from that era that did so on purpose are now considered to be classics. Val Lewton's excellent low-budget horror films made for RKO, beginning with *Cat People* in 1942 and ending with *Bedlam* in 1946, are now hailed as daring examples of breakthrough psychosexual cinema. Though made with nowhere near the same level of competence as the films of Val Lewton, *Black Dragons* has to be given high marks for even attempting the unlikely blend of genres we find in this film. *Black Dragons* combines elements of espionage, horror, phildickian paranoia (almost ten years before Phil Dick sold his first short story), and even quasi-science-fiction.

As the world's foremost expert on the Cinema of Hysteria, given that I made it up, I can assure you that *Black Swan* possesses every trait of the subspecies. First, sex is the electric current that not only drives these movies dramatically and gives them their dreamy power but untethers them from the more practical obligations of storytelling. Second, at the same time that these films are imagistic to the point of being hallucinatory, they're distinguished

In the above film still, one can only wonder if Bela Lugosi is attempting to find a way out of this delirious film.... *(Photo courtesy of Bill Chase)*

from the superficially trippy by riveting central performances that are naked to the point of reckless: Gene Tierney in the neon-noir *Leave Her to Heaven*, Natalie Wood in the fevered *Splendor in the Grass*, Sheryl Lee in *Twin Peaks: Fire Walk with Me*. Without Kim Novak's bruised carnal melancholy and James Stewart's turning his everyman persona inside out, 1958's *Tristan and Isolde*-on-acid *Vertigo* isn't one of the greatest movies ever made, whatever vision and mastery Alfred Hitchcock brought to it; that Hitchcock regretted both casting decisions is indicative of how, for once, he didn't understand his own movie, another thing often true of the Cinema of Hysteria [...]. Years ago I realized that whenever I see *Vertigo* with an audience, the film never casts the same spell as when I watch it by myself. This may be the truest thing about the Cinema of Hysteria, utterly the stuff of dreams and therefore utterly private, which is at odds with not only the communal way in which movies have been watched and responded to for most of their history but with verdicts of good and bad altogether.

That was Erickson talking about *Black Swan* again, in case you were lost.

Everything Erickson says above about sex being "the electric current that not only drives these movies dramatically and gives them their dreamy power but untethers them from the more practical obligations of storytelling" does not apply directly to Lugosi's performance in *Black Dragons*, but it does apply to his more celebrated performances from a decade before, specifically *Dracula* (1931), *White Zombie* (1932) perhaps most dramatically—and hysterically—*The Black Cat* (1934), and *The Raven* (1935). If you crossed out the words *Black Swan* and replaced them with the titles of any of these four films, you would hardly need to change anything else about Erickson's review. Erickson claims that *Bride of Frankenstein* is a good starting point for this strange subgenre called the Cinema of Hysteria, and given James Whale's multi-layered, sardonic script and hyperkinetic directorial style, perhaps he's right. But *The Black Cat*, made a year before *Bride of Frankenstein*, might be even more appropriate. Edgar Ulmer's German Expressionist sensibilities, matched with the surreal script and the dream-like performance of its two stars, Lugosi and Karloff, push the film past the bounds of Poe-inspired melodrama into something far darker and hypnotic. *The Black Cat* is perhaps one of the darkest (and most psychologically perverse) films to emerge

Though seemingly overshadowed by his many costars in this photo, Bela Lugosi's fierce performance and dominant personality are, in fact, the essential cornerstones of *Black Dragons*. *(Photo courtesy of Bill Chase)*

from Hollywood in the 1930s, and it's hard not to see *Black Swan* as being a direct descendant of those Golden Age horror films. I wouldn't be surprised if Aronofsky thought of *Black Swan* in precisely those terms when conceiving the idea in the first place.

Even though the sexual subtext of these earlier films is far less blatant than in *Black Swan*, nonetheless the fact is that not one of the films mentioned above could exist without it. In the 1930s producers hired Lugosi for such films knowing he had the ability to inject that subtext into their films without half-trying. Henry Gates' script for *Black Dragons* references Lugosi's earlier performances, but not overtly. Lugosi's Colomb, for example, seems to be infused with supernatural powers, but for no logical reason. Furthermore, the Lugosi of the 1940s had changed considerably from the Lugosi of the 1930s. He was now a sixty year old man with graying hair and a puffy face. And yet, strangely, the female lead of *Black*

Dragons reacts to him as if he's the Lugosi from ten years before.

At one point Alice Saunders (Joan Barclay) comments to FBI agent Dick Martin (portrayed by the future Lone Ranger, Clayton Moore) about Monsieur Colomb, "Handsome devil, isn't he?" Martin seems offended and jealous, despite the fact that he just met the girl about two minutes before, and says something derogatory about Colomb. Alice replies, "Oh, I don't know. Make it a moonlight night and a park bench— might be exciting!"

Later Alice is sleeping in her bedroom and is almost attacked by some sort of shadowy being that we assume to be Colomb himself. Alice flees the room and runs into Colomb's arms downstairs. Colomb says, "When a young woman's nerves commence to give way, it is time she sought refuge in a strong man's arms." Alice says suggestively, "I just ran into yours." Colomb replies, "Mine might be dangerous." Indeed, it seems as if Alice is more than aware of this and is attracted to him for that exact reason.

Aside from the dual sense of sexual attraction and repulsion elicited by Colomb, sex hovers over the film in other ways. At the end of the film we discover that the six rich white industrialists are all members of a Japanese secret society called the Black Dragons. They allowed themselves to act as guinea pigs for a Nazi scientist named Dr. Melcher (Lugosi, before he changed his name to Colomb). This gambit paid off. Using the death masks of six murdered industrialists as his guide, Melcher employs his experimental plastic surgery techniques to completely transform the six Japanese men into exact duplicates of these murdered Caucasians. However, the second Melcher has completed the surgery, the Black Dragons throw him in a subterranean cell to prevent him from revealing what has occurred. Inside the cell is a second prisoner who the Black Dragons are planning to release. Stupidly, the Black Dragons placed Melcher in the cell without taking away his surgical tools. Melcher removes them from inside his coat and instantly performs surgery on the prisoner! He makes the second prisoner look like himself (and kills him, one presumes?), then performs plastic surgery on *himself* in order to resemble the prisoner who's about to be released. (The fact that the role of Melcher is *also* played by Lugosi would seem to render the necessity for plastic surgery completely negligible, but that didn't occur to the director—or to anyone else—before the cameras rolled.) Melcher changes his name to Colomb, then heads for the States to begin picking off his enemies one by one à la *The Count of Monte Cristo*, a story appropriated for horror films even to this day.

In retrospect, now that we know the true nature of this devilish plot,

we can look back on that first party scene and realize that the worst offense committed by these Japanese fiends is not the rampant destruction
of bridges and key military installations, not their cow-towing to labor
union demands in order to cause chaos throughout this great nation of
ours (a fiendish strategy emphasized more than once in the film), not
even the kidnapping and assassinations of six of the most important industrialists in the United States, but the fact that they seem to be spending most of their free time *pawing our women.*

The subliminal message is clear: These foreigners, both Kraut and Jap
alike, have a mysterious hold over our women. What are we going to do
about it? The fear of foreigners having their way with our sisters and wives
and daughters is explicitly used in a great deal of wartime propaganda,
particularly during World War II. Consider Sam Keen's 1986 book *Faces
of the Enemy: Reflections of the Hostile Imagination* in which we see any
number of "foreigner-as-rapist" propaganda posters made by the United
States, Italy, the U.S.S.R., and Germany, all of which hinge on instilling
the flame of patriotism in the breast of the intended viewer (male, mostly)
who will be so outraged by the horrors depicted that he'll be willing to put
his very life on the line in order to protect his loved ones from the brutal,
ham-fisted attentions of the invading enemy swarm.

As in most wartime propaganda, sex is the real nightmare looming in
the background of *Black Dragons.*

In the beginning there was a kind of romantic patriotic aura
about joining the Black Dragon and young men were wooed to
join it by promises of adventurous careers. However, some of the
soshi, or "brave knights" as they were called, were in reality unemployed samurai who no longer had a role to fulfill after the
restoration of the authority of the Emperor. But while in its early
years the Black Dragon Society undoubtedly provided such patriotic young men with an outlet for their adventure-loving natures,
it also led to a steady growth in the number of rogues and ruffians
in membership in later years. Yet from a practical point of view it
must be admitted that they were of value to their country and that
if they had not been members of the society, they might well have
degenerated into unemployed criminals.

–Richard Deacon,
from Chapter 5 of *A History of the Japanese Secret Service*, 1982[6]

The disorientation inherent in the opening scenes of the film, in which we first eavesdrop on the industrialists' conspiratorial plans, seeps through the following four reels. Compare this approach with more highly regarded films that were altered in the editing room to lessen the confusion originally intended by the filmmakers. William Cameron Menzies, winner of the Academy Award for his art direction on *Gone With the Wind* (1939), directed a film in 1951 called *The Whip Hand* that could very well be a candidate for the Cinema of Hysteria. Or perhaps the Cinema of *Hypernoia*? In its unedited version, the film was about a reporter who tracks down an enclave of escaped Nazis in a small town called Winnoga located somewhere in the Midwest. The town, as well as the people in it, seem to be in the process of decaying, like one of those fictional New England sea ports that so obsessed H.P. Lovecraft in such stories as "The Shadow over Innsmouth." It turns out that this secret society of Nazis are developing a chemical biological warfare agent which they plan to release in the U.S., potentially killing off thousands of Americans. Unfortunately, this version of the film has never been seen. Howard Hughes, the executive producer, decided he didn't like it and ordered reshoots that replaced all the Nazis with Communists. Also added was a prologue in which we eavesdrop on the Communists discussing their plan in great detail. This prologue serves to lessen the paranoia in the film considerably. Since we know what's going on, we also know that the main character is not insane or paranoid. We *already* know what's behind the strange goings-on in the small town. Without the prologue, the audience would be as confused as the protagonist. Apparently Hughes did not want this.

More recently, Alex Proyas' *Dark City* (1998)—which precedes the Wachowski Brothers' *The Matrix* (1999) by a year and yet shares similar themes with the latter film and is superior in almost every way—is rendered far more comprehensible, and far less intriguing, by the add-on of a voice-over prologue delivered by Kiefer Sutherland in which the audience is essentially told what's happening in the film long before the intended revelation of the central mystery.

Moviemakers, particularly producers, are a skittish lot. They don't want to lose the audience due to rampant confusion. But what they don't understand is that confusion often translates into *mystery*, and mystery keeps people in their seats.

I'm not sure the confusion in *Black Dragons* makes it a good movie, but it does make it a *compelling* movie, and one worthy of being placed in the canon of the Cinema of Hysteria.

Thus membership of the Black Dragon eventually ranged from Cabinet Ministers and high-ranking Army officers to professional secret agents, blackmailers and hired killers. They came from all classes of the community and membership increased from a few hundreds at the outset to an estimated 10,000 in 1944. While originally the society's activities were directed almost solely towards obtaining intelligence on Russia and Manchuria, by the end of the 1930s they had been extended to Korea, China, the Philippines, Malaya, Hong Kong, Singapore, India, Afghanistan, Ethiopia, Turkey, Morocco, the United States and many countries in the Caribbean and South America.

–Richard Deacon,
from Chapter 5 of *A History of the Japanese Secret Service*, 1982[7]

One might assume that the overall effect of this film is one of instilling fear against the Japanese. Oddly, however, it has the opposite effect. This is what makes the paranoia in this film so transcendent, so postmodern, so phildickian in nature.

For if a technology exists that can transmogrify any Japanese man into a rich white industrialist, that means that racial profiling is completely useless. Internment camps, as well, are rendered moot. Why bother? The dirty rats can make themselves look like your brother or your son or your husband. Your husband could be one of them right now. How would you know? How could you possibly *ever* know?

In that sense, this film prefigures the cosmic paranoia/metanoia inherent in such 1950s noirish science fiction extravaganzas as *Invaders from Mars* (1953), *It Came from Outer Space* (1953), *Invasion of the Body Snatchers* (1956), and *I Married a Monster from Outer Space* (1958).

The working title for *Black Dragons* was *The Yellow Menace*. The title change was fortunate. Not only is *Black Dragons* simply a better title, but it's also more accurate. After all, the menace in *Black Dragons* is not "yellow" at all. The menace looks just like your average white man. The menace isn't any color. It's a crafty chameleon, rendered completely invisible by Nazi technology.

The invisible peril: the worst nightmare of paranoid schizophrenics from time immemorial.

And the populace of the United States in the winter of 1941-42.

Bela Lugosi's trademarked hypnotic gaze is once again front and center in *Black Dragons*, one of Monogram's most postmodern experiments. *(Photo courtesy of Bill Chase)*

From that day on, part of me yearned to be invisible. In a way, nothing would have been nicer than for no one to see me. Although I couldn't have defined it at the time, I felt that if attention were drawn to me, people would see what this girl had first responded to. They wouldn't see me, they would see the slant-eyed face, the Oriental. This is what accounts, in part, for the entire evacuation. You cannot deport 110,000 people unless you have stopped seeing individuals. Of course, for such a thing to happen, there has to be a kind of acquiescence on the part of the victims, some submerged belief that this treatment is deserved, or at least allowable. It's an attitude easy for nonwhites to acquire in America. I had inherited it. Manzanar had confirmed it. And my feeling, at eleven, went something like this: you are going to be invisible anyway, so why not completely disappear.

–Jeanne Wakatsuki Houston & James D. Houston,
from Chapter 20 of *Farewell to Manzinar*, 1973

Despite the fact that *Black Dragons* was complete fiction, nonetheless it reflected the fears of the populace at that time. Many Japanese Americans were living peacefully with Caucasian Americans on December 6th, 1941. All that changed the next day, and suddenly whole families were shunned and forced to leave everything behind. That elderly Japanese gardener who had been working on your property for years *could* be signaling Japanese submarines in the middle of the night. After all, who says he wasn't?

And that grandfatherly white industrialist might not have had democracy and the American Way as his main priority during World War II, a "paranoid" thought born out by the real life behavior of such two-faced industrialists as Henry Ford, the only American praised by Adolf Hitler in *Mein Kampf*: "It is Jews who govern the stock exchange forces of the American Union. Every year makes them more and more the controlling masters of the producers in a nation of one hundred and twenty millions; only a single great man, Ford, to their fury, still maintains full independence."[8] The truth is that *Black Dragons'* seemingly racist message could just as easily be seen as a metaphor for the hordes of home-grown American saboteurs (most of them Caucasian, not Asian) who were using their powerful positions to help bring about a fascist victory in order to shore up their own profits, as evidenced by such scholarly books as *Who Financed Hitler: The Secret Funding of Hitler's Rise to Power 1919-1933* by James and Suzanne Pool (Dial Press, 1978). This subversive subtext, whether intentional or not, lifts *Black Dragons* above its many contemporary equivalents.

Compare the polymorphous, surreal racism of *Black Dragons* with the straight-forward, naked racism in other 1940s spy films produced by much larger studios like Twentieth Century Fox. Consider, for example, the now-obscure propaganda detective melodrama, *Little Tokyo, U.S.A.* (1942) which stars Preston Foster as hardboiled detective Mike Steele (a precursor to Mickey Spillane's Mike Hammer?) whose beat is L.A.'s "Little Tokyo." Steele, Cassandra-like, attempts to warn his superiors on the LAPD about something treacherous brewing amidst this Asiatic sinkhole of the godless, but none of the upper brass will listen to him, perhaps because the only evidence the detective has to offer is a bit of gossip given to him accidentally by a Japanese child in Little Tokyo coupled with Steele's own uncanny intuition.

For about sixty-five minutes we follow Steele along his quixotic journey through the mean streets of Los Angeles as he races to beat the clock,
trying his best to prevent the murder of his girlfriend, Maris Hanover
(Brenda Joyce), the obligatory plucky journalist, as well as the imminent
takeover of California by these "half-pint connivers." It's possibly one of
the most blatantly racist films ever produced by a major American film
studio and is not readily available today, no doubt for that very reason.
I'm sure 20th Century Fox would prefer to pretend it never existed.

Taking a cue from the earlier Lugosi film, the Black Dragon Society
once again rear their reptilian heads as the main antagonists of the film,
along with a few Nazi spies for good measure. It turns out that the Black
Dragons engineered the bombing of Pearl Harbor with the help of a
vast network of flinty-eyed spies embedded in the farmlands located up
and down the coastlines of California and Hawaii. One gets the impression that almost every single Asian in California secretly answers to the
Emperor of Japan via shortwave radios squirreled away in their modest

bedrooms in Little Tokyo, and the few Asians who aren't loyal end up in the L.A. morgue with their heads chopped off.

By the end of the film Steele has failed in preventing the bombing of Pearl Harbor, but his efforts provide the authorities with the necessary evidence to evacuate every Asian from California and send them to "internment camps." Most World War II historians are not aware that Mike Steele was personally responsible for this proud moment in American history. At the end of the movie we see Our Hero (along with his newscaster girlfriend), standing amidst a pack of nervous-looking Asians about to be shipped off on a bus to Nowheresville. The girlfriend declares that those few Asians still loyal to America are more than willing (indeed, even *proud*) to mail themselves to Manzanar as a sacrifice for the greater good of the country. The implication is clear: Any Asian who's *not* happy about the situation couldn't possibly be a loyal American, so they deserve what they get.

When juxtaposed with overt propaganda films such as *Little Tokyo, U.S.A.*, *Black Dragons* comes off as something more than just the silver screen equivalent of the Two Minutes Hate devised by George Orwell (the Sixty-Five Minutes Hate?). From the perspective of the present, *Black Dragons* comes off as a bemusing exercise in slipstream Dadaism.

For this reason, *Black Dragons* continues to hold some relevance—as well as a small cult following—in the 21st century while a horde of other, more pedestrian World War II espionage films have been rendered forgotten by time and general disinterest. Despite its "hysterical" quality, or perhaps because of it, the postmodern core of *Black Dragons* continues to resonate in an electronic age of metanoia, constantly morphing Internet identities, rampant Hollywood plastic surgery disasters, and political loyalties that shift every second depending on expediency and unenlightened self-interest.

As Tom Weaver writes in *Poverty Row Horrors!*: "A confused script and choppy editing are the downfall of *Black Dragons*, but the film compensates in little ways. Fast-paced, it averages better than a murder a reel, and the way-out plot is appealing in a looney sort of way. It's a great 'time capsule' film, with the 'feel' of the early World War II years captured in what can only be called Monogram fashion."[9]

Very true, but perhaps "*hysterical* Monogram fashion" would be a far more accurate description.

(Endnotes)
1   Jeanne Wakatsuki and James D. Houston, *Farewell to Manzanar* (New York: Houghton Mifflin, 2002), 15.

2   Steve Erickson, "Dancing in the Dark," *Los Angeles Magazine*, January 1, 2011 (website accessed July 10, 2011).
3   Wakatsuki and Houston, *Farewell to Manzanar*, 136.
4   Ibid. 138-39.
5   Tom Weaver, *Poverty Row Horrors!: Monogram, PRC and Republic Horror Films of the Forties* (Jefferson, North Carolina: McFarland, 1993), 54.
6   Richard Deacon, *A History of the Japanese Secret Service* (London: Frederick Muller Limited, 1982), 44.
7   Ibid.
8   Adolf Hitler, *Mein Kampf* (trans. Ralph Mannheim) (New York: Houghton Mifflin, 1971 [1925]), p. 639.
9   Weaver, *Poverty Row Horrors!*, 58.

The Corpse Vanishes was based on
the kidnapping of a real-life bride.
(Photo courtesy of Bill Chase)

Chapter 5

The Corpse Vanishes and the Case of the Missing Brides

by Gary D. Rhodes

Monogram Pictures was not usually given to understatement, particularly when it came to Bela Lugosi. The title of *The Corpse Vanishes* is a fascinating exception. Released in May 1942, the film features Lugosi as Dr. Lorenz, a physician and scientist who abducts women in an effort to keep his aging wife, Countess Lorenz (Elizabeth Russell), alive and well. Three bodies disappear during its running time, along with the kidnapping of a journalist (Luana Walters). And that's to say nothing of at least three bodies Lorenz stole in the days, weeks, months, and perhaps years prior to the film's opening scene. To announce the vanishing of a singular corpse in the film title hardly seems to be an adequate tabulation of Lorenz's crimes.

Shooting on *The Corpse Vanishes* began in early March 1942.[1] Sam Robins and Gerald Schnitzer received credit for the original story, which Harvey Gates adapted into a screenplay. When interviewed in 2012, Schnitzer mentioned that one of the producers provided the idea for the tale: "I vaguely recall discussing the idea with Jack Dietz, who claimed he had read about a socialite bride being kidnapped, headlined in the tabloids."[2] Little else is known of the film's production, which was directed by Wallace Fox.[3] *Daily Variety* joked that producer Sam Katzman had borrowed six coffins from an undertaker to use in the film, promising that they would be returned in perfect condition. Two were damaged, which meant an unhappy Katzman had to purchase them.[4]

The company moved through production and post-production rapidly, giving a preview screening on April 10, 1942.[5] The final cut was released on May 8, 1942, only two months after shooting had begun. Industry trade reviews were largely positive, somewhat surprising given that *The Corpse Vanishes* was just a B-movie, a "programmer" meant to complete the lower half of double features. *Motion Picture Daily* judged it to be "about as eerie an offering as has appeared on the screen," in spite of a merely "competent" production that featured some "inept" acting and dialogue.[6] *Film Daily* told readers:

> Bela Lugosi has made some horrifying horror films in his day, but this one tops them all for suspense and sheer, grim, mad frightfulness. It keeps just within the bounds of the Hays' Office ruling on the limits to which a producer can extend himself in his effort to scare audiences out of their skins.[7]

Daily Variety was equally enthusiastic, predicting "fans who like horror opuses will have a shrieking good time viewing *The Corpse Vanishes*." The trade added that Lugosi's "overplaying" actually constituted a "proper" approach to the story material, an opinion rarely voiced at the time, but widely held in the 21st century.[8]

What was that story material? At first, it might be seen as no more than the sum total of the aforementioned descriptions. Distilled further, it could be said that *The Corpse Vanishes* was just another low-budget mad doctor movie featuring a horror actor past his prime, a star no longer ascendant. As with the other films in the Monogram Nine, however, a cursory viewing is not sufficient. Far more is here than meets the eye.

The Corpse Vanishes marks a few notable firsts, including Lugosi's initial pairing (of what became three films) with actress Minerva Urecal.[9] It was also his first mad scientist role for Monogram, at least if one views his plastic surgeon in *Black Dragons* (1942) as being murderously vengeful, but still very much sane. And unlike its predecessors, *The Corpse Vanishes* opens with urgent action, a bride saying "I do" before abruptly collapsing onto the church floor. Subsequent Monogram Nines like *Bowery at Midnight* (1942) would also throw audiences immediately into the action, a plot device similar to that adopted by later Hollywood blockbusters.

Much more significant, though, is the extent to which *The Corpse Vanishes* activates the past, resulting in the convergence of three important trajectories of horror entertainment: (A) the intrepid and fast-

The Corpse Vanishes marked Lugosi's first screen appearance with actress Minerva Urecal, pictured here on screen right. *(Photo courtesy of Bill Chase)*

talking female newspaper journalist who investigates and documents weird goings-on that, (B) under scrutiny invoke the vampiric more than the scientific, all being the work of (C) a bizarre and insane family. Here is a brew that percolates with more possibilities than any test tube in Dr. Lorenz's laboratory, combining elements of the past into a unique formula that was prescient of horror movies to come.

Ten Days in the Mad-House

Ben Hecht and Charles MacArthur's play *The Front Page* took Broadway by storm when it opened in 1928, in no small measure because of Lee Tracy's portrayal of newspaperman Hildy Johnson. Its plot was simple: a police reporter attempts to capitalize on the pending execution of a condemned murderer while simultaneously trying to quit his job and marry his fiancée. Of the many journalists the play depicted, an article in the *New York Times* observed:

The bored reporter, the bully, the nauseated esthete who finds his shiftless comrades revolting and sprays his desk with disinfectant, the nervous and merciless managing editor – all go through their pace. The skepticism, the callousness, the contempt, the vague dissatisfaction with their lot, the boorishness, the brutal jesting, and the omniscience are not invented.[10]

Hollywood quickly seized on the story, hardly surprising given the appeal that clever dialogue had for studios in the early years of the talkie. Lewis Milestone directed Pat O'Brien as Hildy Johnson in the 1931 film adaptation. Its opening text sets the scene, humorously remarking that *The Front Page* is "laid in a mythical kingdom."

Journalists proved enduring in Hollywood scripts, perhaps because many of them seemed as socially conscious as they were corrupt, as ingenious as they were conniving, as good as they were bad. Though he didn't get to reprise his Broadway role on film, Lee Tracy still found a home in Hollywood, playing Hildy Johnson-inspired reporters in *Doctor X* (1932), *Blessed Event* (1932), *The Strange Love of Molly Louvain* (1932), *Advice to the Lovelorn* (1933), *Behind the Headlines* (1937), *The Payoff* (1942), and – by way of a promotion to newspaper editor – *Power of the Press* (1943). But however much Tracy embodied the screen journalist, the most famous example remains Orson Welles' *Citizen Kane* (1941), whose title character (based on newspaper magnate William Randolph Hearst) famously remarks in 1898, "You provide the prose poems; I'll provide the war." Journalism was yellow, even in black-and-white.

While *The Front Page* encouraged Hollywood to produce sound films about the newspaper business, another, even older tradition is also crucial to consider, that of the woman journalist, the "girl stunt reporter," a role that originated with the real-life exploits of Nellie Bly (pen name of American journalist Elizabeth Cochran Seaman). In 1887, the managing editor of the *New York World* suggested that Bly pretend to be insane so she could get remanded to an infamous asylum on Blackwell's Island. As Jean Marie Lutes notes, "Bly eagerly accepted the assignment."[11] Fooling the experts, who readily condemned her as crazy, she spent ten days inside the institution, where abuse of all kinds was ubiquitous. Bly later asked rhetorically, "Where could Dante have gotten a truer description of the tortures of Hell? Where could Doré have found a greater illustration?"[12] Her series of articles – collectively published in book form as *Ten Days in the Mad-House* (1887) – spurred a grand jury investigation. And her approach pioneered a new form of investigative journalism, one that placed a woman reporter in jeopardy.[13]

Bly's adventures continued in 1889, when she travelled around the globe with only one bag and a small amount of money. Just 72 days after her journey began, Bly successfully reappeared in New York.[14] Making reference to Jules Verne's novel *Around the World in Eighty Days* (1873), the *Chicago Tribune* announced, "Phineas [*sic*] Fogg of fiction has been outdone by the vigorous and sprightly young woman of fact."[15] Once again the famous journalist was triumphant. As Lutes explains, stunt reporters like Bly "boldly challenged the value of the experts' neutral pronouncements, insisting instead on the significance of their own bodies as sources of knowledge."[16] That knowledge came from gut instinct, as well as from hard-earned personal experience.

Girl reporters became popular, so much so that mystery fiction from the 1880s began to feature them. Sometimes they were assistant detec-

Patricia Hunter (Luana Walters) is the intrepid "girl reporter" in *The Corpse Vanishes*.
(*Photo courtesy of Bill Chase*)

Gary D. Rhodes | Robert Guffey

tives, but by the early twentieth century, these women often became lead characters. LeRoy Lad Panek describes them as:

> independent, enterprising, intelligent, knowledgeable, capable, and successful women, women who, in spite of romantic distractions, succeeded in doing things conventionally associated with men. Not only do these women succeed in a traditionally male profession, but they also do so without significant outside help – particularly male help.[17]

Panek provides numerous examples of such novels, including Charles Carey's *The Van Suyden Sapphires* (1905), Reginald Kauffman's *Miss Frances Baird, Detective: A Passage from Her Memoirs* (1906), Leroy Scott's

In *The Corpse Vanishes*, Lugosi's character is at times reminiscent of Dracula. Here he is hypnotizing Dr. Foster (Tristram Coffin). *(Photo courtesy John Antosiewicz)*

Counsel for the Defense (1912), Hugh C. Weir's *Miss Madeline Mack, De-tective* (1914), and Anna Katharine Green's *The Golden Slipper and Other Problems for Violet Strange* (1915).[18]

Given their popularity, girl stunt reporters appeared onscreen dur-ing the early cinema period. "The Girl-Reporter saves the situation and makes a scoop at the same time," the *Moving Picture World* said of these characters in 1912.[19] In *The Insane Heiress* (1910), Nell – a character clearly inspired by Nellie Bly – solves the mystery of an abducted wom-an by pretending to be insane. Once incarcerated in an asylum, she chloroforms a nurse in order to change her disguise and uncover more clues.[20] Then, in 1914, Mary Fuller starred in Edison's serial *The Active Life of Dolly of the Dailies*, playing a "daring" journalist who makes her way up through the ranks of *The Comet*, a newspaper otherwise staffed by men.[21] Charles Ogle, notable for his work as the monster in Edison's *Frankenstein* (1910), played Fuller's editor.[22] Among the serial's twelve chapters were *A Tight Squeeze, A Terror of the Night*, and *Dolly Plays De-tective*. In *The Chinese Fan*, the only surviving episode, an Asian villain kidnaps Dolly and holds her prisoner with another abducted woman. Dolly outwits and physically overpowers an opium-crazed guard, rescu-ing herself and her fellow inmate, as well as providing *The Comet* with a major "scoop."[23]

After the success of *The Front Page*, the girl reporter assumed a new place of prominence in Hollywood, as can be seen in the horror film *Mystery of the Wax Museum* (1933). In it, Glenda Farrell plays Florence Dempsey, whom *Variety* described as follows:

> a hard-striding, hard drinking girl reporter, not so completely hard, however, that she doesn't find tears useful when the mean old managing editor doesn't like the way she's handling a story. Miss Farrell, talking and acting in the pretty darned tough man-ner Warner Brothers pictures admires in its femme players, does a generous bit of dashing about stalking clues and so on.[24]

Put another way, Farrell's gum-chewing, fast-talking character drew heavily on the role played by Lee Tracy in the horror movie *Doctor X*, produced by the same studio. To the extent that Farrell's character need-ed to be distinguished because of her gender, *Doctor X* drew upon the tradition of Nellie Bly. The character Florence Dempsey is a strong wom-an, her name evocative of Jack Dempsey, world heavyweight champion boxer from 1919 to 1926; the same year that Warner's released *Mystery of the Wax Museum*, Jack Dempsey appeared in MGM's film *The Prizefighter and the Lady*. As for Florence, she was a woman, but also one of the boys; at one point, she is even referred to as a "wise guy."

The girl reporter returned many times, including in a series of nine "Torchy Blane" movies produced at Warner Bros. between 1937 and 1939; seven of them featured Glenda Farrell as the intrepid title character. However, the most famous of these movies was Howard Hawks' *His Girl Friday* (1940), a remake of *The Front Page* starring Rosalind Russell in what had previously been the male role of Hildy Johnson. Cary Grant's newspaper editor Walter Burns believes she is a great "newspaperman," a term that Russell's Hildy also uses to describe herself. The following year, Barbara Stanwyck starred as Ann Mitchell in Frank Capra's *Meet John Doe* (1941), a girl reporter who pulls a "circulation stunt," a "fake-a-roo" in which she concocts a letter to the editor that spurs mass public interest, so much so that she has to find someone to pretend to be its author, "John Doe" (Gary Cooper).

The lengthy history of the girl reporter of the screen also resulted in Patricia Hunter (Luana Walters), the hero of *The Corpse Vanishes*. She refers to herself using the non-gender-specific name "Pat"; Keenan (Kenneth Harlan), her editor at *The Chronicle*, and cameraman Sandy (Vince Barnett) do the same. On one occasion, she is called a "newspaperman." Like Ann Mitchell in *Meet John Doe* and Florence Dempsey in *Mystery of the Wax Museum*, Pat nearly finds herself out of a job, even though she is more clever than the men around her. Nevertheless, Sandy derisively jokes that Pat wouldn't recognize a clue "if it bit her." She wants to do investigative journalism, but Keenan demands that she cover society news like weddings, with an eye towards fashions worn by the guests. However, Pat's goal is to unravel the "Case of the Missing Brides," which she must do, not only for the sake of her career, but because the District Attorney's office clearly isn't up to the task. As her name suggests, she is a hunter.

Realizing that all of the kidnapped corpse brides wore the same type of mysterious *Stanhopea* orchid, Pat attempts to interview Dr. Lorenz, the man who originally hybridized the flower. She ignores the locals who fear him, to the extent that she hops on the back of a truck in order to sneak a nighttime ride to his home.[25] After being removed from the vehicle, Pat bravely takes a lift from another stranger, Dr. Foster (Tristram Coffin). When she finally meets Dr. Lorenz and his rude and abusive wife, Pat is undaunted. During the crazy night that follows, she is occasionally scared and even faints once, but none of that dissuades her

Artwork of Countess Elizabeth Báthory de Ecsed (aka "Elizabeth Bathory"), published in the *Cleveland Plain-Dealer* on August 11, 1912.

Patricia Hunter rightly keeps her distance from Countess Lorenz (far left), the most sadistic member of the film's horrifying family. *(Photo courtesy of Bill Chase)*

from getting a "sensational" story. Her tenacity even leads Foster to ask if she is "one of those hard-boiled reporters that we read about or see in the movies?"

To catch Dr. Lorenz, Pat convinces her editor to hold a "stunt" wedding, a "phony" ceremony with cigarette girl-turned-actress Peggy Woods (Gwen Kenyon) playing the bride. As expected, a *Stanhopea* orchid is delivered, but in a twist, Dr. Lorenz kidnaps Pat instead of the fake bride. She survives to tell the tale, in part because she physically overpowers the Countess. Then, in a conclusion not dissimilar to those seen in *Mystery of the Wax Museum* and *His Girl Friday*, Pat marries Dr. Foster. The film ends where it began, at a wedding. "Finally I make a newspaperman out of you and then you have to go and quit," Keenan complains. But Pat no longer has anything to prove: she is as tough and clever as Hildy Johnson and Nellie Bly.

In the Wilds of Transylvania

Many of the fictional characters in Bram Stoker's novel *Dracula* (1897) were deeply interested in, even dependent on, documenting the bizarre events that unfold. His novel unfolds through multiple perspectives, a variety of recorded observations, among them newspaper stories, diaries, and letters. Women write many of these, particularly Lucy Westerna and Mina Harker (née Murray), with the latter explicitly describing the role and even tools of authorship. As she notes in her journal, "I shall get my typewriter this very hour and begin transcribing. Then we shall be ready for other eyes if required." Mina later writes, "I took the cover off my typewriter, and said to Dr. Seward: — 'Let me write this all out now.'" In his own diary, Seward recalls, "as I passed a while ago I heard the click of the typewriter. They are hard at it. Mrs. Harker says that they are knitting together in chronological order every scrap of evidence they have." Investigative reporting can solve crimes; compiling the research into narrative form can convince readers a crime has occurred.

Tod Browning's film version of *Dracula* (1931) does not rely on such reportage, but does not eschew it either. An onscreen newspaper article announces the arrival of the ship on which Dracula (Bela Lugosi) and Renfield (Dwight Frye) have traveled: "Crew of Corpses Found on Derelict Vessel." Later in the film, Martin (Charles Gerrard) reads aloud a newspaper article that records the tale of "two small girls" attacked by the undead Lucy (Frances Dade).

Without Browning's version of *Dracula*, there would not have been a star named "Bela Lugosi." The actor Bela Lugosi would probably have struggled onward in a variety of character roles in Hollywood and might even have achieved a degree of fame. However, Lugosi the horror icon would not have existed. By extension, it seems likely that, while Dracula would have remained an important literary and stage vampire, he would not have proven as enduring without Lugosi, whose appearance and voice have vastly overshadowed Stoker's own description. Of course, Browning's film was produced and it became a box-office success. Typecasting resulted, with Lugosi remembered decades after his death because of Dracula. Of all the many biographical details known about him, perhaps none resonates as strongly as his burial: Lugosi was interred in 1956 wearing one of his vampire capes.

With regard to Lugosi's career, it is possible to see the immediate effect Browning's *Dracula* had, not only in the horror film roles he was offered, but also in his billing. Publicity for a number of movies, among them Robert Florey's *Murders in the Rue Morgue* (1932) and Edgar G. Ulmer's *The Black Cat* (1934) headlined him as "Bela (Dracula) Lugosi," which reminded viewers of what they likely already knew. The actor and role had become synonymous, so much so that in the 1932 short subject *Hollywood on Parade, No. A-8*, Lugosi plays a wax statue come-to-life. He does not portray Dracula in it, as some writers have mistakenly noted; rather, he plays "Bela Lugosi as Dracula." The two were separate, but forever linked in a kind of cinematic and cultural symbiosis.

Given how much the vampire consumed Lugosi, it's somewhat surprising that he did not actually play Dracula onscreen again until *Abbott and Costello Meet Frankenstein* (1948), seventeen years after the release of Browning's film. In fact, after 1931, he didn't play *any* vampire onscreen until Lew Landers' *The Return of the Vampire* in 1943. Horror film roles were plentiful, particularly mad doctors, but not vampires. The undead stayed dead, at least for many years.

This is not to say that studios forgot about Dracula. From 1934 until the beginning of 1936, Universal hoped to cast Lugosi in *Dracula's Daughter* (1936). For a number of reasons, though, the Lambert Hillyer-directed sequel didn't feature any actor as Dracula, its narrative concentrating instead on his vampiric offspring. Lugosi did appear in Tod Browning's *Mark of the Vampire* (1935), an extremely atmospheric film that bears many similarities to the 1931 *Dracula*. Though Lugosi's costume resembles Dracula, his character Count Mora was not actually undead. Instead, Lugosi played an actor pretending to be a vampire.

Enter Sam Robins and Gerald "Jerry" Schnitzer. However much they were inspired by Dietz's memory of a kidnapped bride, their original story for *The Corpse Vanishes* – and Harvey Gates' screenplay based upon it – cited vampire lore repeatedly, more so than any film in which Lugosi had appeared since *Mark of the Vampire*. As *Motion Picture Daily* informed readers in 1942, *The Corpse Vanishes* attempted to "out-Dracula Dracula."[26] This is apparent from the opening credits, which feature artwork of a silhouetted figure wearing what appears to be a cloak or cape; he outstretches a claw-like hand towards a flower.

To be sure, Dr. Lorenz is a physician and scientist. It is quite possible that one of the film's writers appropriated Lorenz's name from Austrian surgeon Adolf Lorenz (1854-1946).[27] Famous for his work with bone deformities and orthopedics, Lorenz became known as the "Bloodless Surgeon of Vienna." His name had earlier appeared in *Dr. Lorenz Outdone*, Lubin's American retitling of Georges Méliès' *Up-to-Date Surgery/Une indigestion* (1902). In it, a surgeon saws off a patient's arms and legs before removing various objects from his stomach cavity. Once the operation is

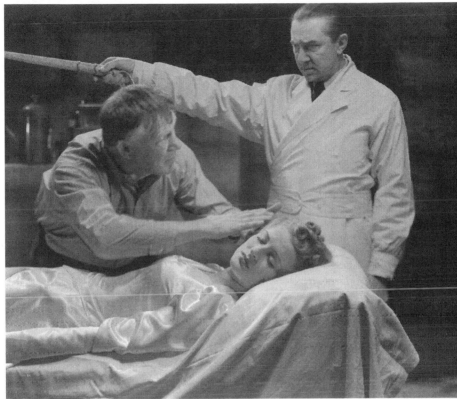

Angel (Frank Moran) takes more abuse from Dr. Lorenz than any other member of the clan. *(Photo courtesy of Bill Chase)*

over, the doctor puts the man back together, but "a leg is placed where an arm should be, and vice versa."[28]

Lugosi's Lorenz is himself a man of science, a subject that interested Browning's Dracula, at least to a degree, as he announces that Professor Van Helsing's name is well known "even in the wilds of Transylvania." In *The Corpse Vanishes*, his wife is Countess Lorenz, whose title conjures the memory of Count Dracula's royal status, one that Dr. Lorenz may or may not share. Their accents suggest Eastern Europe or perhaps, at least in Russell's case, Germany. Dr. Lorenz is also a hypnotist, placing Dr. Foster into a "somnambulistic" state at one point; Dracula possessed the same skills. And to an extent, the kidnapped brides in Lorenz's basement echo Dracula's three Transylvanian wives.

Much like the carriage driver who does not want to take Renfield to Dracula's castle, a taxi driver is too scared to drive Patricia to the Lorenz home, pretending to be "out of gas."[29] After all, Lorenz has the local reputation of being a "strange, spooky guy," one who has imported a special crate of moss, apparently from "somewhere in Europe," the location where he first hybridized the mysterious orchid. Here again the film recalls Dracula, who ships three boxes of earth from Transylvania to England. And like Dracula, who doesn't utter a single word in the Browning film for the first ten minutes, nearly fifteen minutes of *The Corpse Vanishes* pass before Dr. Lorenz speaks.

During the middle of the night, Lorenz wears all black as he hovers over the sleeping Patricia and Dr. Fowler (Tristram Coffin), images reminiscent of the vampire approaching the beds of Lucy and Mina (Helen Chandler) in Browning's *Dracula*. Most visual of all is the fact the Lorenzes sleep in coffins. Dr. Lorenz openly admits that he finds it "much more comfortable than a bed." During one of the kidnappings, Dr. Lorenz hides inside another coffin so as to fool police looking for a female corpse. No film had depicted Lugosi in a coffin since Browning's *Dracula*.[30] Here is one of the most memorable and visually arresting images of Lugosi, the Dracula actor inside a casket, and yet it is also one of the most rare in his film output.

None of this is to suggest that Dr. Lorenz is actually a vampire. In fact, he more closely resembles what Countess Zaleska (Gloria Holden) hopes Dr. Garth (Otto Kruger) will be in *Dracula's Daughter* (1936): a "doctor of minds and souls," someone who "stands between [her] and destruction." Dr. Lorenz kidnaps brides in an effort to, as one character suggests, "sustain his wife in a youthful state." With his hypodermic needle, he extracts blood from his victims' necks and – after mixing it with some other chemical – injects the same into the Countess. "You're beautiful," he tells her, "and I shall always keep you that way." Without regular shots, she is wracked with pain, the effects of a rapid aging process. Even as he is dying, Dr. Lorenz attempts to give her a final injection. Failing to do so has immediate effect. As Dr. Foster has already realized, the Countess looks young, but is probably "seventy or eighty years old."

As much or more than Countess Zaleska, Countess Lorenz is reminiscent of Hungarian Countess Elizabeth Báthory de Ecsed (1560-1614, aka "Elizabeth Bathory" and "Elizabeth Bathori"), who tortured and killed dozens, if not hundreds, of young women between 1585 and 1609. After her death, writers claimed she had vampiric tendencies, bathing in the blood of virgins to maintain a youthful appearance. Dr. Lorenz's injections perform a similar function for his wife, to the extent that he kidnaps brides at the altar. "All of them must be [young]," he insists. Countess Lorenz requires virginal blood just as much as Countess Báthory allegedly did. And Dr. Lorenz acts at her domineering behest.

Accounts of Báthory appeared in the American press at least as early as 1827. In September of that year, the *North American* told readers: "One day she struck [an 'innocent' young woman] in a brutal manner, and the blood of the victim having flown into her face, she ran to a mirror to wipe it off. She fancied that her skin became whiter, more beautiful."[31] In 1894, the *Chicago Tribune* published a similar story, telling readers her "naturally cruel nature was spurred by the frenzied desire to retain her waning beauty at any price."[32] And in 1912, the *Cleveland Plain Dealer* maintained that the blood obtained for Báthory by her lackeys was "always saved, and in this life fluid the woman actually bathed."[33]

The *Plain Dealer* also published an illustration of the murderous Countess admiring herself in a mirror. *The Corpse Vanishes* created a similar image, the Countess admiring her reflection while Dr. Lorenz promises to "always keep [her] that way." In the *Plain Dealer* illustration, the Countess also holds a bloody cane over a defenseless maiden, a depiction of her sadism. Countess Lorenz shares this trait, as can be seen when she strikes Pat, as well as in the cruelty she displays towards members of her extended family.

The Lorenz Family

In the horror film, the American family can become twisted into a horrible inversion of itself. Nowhere is this more evident than in the 1960s and 1970s, beginning with Norman Bates (Anthony Perkins) and his mother in Alfred Hitchcock's *Psycho* (1960) and continuing through Roman Polanski's *Rosemary's Baby* (1968) and George Romero's *Night of the Living Dead* (1968). Depraved families then appeared in Wes Craven's *The Last House on the Left* (1972) and *The Hills Have Eyes* (1977), and – most infamously of all – Tobe Hooper's *The Texas Chain Saw Massacre* (1974). In *Hearths of Darkness: The Family in the American Horror Film*, Tony Williams states that:

> typical American families [in these films] encounter their monstrous counterparts, undergo (or perpetuate) brutal violence, and eventually survive with full knowledge of their kinship to their monstrous counterparts. All these depictions contradict normal idealized family images in mainstream American film and television.[34]

Williams adds that these films belong to a "definable historical context," one that dates to the literature of authors like Nathaniel Haw-

Kidnapped brides – who must be "young" and "pretty" – make "charming" additions to the Lorenz family.

thorne, Edgar Allan Poe, Ambrose Bierce, and H.P. Lovecraft.[35]

Horrifying families also appeared in the nonfiction press, whether in the case of the Manson Family in the late 1960s, or the exploits of the Bender Family in the 1870s. With the help of their two children, John and Elvira Bender murdered at least a dozen travelers who stopped at their hotel in Kansas. Usually daughter Kate distracted the victims while John or John, Jr. slit their throats. A trapdoor dropped the corpses into the basement, where the Benders looted them prior to burying them elsewhere on their property. By the time authorities got involved, the Benders had disappeared, never to be apprehended. The press seized on their story, as did the fictionalized dime novel *The Five Fiends; or The Bender Hotel Horror in Kansas* (1874), which overestimated the family's size by one member.[36]

Tony Williams traces the rise of horrifying families onscreen to Universal Pictures in the 1930s and 1940s.[37] In most cases, these relationships appeared thanks to sequels, the familial becoming the studio's key approach to continuing the narratives of monsters that had (apparently) been killed, as in films like Browning's *Dracula* and James Whale's *Frankenstein* (1931). Examples include *Dracula's Daughter* and Robert Siodmak's *Son of Dracula* (1943), as well as Whale's *Bride of Frankenstein* (1935), Rowland V. Lee's *Son of Frankenstein* (1939), and Erle C. Kenton's *The Ghost of Frankenstein* (1942). As Williams notes, these movies attempted to "externalize tensions emerging from the family."[38] They also represent a porous, even confused notion of what family means. Despite its title, *Son of Dracula* seems to feature the original Dracula, not his offspring. And the title of *Bride of Frankenstein* – as well as dialogue spoken in it – refers not to the betrothed of Dr. Frankenstein (Colin Clive), but instead to the mate he creates for his monster. By contrast, the title of *Son of Frankenstein* definitely refers to Baron Wolf von Frankenstein (Basil Rathbone), the doctor's son.

Despite reliance on the familial, it was actually rare for an individual film of the period to feature a horrifying family. James Whale's *The Old Dark House* (1932) supplies the key example of the 1930s. During a terrible storm, five travelers unexpectedly find themselves stuck at the Femm family home. Horace Femm (Ernest Thesiger) is an extremely nervous sort, one who might be wanted by the police. His gruff sister Rebecca (Eva Moore) is a religious fanatic. Their aged father Roderick (Elspeth Dudgeon, credited onscreen as "John Dudgeon") is allegedly "wicked" and "blasphemous." Butler Morgan is a "brute" when drunk, but the family must employ him to look after the maniacal Saul Femm (Brember Wills), who – during a brief moment of apparent sanity – accuses the others of murdering their own sister years earlier.

That same year, in Tod Browning's film *Freaks* (1932), the title characters represent a non-biological family, but a family nonetheless. "One of us! One of us!", the characters chant, their deep and loyal ties to one another bound by their physical challenges, as well as by their emotional connections. Indeed, their chant is heard when they admit Cleopatra (Olga Baclanova), a "normal" woman, into their family, the result of her marriage to a dwarf named Hans (Harry Earles).

However different *The Corpse Vanishes* is from *Freaks* and *The Old Dark House*, it also features a "family," some of the members related by blood, some not. And it is a family unknown to the authorities, who according to the press are searching for a singular "corpse thief." In his initial dialogue, Dr. Lorenz praises his "little family" for being "so very faithful." And yet the family members increase and decrease at the whims of Dr. Lorenz and the Countess. Perhaps the most unusual is Mike (George Eldredge, credited onscreen as "George Eldridge"). Physically and intellectually, he seems to be a healthy, middle-aged man. In his limited screen time, he is rude to Pat, but only because she wants to interview Dr. Lorenz without having an appointment. Whether he is transporting a newly arrived coffin from the train station or helping to kidnap women, Mike performs crucial tasks for Dr. Lorenz with complete loyalty. He is unusual because he lacks any narrative backstory. Why, in other words, is this man with no known blood ties to the family so deeply enmeshed in Lorenz's crimes?

Mike's limited footage results in part from the amount of attention devoted to Fagah (Minerva Urecal), a mysterious old woman, and her two sons, the mentally challenged Angel (Frank Moran), and the sadistic dwarf Toby (Angelo Rossito, credited onscreen as "Angelo"). The trio lives together in a single room inside the basement of the Lorenz home. Toby leaves the home on occasion with Mike and Lorenz. He also undertakes menial tasks like answering the front door and showing guests to their bedrooms. The Countess calls him a "gargoyle"; Pat calls him a "monstrosity." For his part, Toby takes joy in the suffering of others, gleefully telling Pat, "I guess you'll sleep very good... *maybe*," before laughing openly at what he knows will be a traumatic night.

By contrast, Dr. Lorenz barks at Fagah when she appears on the ground floor of the home: she and Angel belong underground. That said, Lorenz gives Fagah the crucial task of assisting in the transfusions that keep the Countess alive and well. He also leaves the well being of the kidnapped brides to Fagah, who obeys his commands unquestioningly. Like Toby, she refers to Lorenz as "Master"; this terminology (and the power relationships it denotes) recalls the language Renfield (Dwight Frye) uses to speak to the title character of Browning's *Dracula*.

By contrast, Angel seems to have limited duties, if any. He is allowed in the laboratory during one transfusion. But his penchant for admiring the kidnapped brides and caressing their hair has severe consequences. Catching him the first time, Dr. Lorenz whips Angel repeatedly while Toby watches, gloating and snickering in the most sadistic manner. "Why do you beat my son so hard?", Fagah asks. Lorenz replies, "Because he's a beast, an animal. And someday I shall have to destroy him."

Lorenz's threat soon becomes reality. During the night that Pat stays at the Lorenz home, Toby hears Angel getting out of bed. "I know where you're going," he says. "Someday the Master will catch you, then you'll be sorry." Grunting, Angel leaves, sneaking into Pat's bedroom. Later, he follows her in the basement, lasciviously chewing on a turkey leg with a smile on his face. By that time, the Countess has declared that Angel is a "menace" to the family's safety. Lorenz agrees and strangles Angel to death.

Trying to make their getaway at the final kidnapping, the Lorenz family again decreases in size. A policeman shoots Toby, who pleads with Lorenz not to leave him behind. Without hesitation, Lorenz literally kicks him to the curb. In retaliation, the grief-stricken Fagah stabs Lorenz, who in turn strangles her. Once Lorenz is dead, Fagah uses the last of her strength to stab the Countess, who has fallen to the floor after being overpowered by Pat. Disloyalty begets disloyalty, with Countess Lorenz's death not dissimilar to Countess Zaleska's in *Dracula's Daughter*, her jealous servant Sandor (Irving Pichel) shoots her with an arrow after she tries to give Dr. Garth eternal life.

The Lorenz clan also includes those women who have no opportunity to fight back, the kidnapped brides who are vaulted beneath the family home. They are alive, but trapped in a cataleptic state. It is clear that the doctor and the Countess consider them to be relatives, at least of a sort. When speaking excitedly about Peggy, the fake bride, Dr. Lorenz enthuses, "She'll make a charming addition to our family." And the brides are particularly precious in the eyes of the otherwise cruel Countess. When the Lorenzes decide to flee at the end of the film, she shows far more consideration to the kidnapped women than for anyone else. "The brides," she worries, "what will we do without them?"

At first, it seems the Countess' concern for the brides comes solely from their capacity to restore her health. While that is her key interest, the Countess does have another reason, one that Dr. Lorenz shares. Of one of the kidnapped women the Countess remarks, "She's pretty... very young." Later, given Lorenz's "very special reason" for asking Pat to spend the night, the Countess happily informs the reporter, "Some time you too will be a bride." And when examining a photograph of the stunt bride, the Countess becomes particularly excited, perhaps more than at any other point in the film, lustfully exclaiming, "She's a most unusual type ... such fascinating eyes." Dr. Lorenz and the Countess are infatuated with the brides, to the extent that their membership in the family seems sexualized. Along with shared attraction for the victims, the Lorenzes literally share in them physically thanks to the use of their blood.

Conclusion

The Corpse Vanishes remains a fascinating, even if flawed film. For example, no single moment was meant to be more dramatic than Pat's discovery that the minister at the stunt wedding is actually Dr. Lorenz in disguise. His back is to her as she enters the minister's office; she learns the truth only after approaching him. But the camera angle and poor blocking greatly diminish its impact on the viewer, as it's obvious that the fake minister is Lorenz as soon as Pat enters the room.

Nevertheless, *The Corpse Vanishes* is a welter of ideas and influences, appropriating as it does the histories of girl stunt reporters and Hollywood vampires and placing them into an early example of the perverse kind of family that populated horror films of future decades. As with *The Texas Chain Saw Massacre*, for example, the Lorenz family seems to appear out of nowhere, and its storyline remains open-ended, at least to a degree. A policeman hits Mike, but his fate is never explained. The authorities might arrest him, or he might escape. We don't know.

In the end, perhaps Monogram wasn't understated in its choice of title. No corpse vanishes, not even one. Instead, Dr. Lorenz kidnaps women who are actually still alive. But even more than with Mike, their fate forever hangs in the balance. The audience does not learn if all of them are rescued. Do they survive? And if so, have they been forever scarred by their temporary adoption into the Lorenz family?

(Endnotes)

1 "Eight More Features Get Starter's Gun This Week," *Film Daily*, March 10, 1942, 6.

2 Gary D. Rhodes, "Gerald Schnitzer," *Filmfax Plus: The Magazine of Unusual Film, Television & Retro Pop Culture*, No. 129 (Winter 2012), 38. Unfortunately, it is difficult to find the news story Dietz read. Various brides were kidnapped in the 1920s and 1930s, one of them being an heiress named Helen Fisher Drill. See "Abducted Heiress Rescued in West," *New York Times*, April 20, 1931, 40. Other examples of such incidents include "Kidnapped, Swears Bride," *New York Times*, January 9, 1921, 2; "Abducted Bride Escapes," *New York Times*, March 14, 1923, 12; and "Jailed for Kidnapping, He Dodges Wrong Bride," *New York Times*, December 2, 1934, E2. A related story, more similar to the plot of *The Corpse Vanishes* than the others, reported the kidnapping of a bridegroom who "had been kidnapped, chloroformed, and then left by the roadside" while his bride was waiting for several hours at a church in New York. After being rescued and revived, the bridegroom married "twenty four hours behind [the] scheduled time," with the "villain foiled" as in "all good melodramas." See "Villain Chloroforms and Kidnaps Bridegroom; Bride Weeps at Church, but Ending Is Happy," *New York Times*, October 26, 1925, 1.

3 Actor Tristram Coffin later claimed that Elizabeth Russell refused to get inside the coffin for a scene in *The Corpse Vanishes*, requiring the director to use a double. However, viewing the film makes clear that it is Russell in the coffin. See Tom Weaver, *Poverty Row Horrors! Monogram, PRC, and Republic Horror Films of the Forties* (Jefferson, North Carolina: McFarland and Company, 1993), 72.

4 "Hollywood Inside," *Daily Variety*, March 18, 1942, 2.

5 "Chatter," *Daily Variety*, April 9, 1942, 2.

6   Vance King, *"The Corpse Vanishes," Motion Picture Daily*, April 15, 1942, 11.
7   *"The Corpse Vanishes," Film Daily*, April 16, 1942, 6.
8   *"The Corpse Vanishes," Daily Variety*, April 13, 1942, 3.
9   Lugosi would also costar with Minerva Urecal in *The Ape Man* (1943) and *Ghosts on the Loose* (1943).
10 J. Brooks Atkinson, *"The Front Page," New York Times*, August 26, 1928, 95.
11 Jean Marie Lutes, "Into the Madhouse with Nellie Bly: Girl Stunt Reporting in Late Nineteenth-Century America," *American Quarterly*, Vol. 54, No. 2 (June 2002), 217.
12 Nellie Bly, "Among the Mad," *Godey's Lady's Book*, January 1889.
13 For more information on Nellie Bly, see *Deborah Noyes, Ten Days a Madwoman* (New York: Viking, 2016).
14 Noyes, 94.
15 "Nellie Bly's Trip Round the World," *Chicago Tribune*, January 26, 1890, 12.
16 Lutes, 245.
17 LeRoy Lad Panek, *The Origins of the American Detective Story* (Jefferson, North Carolina: McFarland and Company, 2006), 169.
18 Panek, 169.
19 "Saved," *Moving Picture World*, October 19, 1912, 221.
20 *"The Insane Heiress," Moving Picture World*, December 24, 1910, 1492.
21 Other examples of girl reporters in early films appear in Vitagraph's *How Cissy Made Good* (1915) and Kulee's *How Molly Made Good* (1915).
22 *"A Terror of the Night," New York Dramatic Mirror*, May 27, 1914, 42.
23 A copy of *The Chinese Fan* is available on the DVD *Lost & Found American Treasures from the New Zealand Film Archive* (San Francisco, California: National Film Preservation Foundation, 2013).
24 Cecilia Ager, "Going Places," *Variety*, February 21, 1933, 12.
25 Some of the outdoor shots of Pat at the train station were clearly shot in daylight, but the film suggests it is nighttime. Lanterns are lit at the depot, and Foster has his car headlights turned on. Through the windows of Foster's car (as well as Lorenz's home right after their arrival), it definitely appears to be dark outside.
26 King, 11.
27 The name was not the only allusion to a famous person that the script used. Their dialogue also references clairvoyant "Madame Zora." It also seems likely that the name of the film's "Forest Mortuary" was inspired by Forest Lawn Memorial-Parks & Mortuaries.
28 *Complete Catalogue of Genuine and Original "Star" Films (Moving Pictures), Manufactured by Geo. Méliès of Paris* (New York: Star Films, 1903), 26. Available in *A Guide to Motion Picture Catalogs by American Producers and Distributors, 1894-1908: A Microfilm Edition* (New Brunswick: Rutgers University Press, 1985), Reel 4.
29 Tom Weaver sees a parallel between the taxi driver in *The Corpse Vanishes* and the inn keeper in *Dracula*. See Weaver, 71.
30 At one point in *Mark of the Vampire*, the fake vampire Count Mora is at rest, but the shot does not clearly show him inside a coffin.
31 "The Castle of Cseisthe, in Hungary," *North American; Or, Weekly Journal of Politics, Science and Literature*, September 1, 1827, 123.
32 "One Woman's Secret of Beauty," *Chicago Tribune*, October 6, 1894, 16.
33 "The World's Greatest Murderers, XVI–Elizabeth of Transylvania," *Cleveland Plain Dealer* (Cleveland, Ohio), August 11, 1912, 3.
34 Tony Williams, *Hearths of Darkness: The Family in the American Horror Film* (Madison, New Jersey: Fairleigh Dickinson University Press, 1996), 13.
35 Ibid, 30, 27.
36 For more information on the Benders, see Phyllis de la Garza, *Death for Dinner: The Benders of (Old) Kansas* (Unionville, New York: Silk Label Books, 2014).
37 Williams, 30.
38 Williams, 50.

In *Bowery at Midnight*, John Archer asks his Psychology professor, Bela Lugosi, for advice on a research project... with disastrous results. *(Photo courtesy of Bill Chase)*

Chapter 6

Slipstreaming with Karl Wagner and/or Professor Frederick Brenner

The Multiple Realities of *Bowery at Midnight*

by **Robert Guffey**

Slipstreaming in the Bowery

Bowery at Midnight (1942) could very well be one of the earliest examples of a "slipstream" film in American cinema. What is slipstream? Slipstream is an ever-burgeoning literary genre that refuses to be nailed down. The word was first created by science fiction writer Bruce Sterling in the late 1980s to identify what he perceived as a trend in postmodern fiction in which the underlying strangeness of the twentieth century was portrayed in an eccentric, fluid manner that transcended standard genre labels. Writers as varied as Italo Calvino (*Cosmicomics* and *Invisibles Cities*), Steve Erickson (*Rubicon Beach* and *Tours of the Black Clock*), Kelly Link (*Stranger Things Happen* and *Magic for Beginners*), Thomas Pynchon (*Gravity's Rainbow* and *Mason and Dixon*), and Jeff VanderMeer (*City of Saints and Madmen* and *Borne*) are often cited as being preeminent examples of "slipstream." Though the term is difficult to pin down, Sue Lange of Flashlightworthybooks.com made a brave attempt to define the genre as follows:

> Slipstream is uncomfortably defined as fiction that crosses the divide between mainstream and the speculative literatures of science

John Berkes (center) is about to be betrayed by his partners in crime, Wheeler Oakman (left) and Bela Lugosi (right). *(Photo courtesy of Bill Chase)*

fiction, fantasy, and horror. Personally, I like to think of slipstream as simply weird. It feels weird in a way that's weirder than a standard weird sf/f/h story. Physical laws are broken but no one wonders about them. The science is not rigorous or even questioned. The typical strange characters of speculative fiction [...] are not usually present so you can't count on them to impart the weirdness. The humans themselves must do that, but they don't do it by being weird. They are usually the very model of normalcy. They are average, common humans like you and me. It's their very normality in the face of strange circumstances that marks a slipstream story.[1]

If we trace this "eccentric, fluid" style of storytelling through the DNA of world cinema, it's not hard to begin citing such wonderfully surreal examples as Robert Wiene's *The Cabinet of Dr. Caligari* (1920) or Carl Dreyer's *Vampyr* (1932). However, if we were to focus solely on *American* cinema, I would argue that it would be quite difficult to trace this trend further back than the Poverty Row horror films of the 1940s. *Bowery at Midnight* is a perfect example of this type of storytelling—perfect mainly because it's so imperfect, and thus dream-like in its construction.

Bowery at Midnight was produced by Sam Katzman for the infamous Poverty Row studio known as Monogram which churned out hordes of poorly made B films throughout the '30s, '40s, and '50s. In 1953 it rechristened itself "Allied Artists" in an effort to attract more bankable talent and under that name remained in business until 1975 when its final film, *The Man Who Would Be King*, was released with Michael Caine and Sean Connery featured in the starring roles.

Back in 1942, however, Monogram was only interested in making B films as fast as inhumanly possible. *Bowery at Midnight*, for example, was filmed in fourteen days. It's a strange hybrid of the nascent subgenre of film noir (a term that wouldn't actually come into existence until the 1950s), science fiction, and horror. As Tom Weaver wrote in his 1993 book *Poverty Row Horrors!*:

Say whatever you want about the old Monogram horror films, but never make the mistake of saying they were unimaginative. If anything, there was often too *much* imagination lavished on some of their films (*Black Dragons, Bowery at Midnight, King of the Zombies,* more) which combined themes that few other studios would have dreamed of pairing in a motion picture.[2]

In *Bowery at Midnight* Bela Lugosi stars as psychologist Frederick Brenner, a college professor who moonlights as "Karl Wagner," the proprietor of a soup kitchen called the Friendly Mission. Ostensibly, Wagner is spending his evenings doing charitable work, such as feeding the homeless in the bowery. In reality, however, this soup kitchen is just a front for Brenner's illegal operations, which includes robbery, wholesale murder and drug smuggling (though that last offense isn't made explicit). In the publicity for the film, Monogram claimed that Lugosi was playing a double role in this film, but that's not quite true. It's clear from Brenner's later actions that he's almost certainly insane (typical for a psychologist, of course), but there are no indications that Brenner suffers from a split personality. He's aware of his double life and does everything he can to prevent the police from discovering that Brenner and Wagner are the same individual.

The movie begins with felon Fingers Dolan (John Berkes) breaking out of a federal penitentiary—in reality the front gates of Monogram Studios, which are still standing to this very day. One need only stroll down to 4376 Sunset Drive in Los Angeles to see the very same wall that appears in the first shot of this film. Since 1971 these have been the front walls

Not one of these All-American college students realizes that their psychology class is being taught by a murderous sociopath (a situation that may not be as uncommon as one might think). *(Photo courtesy of Bill Chase)*

of KCET, the PBS station, but in April of 2011 the building was sold to the Church of Scientology. Apparently, Monogram didn't have the budget to build a prison set, so someone decided that the front gates of Monogram were close enough to a prison to be an appropriate stand-in.

After giving the authorities the slip, Dolan makes his way to the Friendly Mission where Wagner recognizes him. Within minutes, Wagner has initiated Dolan into the ranks of Wagner's secret team of criminals. In the next scene, Wagner and two other criminals—Fingers Dolan and a hired killer named Stratton (Wheeler Oakman)—are breaking into The Atlas Jewelry Company. After Dolan successfully cracks open a safe filled with precious jewels, Wagner orders Stratton to shoot him on the spot. Wagner has done this before. Later in the film a police detective remarks that this is one of Wagner's modus operandi: committing robberies, then assassinating one of his compatriots and leaving the corpse behind. In my favorite scene in the film, Wagner is planning a heist of a jewelry store in broad daylight. Wagner and one of his henchmen, a transient named Charley (Vince Barnett), are standing on a high rooftop across the street with the intent of creating a distraction. What Charley doesn't know yet is that *he's* the distraction. Unexpectedly, Wagner pitches Charley off the roof. As a crowd forms around the dead body, one of Wagner's stooges strolls into the jewelry store across the street and makes off with a load of loot. Of course, the Friendly Mission offers Wagner a near-endless supply of transients and ne'er-do-wells, so the kindly professor isn't in danger of running out of potential recruits any time soon.

The next major character to whom we're introduced is Sgt. Pete Crawford, portrayed by Dave O'Brien who also starred in two previous Lugosi films, 1940's *The Devil Bat* and 1941's *Spooks Run Wild*. Crawford gets involved in a shoot-out with criminal Frankie Mills, portrayed by Tom Neal (who will later become far more famous for his starring role in Edgar Ulmer's 1945 film *Detour*, which many scholars consider to be one of the best films noir ever made—some say *the* best). Mills, like the ill-fated Fingers Dolan, hides out in the Friendly Mission. Wagner's nurse, a beautiful young woman named Judy Alvern (Wanda McKay), notices that Mills has been shot and offers to treat the wound without even asking Mills what happened or why. Apparently this is standard operating procedure at the Friendly Mission (per Wagner's orders, perhaps?). Unfortunately for Mills, he too is spotted by the eagle-eyed Wagner and is soon embedded in the mastermind's subterranean band of criminals.

No true film noir would be complete without the connective tissue of coincidence binding the tale together. As Mickey Spillane writes in his 1953 novel *Kiss Me, Deadly*, referring to his famous detective character, Mike Hammer, "Some people are accident prone. You're coincidence prone."[3] In fact, every major character in *any* film noir is coincidence-prone. It just so happens that Judy Alvern, the young lady who works as Wagner's nurse, is also the girlfriend of Richard Dennison (John Archer), one of Wagner's/Brenner's students in his psychology class at the local University. Richard tries to convince Judy to give up her volunteer work at the Friendly Mission. It's very clear that Richard hails from an upper class background and considers Judy's "bleeding heart" attitudes toward the poor to be a load of liberal nonsense that can only be cured by accepting his proposal of marriage. ("Judy, I—I want you to give up that silly job," Richard says. "Saving humanity—it's ridiculous!") Judy accuses Richard of knowing nothing about the real world and essentially tells him to hit the pavement. Judy's words have some effect on Richard. The next day, after Brenner's psychology class, Richard tells the professor that he intends on writing a paper about the psychology of the underprivileged. The professor halfheartedly urges him to pursue the project, not knowing that the poor fool intends on conducting his research at Wagner's Friendly Mission.

Not surprisingly, Richard recognizes Brenner at the Mission later that night. At first Wagner tries to deny that he's the same man as Brenner, then quickly gives up and ushers Richard into his secret underground headquarters where he introduces the young man to some of his cohorts, including Frankie Mills. Richard assumes that the professor is conducting some kind of massive psychological study using the Mission as a cover, then realizes his assumptions are rather off-base when Wagner orders Mills to kill Richard for uncovering his secret. Mills doesn't hesitate to shoot the little rich boy through the head with a revolver.

Wagner disposes of the body in the usual manner: He gives the corpse to one of his minions, Doc Brooks (Lew Kelly), a doddering old drug addict who had at one time been a great surgeon but is now reduced to being Wagner's caretaker in return for a steady supply of narcotics. Wagner thinks that Brooks is burying these corpses in a secret room hidden beneath the *first* secret room.

Plunged into Multiple Realities

This is a film about multiple realities, hidden layers, both metaphorically and literally. Not only does Wagner contain layers of different identities hidden within himself, but so does the Friendly Mission. On the surface the Friendly Mission is just that: a respite for the downtrodden. Beneath the surface it serves the exact opposite purpose by exploiting the very weaknesses in the underclasses that it ostensibly seeks to treat. In this sense, Wagner's Friendly Mission is comparable to the New-Path facility in Philip K. Dick's 1977 novel *A Scanner Darkly* (another tale that combines various genres into a story about dual identities and the exploitation of the lower classes). On the surface New-Path seeks to reform drug addicts, when in reality it uses them to farm the very illegal substances from which they need to be cured. The social message of *Bowery at Midnight* similarly contains hidden layers, just like the architecture of the Mission itself.

The Friendly Mission in *Bowery at Midnight* is the ultimate validation of every conservative nightmare. Ask any conservative or libertarian what they think about welfare programs that seek to alleviate the suffering of the poor, and almost all of them will try to tell you that these programs do little to help the underclass, but instead entrap them in a backwards system of eternal dependence on the state and encourage fraud and criminal behavior while doing so. *Bowery at Midnight* seeks

Bela Lugosi's charitable works in the bowery are about to take a nasty turn as he attacks costar Wanda McKay in this publicity still for *Bowery at Midnight*. *(Photo courtesy of Bill Chase)*

to reveal to us a disturbing reality: that the poor will stick shivs in the backs of their compatriots for a buck if given half a chance, and anyone crazy enough to want to alleviate the plight of the homeless is either a confidence man or dangerously naïve like Richard's girlfriend, Judy. At the same time, as the story unfolds further, one can't help but wonder if the screenwriter, Gerald Schnitzer, sought to slip an even more subversive message beneath the seemingly reactionary foundation.

This larger intent is confirmed in a 2012 interview with Schnitzer conducted by Gary D. Rhodes in the pages of *Filmfax* #129:

> My idea was lost, I think, thanks to low key lighting of the sign above the shelter that read: 'Not What Is Your Creed, But What Is Your Need.' So, here are the poor and the wretched seeking peace, only to find hell, orchestrated by an upstanding suburbanite who seems to live a balanced married life, in the suburbs with a two-car garage and a manicured lawn... meanwhile he is playing havoc with the poor and the wretched.[4]

The slipstream merging of Bela Lugosi's Gothic screen persona with that of a contemporary crime drama is perfectly represented by this unique publicity photo for *Bowery at Midnight*. *(Photo courtesy of Bill Chase)*

Fear the Unknown

Many horror films are reactionary at their very core. They have to be. The ultimate message of many horror films is simple: Fear the Unknown. This message can be extended into real life in ways that are clearly unhealthy and disturbing. How much xenophobia fuels the classic werewolf and zombie story structure? It's a good question, one that might need a completely separate book to explore thoroughly. Nonetheless, we can touch on this question somewhat in the context of slipstream fiction, and particularly in the context of *Bowery at Midnight*.

Not only is *Bowery at Midnight* a crime noir, but it's also a zombie flick. Indeed, one could argue it's one of the earliest zombie flicks. The first zombie feature film ever made was the Halperin Brothers' *White Zombie* (1932) in which Lugosi stars as Murder Lengendre, a voodoo master who revives dead Haitians to perform manual labor in his sugar plantations. It's appropriate, therefore, that exactly ten years later Lugosi should star in yet another zombie film. And yet in *Bowery at Midnight* Lugosi is not the mad man reviving the dead, it's his squirrelly minion, Doc Brooks.

As Schnitzer said in the aforementioned *Filmfax* interview:

> My idea was to 'foreclose the mortgage' on Lugosi's fog-enshrouded, proverbial castle and put him into a fresh environment like L.A.'s downtown skid row. I tried to modify his typical scary persona at the start, but Lugosi is Lugosi and will always cast his Dracula genes, even in the American suburbs. Producers and theatre owners alike turn pale when you change the format.[5]

Schnitzer, therefore, was attempting to peel back several layers of artifice from Lugosi's screen persona, at least as far as he could manage within the constraints in which he was forced to work. By extension, he was also attempting to peel back layers of artifice from the harsh reality of 1940s America.

Realities within realities. Personalities within personalities. Secrets within secrets. Lies within lies. Genres within genres. Beneath the Friendly Mission lies a secret room where Wagner plots all his deviltry. Behind this secret room is another one in which Brooks buries Wagner's many victims. However, unbeknownst even to Wagner, a *fourth* secret room lies beneath the third secret chamber. The entrance to this mysterious chamber is beneath one of the makeshift graves. What looks like a grave is really a door into a whole separate reality, a separate genre hid-

Frequent Bela Lugosi costar Dave O'Brien (who can also be seen in 1940's *The Devil Bat* and 1941's *Spooks Run Wild*) tries to get to the bottom of a mysterious string of murders by interrogating Lugosi and Wanda McKay. *(Photo courtesy John Antosiewicz)*

den within the crime noir genre the audience thought they were dealing with from the very first reel. In this *sub*-subterranean realm Doc Brooks performs experiments on Wagner's victims, discovering a method by which to bring these poor unfortunates back to some semblance of life. We see only brief glimpses of the mindless brutes shuffling around inside that tiny chamber, condemned to an undead existence, trapped by the drug-addled servant of a criminal mastermind—not even the mastermind himself. That's how lowly these particular zombies are. Like the undead Haitian plantation workers in *White Zombie*, these corpses have also been plucked from the ranks of the lower classes. The metaphor here should be obvious.

In 1980 Dennis Etchison published a brilliant short story entitled "The Late Shift" in which corpses are revived by a mysterious corporation for a period of three to four days in order to perform mindless tasks such as working as a cashier at the local 7-11 or handing out tickets at an all-night porno theatre. In this story Etchison uses the traditional zombie tale to say something very unsettling and subversive about capitalism, an unforgiving system that frowns upon "dead time" of any sort, time in which one is not being truly "productive" or sacrificing one's blood for the sake of the corporation to which one has pledged one's very life.

One could argue that *Bowery at Midnight*—as well as *White Zombie*—prefigures the central question of Etchison's story by several decades, if not in its satirical intent then at least in its use of the zombie to make a commentary about the seemingly hopeless position the underclasses occupy in a capitalist system, a system in which the rich get richer and the zombies get... well, deader.

Richard Dennison represents what happens when one makes the mistake of crossing over to the wrong side of the tracks, even if only out of mere curiosity. The rich have their world, the poor have theirs. Rich psychology students who want to disguise themselves as the poor in order to write a research paper can't expect to end up like Joel McCrea in Preston Sturgess' 1949 film *Sullivan's Travels*: hitched to Veronica Lake with a hit movie under your belt. No, instead you can expect to be shot full of holes and your "dead time" put to good use by an industrious soul like ol' Doc Brooks. In this case, Richard is amongst the gibbering dead who kill and consume Wagner at the end of the film when Brooks leads Wagner down into his secret chamber in order to save the professor from the police. The professor is indeed saved by the police, but not before being ripped to shreds by Brook's horde of zombies while the cops, including the fair-haired Pete Crawford, just stand by and watch the gory scene unfold. "Well, that takes care of the professor!" Crawford says with a jovial smile on his face, seemingly not at all surprised by the zombies lurking in Wagner's *sub*-sub-level basement.

The Rich Eat What They Want

Most crowd-pleasing B-thrillers from the early 1940s definitely did not end with the young rich hero being fatally shot, surgically transformed into a mindless zombie, and feasting on the villain's remains. What's even stranger is the film's out-of-left-field epilogue in which we see Richard lying in bed at home, wearing a robe, and reading the newspaper. His girlfriend, Judy, is waiting on him hand-and-foot. We're led to assume that Judy has now changed her mind, and has accepted Richard's engagement proposal. Richard is in bed healing from his traumatic experience in the bowery. How could the man "recover" from having been fatally shot and transformed into a zombie? One might

Our Boys In Blue, accompanied by Wanda McKay and Lew Kelly, do not appear at all eager to save Bela Lugosi from a subbasement filled with ravenous zombies. *(Photo courtesy John Antosiewicz)*

assume that this scene was tacked on at the end because someone at the studio felt the film was far too grim and needed a happier ending. (Similar concessions were made in other 1940s noir films, Fritz Lang's *The Woman in the Window* being one of the most prominent examples.) And yet, perhaps the scene has a deeper meaning. We could conclude that the scene offers us the concluding argument to the conservative nightmare laid out previously: Judy has now seen the error of her ways. Richard was right. No good can come of volunteering one's services for the benefit of those lousy transients in the bowery. Staying home all day and waiting on your rich husband is a more satisfying existence. One can almost see Richard emerging from his zombified state and saying to Judy, "See? I told you so! It just doesn't pay to help the poor! They want to be this way... otherwise they'd do something about it themselves!" And Judy nods and laughs and says, "Yes, Richard, dear!" Fade out and fade to black.

Instead we get this weird little dénouement in which Richard, the ex-zombie, is propped up in his lavish bedroom feasting on eggs while bantering with his new wife. The cops didn't even book him for taking part in the wholesale torture and dismemberment of Prof. Brenner? Apparently not. Needless to say, it *does* pay to be rich. This final *non sequitur* leaves one with a disturbing notion.

See that rich young lad walking confidently down the street? Why, just yesterday he was a zombie. I heard he ate his college professor and got away with it. And get a load of his wife. Some guys get all the luck: good looks, money, a beautiful wife. Too bad he had to die so soon. Hey, I wonder if his ball-and-chain ever thinks about the fact that he's a corpse when she's cooking him his scrambled eggs in the morning? What does she care? That dame's set for life. Some chicks will put up with anything from a guy as long as he's loaded. It makes you wonder how many of these other rich bastards are cannibalistic zombies. Makes you wonder indeed....

Monogram as Trailblazer

In the final analysis, *Bowery at Midnight* is an insane little film that receives bonus points for its bravery and dream-like atmosphere. The same atmosphere that David Lynch takes such pains to create in surreal, slipstreamy films noir like *Lost Highway* (1997) and *Mulholland Drive* (2001) is generated by some of these low budget 1940s gems completely on accident—or, rather, the atmosphere seems on the *surface* to be generated completely on accident. One could argue that the imaginations of these early filmmakers are less inspired than an idiosyncratic artist like Lynch, but at the end of the day who's to say which method is best: that of the *intuitive* slipstream artist, or the *accidental* slipstream artist?

To answer that question, it's crucial to point out that judging from Gerald Schnitzer's own words—the aesthetic we now call "slipstream" was embedded in *Bowery at Midnight* from the very beginning, during the feverish forty-eight hour period in which Schnitzer belted out the screenplay: "Normally—a euphemism for hardly ever—we'd get a couple of weeks [to complete a screenplay]. I wrote [*Bowery at Midnight*] in less than two days, around the clock at home, listening to my infant son calling my wife, or anyone, for his four o'clock bottle."[6] While creating that hard, that intensely, sometimes the subconscious takes over the creative process. Clearly, Schnitzer intended the film to be a mixture of various genres for the express purpose of—as he said himself—melding Lugosi's Gothic persona with the horrors of the modern day world to create the kind of distorted social realism at which film noir excels. Even though the word did not yet exist, Schnitzer's intent was unquestionably to create a "slipstream" film. The ancillary High Strangeness of *Bowery at Midnight* no doubt rose unbidden from the depths of Schnitzer's unlocked brain as his fingers raced across his well-worn Smith-Corona typewriter.

As mentioned in a previous chapter, Ray Bradbury's most common piece of advice for young writers (and for himself) was always "DON'T THINK." When one doesn't think, dreams slip out onto the page in ways the creator could never have planned. The tight schedules of these low budget films, combined with the devil-may-care attitudes of producers such as Sam Katzman, allowed artists like Schnitzer to practice his craft in chaotic, anarchistic ways that no major Hollywood studio would have tolerated in the early 1940s. For that reason, above all, the Monogram Nine stand out as progenitors of a new kind of "slipstream cinema," cross-genre experimentalism that would not be fully explored in Hollywood until at least twenty years in the future.

(Endnotes)

1   Sue Lange, "The Best of Slipstream Stories," *Flashlight Worthy* (website accessed June 27, 2017).

2   Tom Weaver, *Poverty Row Horrors!: Monogram, PRC and Republic Horror Films of the Forties* (Jefferson, North Carolina: McFarland, 1993), 36.

3   Mickey Spillane, *Kiss Me, Deadly* (New York: E.P. Dutton, 1952), 39.

4   Gary D. Rhodes, "Gerald Schnitzer: Monogram Screenwriter for Bela Lugosi and the East Side Kids," *Filmfax*, No. 129, 2012, 39.

5   Ibid.

6   Ibid. 39-40.

In the early 1940s, Bela Lugosi made the most of his temporary imprisonment at Monogram Studios. Similar to the way he would later describe his unending identification with the role of Dracula, Lugosi no doubt considered his association with Monogram to be both "a fortune" as well as a "curse," in the sense that Monogram granted the actor star status, but at what cost? This particular publicity still from *The Ape Man* perfectly encapsulates Lugosi's uneasy relationship with the Poverty Row studio. *(Photo courtesy John Antosiewicz)*

Chapter 7

Alienation and the Ape
(or)
The Ape Man: A Tale of Artifice, Lies, False Fronts, and Rampant High Weirdness

by Robert Guffey

By March 19, 1943, the day that William Beaudine's *The Ape Man* was released in theaters all across the United States, there was already a rich history of American films, short stories, novels, and comic books dealing with the theme of humanity's relationship to the ape. Given the religious strictures that held sway in the United States in the latter half of the nineteenth century and the first half of the twentieth century, it's not surprising that this topic—so clearly inspired by Charles Darwin's Theory of Evolution as laid out in Darwin's *On the Origin of Species*, a revolutionary book published to howls of both acclaim and disgust in 1859—was often considered taboo. In schools across the United States, Darwin's Theory of Evolution was not allowed to be taught because many Christians believed that Darwin's book contradicted the Bible's version of humanity's origins. In some areas of the American South, such a ban on Darwin's Theory was still in operation as late as 1967. As a result, the topic of man's evolutionary connection to early primates was displaced from the classroom into far less academic contexts, such as the pages of popular magazines and darkened movie theatres in which the taboo could be acknowledged in a far more socially acceptable context, i.e., in the form of fiction.

Many of these stories manifested in the form of horror or outlandish fantasy, perhaps to further distance the topic from its potentially offensive real world source. In the January/February 2012 issue of *Video Watchdog Magazine*, I published an extensive article about the history of these "ape men" movies entitled "Charles Darwin and the Suppressed Science of Dr. Mirakle," focusing particularly on Robert Florey's expressionistic *Murders in the Rue Morgue* (1932). The article traces this cinematic obsession with fantastical "ape men" from Wallace Worsley's *A Blind Bargain* in 1922 all the way to the original *Planet of the Apes* series of the 1960s and '70s. Though I briefly touch upon Beaudine's *The Ape Man* over the course of this comprehensive survey, in truth the film deserves to be studied in far greater depth. Despite its bottom-of-the-budget origins, this film perhaps says more about America's relationship with Darwin's Theory of Evolution and the horror genre itself in the midst of World War II than any other film of the *fantastique* produced in that tumultuous period.

At its core, *The Ape Man* is a film about artifice, lies, and false fronts. It's a con job that admits it's a con job. It's the cinematic equivalent of a magician opening up his box of tricks and revealing the true nature of his illusions for a stunned and disenchanted audience. It's a film that refuses to play by the rules, to its own detriment, and yet this transgressive attitude makes it seem far more compelling from the perspective of 2019 than many other high budget, A-level films produced by major studios at that same time. Like many other Monogram horror films produced during the Second World War, *The Ape Man* inexplicably continues to attract new generations of admirers. Any rational film critic can only shake his head in disbelief at this strange turn of events. What is it about these low budget B-films that speak to the twenty-first century mind?

We begin with Bela Lugosi. Even in the 1930s, during Lugosi's heyday, Lugosi's acting techniques were considered broad and overly theatrical. According to Lugosi himself, during the filming of *The Thirteenth Chair* (1929) director Tod Browning taught Lugosi how to tone down his acting style, reminding him that he was no longer projecting to those sitting in the back row of an auditorium but instead for a camera standing only a few feet away. Lugosi gradually learned to alter his techniques. Nonetheless, by the time of Lugosi's death, his name had

Bela Lugosi is about ready to crack the whip on his reluctant accomplice, Henry Hall, as sister Minerva Urecal anxiously watches. *(Photo courtesy John Antosiewicz)*

almost become synonymous with Bad Acting. But times change, as do the tastes of audiences. All the personal quirks that made Lugosi an anathema to mainstream success in the 1940s and '50s have become the very elements that draw post-postmodern audiences back to his performances, even those performances that were considered laughable when they were contemporary—indeed, *particularly* those performances.

Many people were unable to detect recognizable figures in the earliest Impressionist paintings of the 1870s, thinking them to be little more than paint splotches randomly applied to canvas as opposed to a well thought-out work of art. I would argue that Lugosi's performances are tantamount to Impressionist paintings or even the avant-garde Pop Art paintings of 1960s artists such as Andy Warhol and Roy Lichtenstein. Every element that hostile mainstream critics criticized in Warhol and Lichtenstein's paintings are present in Lugosi's most memorable performances, which are consistently larger than life, over-indulgent, brash,

BELA LUGOSI AND THE MONOGRAM 9

colorful, in-your-face, purposely artificial, purposely extravagant, performances that go out of their way to elevate trash to High Art, not unlike Warhol's soup cans or Lichtenstein's overblown comic book panels. (In light of this comparison, perhaps it's no surprise that Warhol created a famous silkscreen of Lugosi in 1963, a scene from Tod Browning's *Dracula* entitled *The Kiss*.)

In the 1960s, influential film critics of the French New Wave began to elevate American B-film directors such as Budd Boetticher and Jacques Tourneur to the status of icons, quite rightly noting consistent themes in their films that were often far more illuminating and subversive than the mainstream pablum that had been produced by their contemporary A-film directors. Boetticher's "Ranown" series of Randolph Scott westerns was reevaluated and deemed to be High Art, as were the 1940s B-horror-films produced by Val Lewton such as Tourneur's *The Cat People* (1942) and *I Walked with a Zombie* (1943). Though the Monogram Nine do not share a single director, as do the "Ranown" westerns of Randolph Scott, nonetheless I think the Monogram Nine deserve to be included in a similar category.

In a replay of his far more atmospheric death scene in Robert Florey's *Murders in the Rue Morgue*, Bela Lugosi is fatally attacked by Emil Van Horn while Louise Currie can only look on in horror. (Photo courtesy John Antosiewicz)

Whether these films should be considered Art by accident or design is almost beside the point. The fact is that it can be demonstrated that these nine films were often ahead of their time and experimental to a degree that would have been almost impossible at any of the mainstream studios operating in Hollywood at that time. The fact that all nine of these films were specifically tailored to the talents of Lugosi gave them a consistency they may otherwise have lacked, but this consistency could not be described as repetitious in any way. The variety of subjects and genres explored over the course of these nine films are actually quite broad, while remaining within the increasingly fluid horror genre boundaries no doubt dictated by the films' producer, Sam Katzman.

The Ape Man was the sixth in a series of horror films produced by Katzman at Monogram during the early 1940s to feature Lugosi in a starring role. All nine of these films were meant to appeal to the same massive audience that had made such hits out of Universal horror flicks such as *Son of Frankenstein* (1939), *The Invisible Man Returns* (1940), and *The Mummy's Hand* (1940). Unlike the Universals, however, the Monogram films almost always cross genre boundaries with such delirious abandon that one sometimes wonders if intentional avant-garde techniques were being employed by those behind the cameras. I believe it can be demonstrated that this was indeed the case. Whether this was the *specific intention* of the filmmakers is wholly irrelevant. What matters is what's on the screen, and how the content of these often overlooked films fit into the context of twenty-first century American society. *The Ape Man* is as good a film to use as an example of the Monogram Nine's contemporary relevance as any other in the series, directly because of the many elements that were considered defects when the film was first produced.

As mentioned before, *The Ape Man* was released in March of 1943, sandwiched between two mainstream Lugosi horror flicks: Roy William Neill's *Frankenstein Meets the Wolf Man* (Universal, 1942) and Lew Landers' *The Return of the Vampire* (Columbia, 1944). Though both of these films can boast considerably more atmosphere and polish than *The Ape Man*, neither of them can be said to exploit cutting edge theatrical and literary techniques that were being explored only by the most sophisticated artists of World War II America, and yet such techniques can be found all throughout *The Ape Man*. Though this might sound like an outlandish statement at first, a careful examination of *The Ape Man* will bear out its essential truth.

The central Darwinian subject matter of *The Ape Man* was, as previously mentioned, already old hat in 1943. By March of '43 the audiences of America had already been subjected to *The Wizard* (1927), *Island of Lost Souls* (1932), *The Gorilla* (1939), *The Ape* (1940), *The Monster and the Girl* (1941), *The Strange Case of Dr. Rx* (1942), and *Dr. Renault's Secret* (1942), among several other similar films. So it's not the subject matter of *The Ape Man* that's avant-garde, it's the techniques employed by the writers and directors to explore that subject matter.

In the 1920s German playwright Bertolt Brecht introduced what he called the Theory of Alienation in his stage plays. Brecht, a committed Marxist, believed that the "suspension of disbelief" built into almost any form of popular entertainment was nothing more than a palliative, a kind of opium imposed upon the proletariat by their capitalistic masters. In Brecht's view, one way to break the masses out of this trance was to completely remove the "suspension of disbelief" from the audience in the theatre by alienating them from the events occurring on stage, to completely remove the "entertainment" (at least as the word "entertainment" is popularly understood) component from the equation. The way Brecht managed to do this was by building into his plays disruptive moments that would break the traditional flow of his storyline and advertise to the audience that none of this was to be believed, that all of this was mere fiction, tantamount to a hypnotist suddenly clapping his hands in the face of his swooning subject, then putting the subject back to sleep, then repeating the process all over again. Brecht's intent was to constantly keep the audience members on their toes, to force them to think for themselves, to *participate* in the events unfolding on stage, just as he wanted them to participate more actively in the political events of the world around them.

According to Phoebe von Held, author of *Alienation and Theatricality*:

> As early as 1920, Brecht articulates a preference in his journal entries for a kind of acting that does not pretend to replicate nature, but self-consciously displays its artifice. The theatricality conditioned essence of acting is not denied but brought into relief. He describes the acting of Paula Banholzer ('Bi') as follows:
>
> 'A queen is a queen, terror is terror, but Bi remains Bi. She has style, but she never attains the effects of nature. [...] She does not imitate nature: she acts!'
>
> A fundamental structural principle of Brecht's later theory of alienation becomes apparent here. Nature and aesthetics are recognized as two separate spheres. Moreover, that separation is accentuated in representation. Dramatic character and actor are

held at a distance from each other, producing an overt dualism. Bi does not become a queen, but her acting reveals its artificial constitution. Whilst appreciating in acting a visible residue of artifice, which later becomes one of the characteristics of the alienation effect, Brecht is already calling for an aesthetic of estrangement at the level of dramatic text [...]. In *Excerpts on Dramaturgy*, the sensibility of alienation that Brecht propagates is typified by a sense of wonder and astonishment:

'The most important rule for the poet is to figure out the peculiarities within his materials [...]. The more miracles he can show the spectator, the richer his work. [...] If a man appears on the stage, who cannot appear, this can become an effect instead of a mistake, provided the poet does not cowardly remain silent about why he appears nevertheless, or at least: how strange he (and all of us) find it, that this man appears. Audaciousness is better than comprehension; silent astonishment better than explanation.'

Brecht is interested in an effect of estrangement caused by unexpected, peculiar, or seemingly nonsensical stage events that disrupt the flow of the plot and thereby instigate astonishment. The audience is prompted to search for another level of insight. The passage above foreshadows the idea that aesthetic estrangement may sharpen the spectator's perception, or that it may provoke inquisitiveness. This is a principle typical of Brecht's later approach to alienation. But the emphasis here is still more on the all-consuming effect of estrangement, on the deferral of signification rather than on consequential recognition. The spectator must be overwhelmed by a sense of miraculous bewilderment [...]. Chaos, incomprehensibility and strangeness rank higher than transparency [...].[1]

Not only does Brecht's overall summation of Banholzer's acting style perfectly mirror Lugosi's technique, but the above description of Brecht's avant-garde Theory of Alienation applies as much to Lugosi's Monogram films as it does to acknowledged masterpieces of the stage such as Brecht's *The Threepenny Opera* (1928/29). That the former are considered to be prime examples of trash cinema and the latter the zenith of High Art does not matter at all. As Brecht himself once said, "Sometimes it's more important to be human than to have good taste."[2] Brecht didn't care about good taste or conforming to the strictures of what mainstream theatre critics considered to be legitimate art. He was interested in instilling a particular *effect* in the minds of the bourgeoisie; whether that effect was brought about by a critically acclaimed stage play or a B-level film churned out in a week by a Poverty Row studio probably would not have mattered to him. That William Beaudine's *The Ape Man* is a perfect example of the Theory of Alienation being surreptitiously slipped into a Hollywood production intended for mass consumption may have surprised him; on the other hand, it may not have surprised him at all. Brecht himself need not have been involved in the production of any one particular play or film for the Theory of Alienation to have been employed in the creation of the work. It can be demonstrated that several other Hollywood films, productions ostensibly financed to accomplish little else than the transitory titillation of America's dulled senses, were also created based on Brecht's unique theories.

An excellent example is Orson Welles' *The Lady from Shanghai*, released by Columbia Studios in the United States a full five years after *The Ape Man* (perhaps a prime indicator of *The Ape Man's* many prescient qualities). Like *The Ape Man*, *The Lady from Shanghai* had very humble origins indeed. The film was based on a 1938 pulp novel entitled *If I Die Before I Wake* by Sherwood King. When Harry Cohn, the head of Columbia, approved Welles' pitch to adapt the novel into a film, the movie mogul no doubt thought he would be getting a crowd-pleasing thriller. Instead, he received a Brechtian Hall of Mirrors *disguised* as a popular thriller. Brecht's Theory of Alienation permeates the film. Welles does everything he can, as screenwriter, director, and star, to alert the audience to the utter absurdity of the plot unfolding before their eyes, perhaps most blatantly in the darkly comic courtroom scene in which bit players in the background continually sneeze and putter about while the defendant's life hangs in the balance. This would have been an emotionally charged scene in any other Hollywood thriller. Welles transforms the scene into a farce in an attempt to break the audience out of their celluloid-induced hypnosis.

In her 1985 book, *Orson Welles: A Biography*, Barbara Leaming explicates Welles' considerable debt to Brecht's theories:

> Gravely disappointed at not having been able to work with Brecht, Orson had, by way of compensation, made a film that very subtly embodied key principles of Brechtian theatrical theory: most notably the actor's distance from his role, which also prohibits the spectator's identification with the action. Orson's having recently read and assimilated Brecht in preparation for their collaboration explains the peculiar presence of the otherwise incongruous (and hitherto mysterious) Chinese theater sequence toward the end of

Voyeuristic tendencies seem to abound in *The Ape Man*'s odd cast of characters, as symbolized by this publicity still featuring Bela Lugosi and Minerva Urecal. *(Photo courtesy John Antosiewicz)*

The Lady from Shanghai. In that sequence, Orson's sailor boy, Michael, while fleeing from the police, slips into the auditorium of a Chinese theater, where a performance is under way onstage. If at first Michael seems distinctly out of place among the entirely Oriental audience, the other members of the audience seem surprisingly unfazed by his presence—even when he is joined by the femme fatale Elsa (Rita Hayworth). In a celebrated essay on Chinese acting (published in English translation in 1936) Brecht had argued persuasively that the Chinese theater epitomized his theory of 'the alienation effect.' Because of the alienated style of acting employed in Chinese theater, 'the audience can no longer have the illusion of being the unseen spectator at the event [...].'

Under Orson's careful direction, so strangely distanced are the performances in general that, in what has often been taken as a major artistic defect of the film, it is rather difficult for audiences to identify with them. 'The artist's object is to appear strange and even surprising to the audience,' writes Brecht of the Chinese actor—a notion that might equally apply to the singularly *strange* performances one discovers in *The Lady from Shanghai*. The Chinese theater sequence is then Orson's distinctly ironic indication that this *strangeness* is hardly ineptitude (as many spectators, critics among them, have mistakenly presumed) but fully intentional: an exploration of the artistic possibilities of the sort of alienated acting that is so clearly antithetical to the naturalistic style that Hollywood held to be the norm [...] If *The Lady from Shanghai* has been generally underrated in film history, it is in part because its expressly Brechtian aspirations have been consistently overlooked. An awareness of the filmmaker's subtle application of Brechtian theory makes it possible historically to assimilate this major film as it has not been in the past [...].

Brecht is generally thought to have acquired this privileged term (i.e., "the alienation effect") from the Russian formalist critic Viktor Shklovsky's key concept of estrangement (*ostraneniye*) in art, whereby the artist views things from a new, and therefore especially revealing, angle. But so *entirely* new is this angle that the spectator may take some time to adjust himself to its utter strangeness [...]. For Shklovsky, and in turn for Brecht, the process of estrangement applies *both* to form and to content: that is, it is not simply reality (content) that is viewed afresh in the successful work of art, but art (form) itself. The artist must do away with artistic clichés, stale modes of perception, by inventing forms capable of viewing the world in original, oblique, perhaps somewhat startling ways.[3]

Welles was not the only major director of the 1940s to be enchanted by Brecht's theories. Charlie Chaplin applied Brecht's Theory of Alienation to his 1947 film, *Monsieur Verdoux*. In fact, Brecht's influence, though not pervasive, has been consistent in cinema ever since the postwar era. Jean-Luc Goddard (*Pierrot Le Fou*, 1965), Rainer Werner Fassbinder (*Katzelmacher*, 1969), Lindsay Anderson (*If...*, 1968 and *O Lucky Man!*, 1973), Pier Paolo Pasolini (*Salò, or 120 Days of Sodom*, 1975), Peter Greenaway (*The Cook, the Thief, His Wife and Her Lover*, 1989), Hal Hartley (*Trust*, 1990), Lars Von Trier (*Dogville*, 2003), and Todd Solondz (*Palindromes*, 2004) have all enthusiastically embraced Brecht's techniques in their work. Of course, the first director to have embraced Brecht's techniques was G.W. Pabst, who adapted Brecht's *The Threepenny Opera* to film in 1931 (the same year Lugosi made his cinematic debut as Dracula). Is it so improbable, therefore, that Brecht's techniques may have trickled down to Poverty Row by 1943?

It's very possible that the screenwriters (Karl Brown and Barney A. Sarecky) and the director (William Beaudine) hired by Monogram to bring *The Ape Man* to life were not at all aware of Brecht's theories. After all, you might ask, is it possible that the director of such low level programmers as *Bela Lugosi Meets a Brooklyn Gorilla* (1952) and *Billy the Kid Versus Dracula* (1966) could have any artistic aspirations whatsoever? Of course it's possible. Examples of such temerity abound in Hollywood. A little over a decade after Beaudine was the king of Poverty Row, Roger Corman (responsible for such low-achieving productions as *It Conquered the World*, 1956, and *Attack of the Crab Monsters*, 1957) openly acknowledged his debt to Federico Fellini, Ingmar Bergman and Francois Truffaut over and over again.[4] Many years before *The Ape Man*, during Hollywood's silent era, Beaudine's artistic aspirations had manifested in such well-respected films as *Sparrows* (1926) starring Mary Pickford. Beaudine's own Poverty Row contemporaries, Edgar Ulmer and Frank Wisbar, definitely had artistic aspirations when they directed such B-movie classics as *Detour* (1945) and *Strangler of the Swamp* (1946). Just because a director or a writer found himself toiling away on Poverty Row doesn't mean that such practitioners were completely unaware of the larger artistic world around them. Indeed, they were probably *painfully* aware of it and doing everything they could to elevate their productions in order to get noticed and perhaps propel them to something higher. This certainly worked for such Poverty Row directors as Joseph Lewis, who soon graduated from Lugosi's first Monogram film, *Invisible Ghost* (1941), to such successful studio films as *My Name Is Julia Ross* (1945) and *So Dark the Night* (1946). Seeing this ascent, why wouldn't a resourceful and canny director like Beaudine try to do anything he could to set himself apart from the gaggle of Poverty Row directors churning out interchangeable westerns, gangster melodramas, slapstick comedies, and the like? Why not roll the dice and inject pure experimental absurdism into the proceedings? After all, what was there to lose? In early 1940s Hollywood, you had to go out of your way to descend any lower than Monogram Studios.

Conversely, it's also possible the filmmakers of *The Ape Man* picked up Brecht's techniques through pure osmosis—or, perhaps even more intriguing, simply recreated Brecht's techniques without being aware of the source material at all. If anyone was going to reinvent the wheel, and do it in such a way that the wheel is now somewhat crooked and weirdly ineffectual, it would be the artisans of Monogram Studios.

What traces of Brecht's theories can be detected in *The Ape Man*? Not only do Brecht's specific techniques show up throughout the course of the film, but the Brechtian themes of artifice, lies, and false fronts abound throughout the film as well. Therefore, the themes imbedded in the storyline echo the techniques being used to bring the story to life.

Let's focus on Zippo, shall we? Within the first two minutes of the film, a mysterious man played by Ralph Littlefield (called "Zippo" in the credits, though that name is never used within the film itself) emerges from a crowd to give the hero of the film, a newspaper reporter named Jeff Carter (Wallace Ford, perhaps best remembered now for his role as Phroso the Clown in Tod Browning's *Freaks*, 1932, and who worked with Lugosi twice before in *Night of Terror*, 1933, and *The Mysterious Mr. Wong*, 1935), a very hot tip for a story. Zippo tells Carter that the story he has for him is "a good story... a great story... a pip!" At the end of the film—very much out of left field—Zippo reveals himself to Carter as the author of the film in which, presumably, all the characters are trapped against their will.

Zippo is the paradoxical lynchpin of the narrative: His actions are both entirely separate from the events of the film and yet, according to the logic of the story, are also what set everything in motion in the first place. As revealed by the ending, Zippo is a composite character of the actual writers of the film, Karl Brown (who supplied the original story) and Barney Sarecky (who wrote the screenplay). One's mind boggles at the possibility of having the actual screenwriter portray the Zippo character under his own name, but perhaps that wouldn't be Brechtian enough at all. It's far too literal. Instead, the screenwriter creates a fictional character who passes himself off as the actual screenwriter. More artifice. More lies.

Artifice, lies and dissimilation permeate the film from beginning to end. The first time we see Zippo, he is standing near a baggage checkout counter at a dock only a few feet away from Our Hero, Jeff Carter. Zippo is reading a newspaper in front of the counter, while behind the counter sits a uniformed customs official. We see Zippo perusing the following headline:

DOCTOR BREWSTER DISAPPEARS!

Famous Gland Expert
Vanishes Without
Leaving Trace
Randall Fears Colleague
Victim of Amnesia; Sister
Returning From Europe

Zippo shows the front page to the customs official and says, "Well, what do you think about that?" Zippo pulls the newspaper back only a fraction of a second later, not giving the customs official time to even glance at it. Zippo walks away before the employee can even respond. He doesn't care about the response, of course, because he's the author of the story and already knows everything that is about to unfold.

Zippo then walks over to Our Hero and says, "You're here to meet Agatha Brewster?" Agatha (Minerva Urecal) is the sister of the missing Dr. James Brewster (Bela Lugosi) mentioned in the newspaper headline. As with the ship employee, Zippo does not let Carter answer the question. He simply urges Carter to follow up on the story printed in the newspaper, then slinks away into the crowd.

One of Carter's fellow reporters, standing beside Carter, asks about Zippo. Carter just shrugs and says, "Some screwball, I guess," which echoes the last line of the film, in which Zippo admits that the movie was "a screwy idea."

A few moments later Zippo appears out of nowhere again, seemingly disrupting the flow of the film while simultaneously moving it along, and points out Agatha Brewster to Carter amongst the crowd of arrivals leaving the newly docked ship. "That's her there," says Zippo, "with the fur piece."

It's important to point out that the character of Zippo may appear to be the clumsiest of plot devices, but if so he's a plot device that the writers must have gone out of their way to shoehorn into the screenplay. After all, the plot so far could easily have moved along without Zippo's presence. It would not have been that difficult to have Carter be the character to spot the newspaper story about Agatha Brewster's missing brother and decide to pursue the story all on his own, without Zippo's help. Therefore, Zippo's inclusion indicates a purpose on the part of the filmmakers beyond the simple mechanics of plot. There must be another reason why Zippo has been inserted into an otherwise typical Hollywood potboiler.

Back to the story: Carter approaches Agatha Brewster and asks if she would agree to an interview about her ghost hunting experiences in Europe. Agatha lets him know in no uncertain terms that she's not at all interested in granting such an interview. After Agatha leaves the scene, Zippo appears once more and says to Carter, "Don't let her give you the brush off. It's a good story." Is Zippo referring to the story of Agatha's missing brother or, far more Brechtian, to the story of *The Ape Man* itself? Perhaps both?

While Zippo is speaking to Carter, we hear what Agatha is being told about her missing brother by Dr. George Randall (Henry Hall), James

Ralph Littlefield, whose God-like character is called "Zippo" in the screenplay (of course, the word "Zippo" is often associated with the concept of "nothing" or "nonexistence"), takes center stage to the right of *The Ape Man*'s ostensible hero, Wallace Ford. *(Photo courtesy John Antosiewicz)*

Brewster's colleague. We learn from Randall that the two seemingly respectable scientists have been engaged in illicit experiments for the past six months while Agatha was away in Europe. Randall explains that Agatha's brother decided to use himself as a guinea pig; though Brewster's still alive, he would be better off dead. He further explains that their experiment was, unfortunately, a "great success." This is a telling line, and contradicts previous write-ups on this film that complain that the purpose of Brewster and Randall's experiments is never explained. Obviously, the purpose of their experiment is explained in that very line: "Unfortunately, it was a great success." Since James Brewster has been transformed into a half-man/half-ape, the purpose of the experiment clearly must have been to turn a human into an ape. Why anyone would want to do this is up in the air, unless it was to prove some sort of evolutionary kinship between the two.

Symbolic signifiers of false fronts and lies begin to pile up on the audience when Agatha and Randall arrive at the Brewster estate. We see Randall and Agatha pass through a secret entrance hidden behind an innocent looking fireplace, then descend a set of stairs that lead to a basement laboratory where Brewster (or what has become of Brewster) is hidden behind a sliding wall panel. Brewster appears to have devolved into half-man/half-ape and is curled up inside a cage with what is clearly a man *dressed* as an ape (the actor Emil Van Horn wearing an ape suit). The fact that Emil Van Horn wore the same exact ape suit in W.C. Fields' *Never Give a Sucker an Even Break* (Universal, 1941), one of the most surrealistic comedies ever produced by a mainstream Hollywood movie studio, might be a clear indication of the filmmakers' intentions with *The Ape Man*: secrets behind fake fireplaces, secrets behind fake walls, secrets hidden within costumes that look more artificial than real. The whole thrust of the film appears to be to highlight the artificiality of life, both real and *imagined* life—the artificiality of Hollywood entertainment and the artificiality of interpersonal relationships in this simulacrum of what we call the real world.

More artificiality: Lugosi as Brewster asks Randall to be released from his prison, despite the fact that the lever that controls the lock mechanism is located within arm's reach of the cage. Was this just poor planning on the part of the filmmakers, or was this subtly absurd detail included on purpose? (Keep in mind that it wouldn't have taken much effort to move the prop a few feet further away from the cage.)

As Brewster leaves the cage at last, his ape companion attempts to leave with him. Brewster turns on the primate, lifts his arms above his head, and begins growling at him like a real ape, forcing him back into the cage. While Brewster roars, we suddenly see Zippo peering down through a basement window at the whole scene. Perhaps admiring his handiwork?

Not long after that, Brewster collapses into a chair and moans, "What a mess I've made of things." Of course, we know Brewster didn't make a mess of things at all—Zippo did. In fact, Zippo's the one who made Brewster think *he's* the one who made a mess of things. And the guilty party is hovering only a few feet above Brewster, staring down dispassionately at him like a curious god.

When we switch locations to the newspaper office that employs Our Hero, Jeff Carter, we are treated to several scenes highlighting the artificiality of interpersonal relationships. Carter is told by his boss that he's going to be teamed up with a new photographer, Billie Mason (Louise Currie). While Carter is under the impression that Billie is a man, he's quite amiable and professional toward his new partner. When he discovers that his partner is a woman, his attitude completely flips. As in many other horror/science fiction films, the female protagonist has a first name that can be confused with that of a man. This happens in many films of the *fantastique* throughout the decades, from *The Ape Man* in 1943 to *The Thing* in 1951, *The Beast from 20,000 Fathoms* in 1953, *Them!* in 1954, *It Came from Beneath the Sea* in 1955, *Tarantula* later that same year, among numerous others. This allows for several moments of wacky misunderstandings (that are intended to be humorous) in which the male protagonist (who, upon meeting the female for the first time, is strategically and improbably turned away from her) addresses the female by her first name, turns around, and is then confused/disappointed/flustered when he discovers his new partner is a woman. In this particular case, Carter spends almost the entire film trying to prevent Billie from taking part in the action, ostensibly because he doesn't believe she can keep up with him, though there is a slight suggestion that he's more concerned for her safety than anything else. The only way we can infer this, however, is that in the last scene of the film Carter threatens to spank Billie for disobeying his orders and getting herself kidnapped by Dr. Brewster. In 1940s American cinema, a man threatening to punish a woman via spanking usually indicates that nuptials lie in the very near future. (This, combined with suggestive scenes of Billie whipping a groaning ape man while wearing her 1940s six-inch stiletto heels straight out of a latter day Dave Stevens pin-up, provides enough sexual subtext for the appropriately bent of mind.)

Leaving aside the general state of sexual politics in 1940s cinema, the misidentification of Billie as a man actually fits into the overall theme of the film. As stated earlier, the entire film is made up of lies and false fronts (both literal and metaphorical). In this case, the false front of Billie being confused for a man is entirely unintentional on Billie's part, though once she understands that a mistake has been made she allows it to go on for a few moments longer than necessary (presumably to toy with Carter, or at the very least to teach him a lesson). Throughout the film, things are not what they appear to be on the surface. "Billie" is not a man; Carter is immediately mistaken by Billie to be "4-F" (i.e., unfit for military service) when in fact he's due to join the military in one month; Dr. Randall appears to be a respectable scientist, but is actually guilty of aiding and abetting several brutal murders; in the eyes of the world Dr. Brewster is missing, but in fact is living in self-exile beneath his own home; Zippo is not even really a character (since in truth he exists *outside* the reality of the film); and Agatha Brewster claims to be a ghost hunter, but is she really?

The case of Agatha Brewster is a fascinating one, and further nails home the Brechtian undertones of the entire film. When Carter and

Billie arrive at the Brewster house to try to interview Agatha about her recent year-long adventure investigating various haunted houses in Europe, Urecal alters her entire manner of speaking. This is clearly on purpose; it was no doubt a conscious choice on the part of the actress, perhaps suggested to her by the director (or the script itself). Brewster does not act the same around Carter and Billie as she does around her brother and Dr. Randall. When Carter begins asking her about supernatural phenomena, she launches into over-exaggerated mannerisms, more like a performer than a sincere investigator into the paranormal. Keep in mind that, despite the fact that *The Ape Man* is ostensibly a Monogram horror film, nothing remotely supernatural occurs in the story. In the universe of *The Ape Man*, there's no suggestion that ghosts are a real phenomenon. It's clear from Agatha's subtle transformation in front of Carter and Billie that she's behaving like an actress on a stage. She doesn't really believe anything she's saying. Carter mentions to Billie that Agatha is famous for being a ghost hunter and has written several well-known books on the subject. Though he never says this aloud, Carter undoubtedly thinks that Agatha is a fraud. At one point, while Agatha is giving the pair a spiel about the existence of ghosts, Carter throws Billie a wink to make his true attitude known to both Billie and the audience.

"All houses are haunted," says Agatha. "All persons are haunted. Throngs of spirits follow us everywhere. We are never alone. This room is crowded right now."

Though Carter thinks Agatha is either crazy or lying, though Agatha is almost certainly a fraud, I would argue that Agatha is nonetheless right. All persons in her universe are indeed haunted. Has not Zippo been haunting Carter and the other characters throughout the story? "Throngs of spirits follow us everywhere." They do indeed. And those spirits are sitting in the audience below, eating popcorn, watching the action unfold before their fascinated and/or bored eyes. The characters in the film can't get away from these spirits. Whenever a scene changes, the spirits follow. "We are never alone." When you're an actor trapped in an artificial reality created by some idiot named Zippo, this couldn't be truer. "This room is crowded right now." When Agatha says this, Billie glances about the room, as if wondering why she can't see these supposed spirits. And though she can't see them, Zippo apparently can. As mentioned before, in the very last scene of the film Zippo breaks the fourth wall, turns toward the camera, and directly addresses the audience watching the film. Zippo, therefore, is the only being in the film who knows he's inside an artificial construct being observed by ghosts called "moviegoers." I would argue that this relatively esoteric level of meaning was actually intended by the screenwriters. Zippo's inclusion alone is suggestive of this.

Zippo continues to "haunt" the other characters throughout the film, and even laughs at them and openly mocks them when they're in great emotional pain. For example, when Dr. Brewster emerges from his hideout behind the fireplace to eavesdrop on Agatha's conversation with Carter and Billie, we see Zippo observing all of this with visible amusement through a basement window. This, despite the fact that Zippo couldn't possibly see any of the action from a window overlooking the basement; the action that he's observing is taking place near the front of the house and is nowhere near the basement. Once again, this purposely disrupts the narrative flow and highlights the artificial nature of the entire moviegoing experience.

We next see Zippo as Carter and Billie slide into their car to leave the Brewster estate. Zippo asks Carter, "Hey, you going into town?" despite the fact that he already knows the answer. Carter says, "Yeah," to which Zippo replies, "Fine, go right ahead." Of course, Zippo is happy with Carter's plans since Zippo is the one who planted them there in the first place. Carter turns to Billie and sarcastically asks if Zippo is one of the ghosts to which Agatha Brewster was referring. Zippo is indeed one of those ghosts, in the sense that he constantly hovers over the action and knows everything that will occur within this strange pocket universe known as *The Ape Man*. The *real* ghosts, however, are the ones who have the ability to hover over Zippo as well, watching his every move just as he does to the other characters in the film. In the world of *The Ape Man*, the moviegoing audience is like the outermost shell of a Russian doll. Or *are* they the outermost shell? The implications of these multiple layers can be quite disturbing indeed, if taken to their illogical extremes....

Layers within layers. Men within apes. Apes within men. Emil Van Horn inside an ape. An ape inside Emil Van Horn. Bela Lugosi inside Dr. James Brewster. Dr. James Brewster inside Bela Lugosi. Fictional characters within actors. Actors within fictional characters. After Carter and Billie drive away, we return to Dr. Brewster's basement where we see the ape inside the cage mimicking the bad behavior of his human master, Brewster, indicating that (at least in this case) humans can often be far worse than their primate ancestors. Brewster releases the ape from his prison, symbolically releasing the ape from deep within himself as well. Brewster has made a decision. The only way to reverse his unfortunate

Though burdened with an absurd screenplay, Bela Lugosi nonetheless manages to deliver a customarily passionate and strong-willed performance in *The Ape Man*. *(Photo courtesy John Antosiewicz)*

condition is to extract spinal fluid from a living person, a procedure that would require murdering the donor. Because Dr. Randall has refused to help Brewster do this, Brewster decides to take matters into his own (semi-human) hands. For the first time in months, Brewster leaves the comforting womb of his underground laboratory. We see Brewster and the ape leave the laboratory via a second set of stairs in the back of the basement, which means there's more than one hidden entrance within the Brewster estate. One wonders how long these hidden passageways have been there, and if they were present for more than a single generation, what was this secret basement used for in the past? Perhaps James wasn't the first Brewster to engage in anti-social behavior that needed to be concealed from others? At any rate, this is another clear signifier of the many secrets and false fronts that exist within Brewster's house, his mind, and the entire film itself.

We next see Brewster climbing through the window of Dr. Randall's office. Brewster chooses not to use the front door. Again, Brewster's methods of ingress and egress are almost always via back routes and secret passageways. Randall is surprised to see his colleague outside the basement. Up to this point, Randall no doubt believed he could continue to live his double life (respectable doctor/criminal co-conspirator) without having to worry about the two halves overlapping. As long as Brewster remained safely exiled within his basement, Randall would never have to face the consequences of his questionable acts. Now, Brewster's sudden appearance poses a problem for Randall. Brewster tries one last time to convince Randall to help him attain the spinal fluid he needs. Randall says, "Do you realize what you're asking me to do? Murder!" Without hesitation, Brewster replies, "Oh, call it what you like!" This, of course, implies that murder is acceptable as long as one calls it something else. More false fronts. More lies.

This scene is over brimming with lies and their consequences. Randall summons his butler into the office, but fails to tell him that Brewster is hiding behind a partition in the back of the room; in this instance he lies by omission. Soon, a police detective arrives on the front doorstep, wanting to ask Randall questions about the missing Dr. Brewster. Randall is forced to leave Brewster alone in his office while he contends with the detective. Though Randall could easily prevent the killing spree that is about to ensue by telling the detective about Brewster's presence in his office, Randall refuses to do so.

As the detective bombards Randall with a series of questions, Brewster takes this opportunity to lure Randall's butler back into the office. Brewster commands the ape to attack the butler, from whom Brewster extracts the precious spinal fluid he requires in order to regain his old life. Brewster, of course, never stops to ponder the paradoxical irony of committing an inhuman act in order to regain one's humanity. It's an impossible task from the beginning, but Brewster's obsession drives him onward.

From a Brechtian perspective, it's important to underscore the fact that Brewster's first victim is a servant. A committed Marxist like Brecht would not have missed the significance of an ethically-challenged, upper-class scientist casually deciding to kill the help for the express purpose of being able to walk upright again.

Brewster and the ape flee the scene with the fluid in hand. After the detective leaves, Randall discovers the corpse of his servant and calls the police back to his office. Even after reporting the murder, Randall still refuses to tell the officers the truth about Brewster.

The next day, Randall shows up on Brewster's doorstep. We see Brewster observing Randall through a hidden camera. Just as Zippo secretly observes all the characters in the film from afar, Brewster engages in the same voyeuristic behavior. Just as the ape mirrors Brewster's questionable behavior, Brewster himself mimics the behavior of his own master (or, more accurately, creator).

Randall admits to Brewster, "I lied to the police yesterday," yet refuses to cooperate any further by helping Brewster inject the dead servant's spinal fluid into Brewster's body. When Agatha pulls a gun on Randall, seeming not at all like the spiritual spinster who wove such elegant tales about spirits for Carter and Billie only the previous day, the doctor reluctantly agrees to the brother and sister's demands. When Agatha pulls the gun on Randall, we see Zippo once again staring down at the scene from the basement window with a sympathetic expression on his face, as if he doesn't enjoy seeing his children act this way. But what else can be done? After all, certain genre conventions are inviolate in popular entertainment. The script had already been written, and the characters are predestined to behave in this exact manner.

As Randall injects Brewster with the stolen spinal fluid, we see Zippo wince and turn his face away. Apparently, God can't stand the sight of needles.

In the 1995 book *Bela Lugosi* edited by Gary and Susan Svehla, Mark A. Miller writes:

> Throughout the [...] film, Littlefield [Zippo] is seen almost everywhere, with no explanation of his identity. His reaction shots,

cut into the film at what should be dramatically important moments, almost seem designed to ridicule Lugosi. For instance, in Lugosi's basement lab, when Dr. Randall is giving him a human spinal fluid injection for the first time, the film cuts to Littlefield outside, watching the proceedings through a window, as he smiles and winks to the viewer. Then, after the injection, Lugosi nervously paces and tries to straighten his back, hoping he is cured. This is one of the few opportunities for Lugosi to have a dramatic moment, but his pantomime is performed in vain because the sequence includes an insert of Littlefield apparently laughing to himself as he watches.[5]

One could take this criticism even further. It's clear that Zippo is not only laughing at Brewster's plight, but he's also very clearly mimicking the doctor's ape-like movements, which indicates that these scenes were shot *after* Lugosi's were already in the can. Obviously, Littlefield could not have mimicked Lugosi's performance without having seen it first. I doubt, however, that Zippo's antics were meant to demean Lugosi personally. Zippo's character is meant to demean the entire audience, the system that would demand that films like *The Ape Man* be made in the first place. The filmmakers are without a doubt aware of the flaws built into this film and the entire Hollywood industry in general; I would argue that they succeed in using these obvious flaws to their advantage as much as would be humanly possible under the circumstances. Lugosi, too, uses these flaws to his advantage. As film historian Gregory Mank once said of such films as *The Ape Man*:

I always have an image in my mind when I think of a Poverty Row horror film. I picture some really cheap Hollywood producer wearing plaid pants and smoking a cigar, and he's holding some very distinguished actor by his ankles over the top of this deep, horrible, fiery pit. And then he drops the actor into the deep, fiery pit, which is the abyss of the absolute worst, cheapest, lowest form of Hollywood budget filmmaking. Then what this distinguished actor has to do is basically get up, claw his way out of this almost bottomless abyss, come up to the top, pull himself out with his dignity intact and virtually smelling like a rose. It's almost a miracle to watch one of these films and see the various actors, many of whom we admire and love, pull this stunt over and over again. It's a show business miracle.[6]

I would argue that Lugosi pulls off this very stunt in all of his Monogram films, but especially in *The Ape Man*.

Back once more to the plot: At around the same time that Brewster discovers the effects of the spinal fluid injection will not last for more than a few minutes, unless he attains more, Jeff Carter reappears on the doorstep of the Brewster household. When Agatha answers the door, she asks him why he didn't call ahead first. Carter lies and says that her line was busy. Carter doesn't stay in the house long. After he's left, he hangs around outside just long enough to see Dr. Randall leaving the Brewster estate. Like Brewster, Carter is now also mimicking Zippo's voyeuristic tendencies. To highlight this connection, the filmmakers include a shot of Zippo spying on Carter from some distance away and smiling approvingly. Carter now suspects a connection between the Brewsters and the mysterious murder of Randall's butler.

That night, realizing he needs more spinal fluid, Brewster and his ape go on a killing spree throughout the town. We see the pair murder a milkman, a shopkeeper, and a young woman sleeping in her bed. Just as Brewster and the ape are about to descend upon yet another victim, a beautiful woman walking the streets alone at night, Zippo suddenly emerges from an alleyway and says to the potential victim, "I wouldn't go down that way if I were you." At first the woman seems reluctant to follow the stranger's advice, but then Zippo gently grabs her by the shoulders and guides her away from the hiding place of Brewster and his ape. "Well, don't ask questions," he says, "c'mon."

Knowing the woman's fate, Zippo/God decides to intervene. One could assume from this act that Zippo/God is a pretty nice fellow. But this begs the question: Why didn't Zippo/God prevent the deaths of the four previous victims? He saved one person, seemingly at random, but allowed four others to die simply to provide some requisite melodrama and vicarious cheap thrills for the benefit of the paying movie crowd. Similar ethical dilemmas on the part of the God-author are examined in later works of metafiction (i.e., stories in which the author includes himself as a character in the story) such as Kurt Vonnegut's 1973 novel *Breakfast of Champions*, Grant Morrison and Chas Truog's 1980s comic book series *Animal Man* (see, in particular, *Animal Man Book 3: Deus Ex Machina*), and several Steve Erickson novels such as *Arc d'X* (1993), *Amnesiascope* (1996), and *Shadowbahn* (2017). In fact, the use of metafiction in literary works of the *fantastique* can be traced all the way back to Gaston Leroux's *Phantom of the Opera* (1910). Not only does *The Ape*

Man continue this tradition, but also points the way toward the far more transgressive works of metafiction mentioned above.

After saving the unnamed woman from certain death, Zippo next appears outside the Brewster home and watches silently as Carter breaks into the house to uncover some hard evidence connecting the Brewsters to the mysterious killing spree sweeping across the city. Though Carter has expressly told Billie not to follow him, she ignores his orders and shows up on the estate anyway. Both enter the Brewster residence without realizing the other is creeping around inside. This results in Billie accidentally knocking Carter unconscious, which gives Brewster the prime opportunity to kidnap Billie and drag her downstairs to his laboratory where he undoubtedly plans to steal her spinal fluid. For no apparent reason, Brewster's ape is angered by the sight of Brewster manhandling Billie (despite the fact that the ape helped Brewster kill at least one other woman before this point), erupts from his cage, and murders Brewster in much the same way that Erik the Ape does away with Lugosi's Dr. Mirakle in Robert Florey's *Murders in the Rue Morgue.* Meanwhile, having recovered from Billie's blow to the back of the head, Carter summons the police to the Brewster house, then desperately attempts to find some way to open the secret entrance behind the fireplace. Carter is becoming more and more frantic, as he can hear Billie screaming somewhere down below him. Now that Brewster is dead, the ape has turned on Billie—which is peculiar, since he apparently killed Brewster to prevent him from hurting Billie in the first place. Perhaps, as in numerous other Golden Age Hollywood films that feature out-of-control primates, the ape has far more amorous intentions in mind for Billie? Alas, we'll never know the answer to that question, as the police show up just in the nick of time and force Agatha to open the secret entrance. The second the hidden door is revealed, the Truth comes lumbering up from the darkness in the form of a murderous ape and, for all its troubles, promptly gets gunned down by the cops. This happens to Truth sometimes, both in the real world as well as in the cinematic one.

What follows is the ultimate revelation, mentioned previously, in which Carter threatens to spank Billie but good, at which point Zippo appears in the driver's seat of Carter's convertible and says, "Don't be a dummy." Carter demands to know who the hell Zippo is, and receives the following response: "*Me*? Oh, I'm the author of the story." Seconds after this revelation, Zippo turns toward the camera, breaks the fourth wall, and says to the audience, "Screwy idea, wasn't it?" He then roles up the window of the car, on which pieces of white tape have been placed to spell out the words "THE END." One can't help but wonder what Carter and Billie did immediately after the end of this scene. They must have been quite shocked to be told that they were merely characters trapped in someone else's fiction. Or did they just assume that Zippo was nuts and move on with their lives? Imagine having the once-in-a-lifetime opportunity to meet God, discover that he appears to be some sort of village idiot who randomly decides which humans will live and which will die, then dismiss the entire incident as the ravings of a madman, and casually move on with one's life. Did Carter go off to fight the Axis Powers like a good Amurrican boy, wondering in the back of his mind if the entire war was a not-so-cleverly constructed piece of fiction manufactured by that weird Zippo guy driving around the United States in a falling-apart jalopy with the words "THE END" perpetually taped to the window? That would be a weird burden to carry around with you while you're in a foxhole being shot at by Nazis in Eastern Europe. Would some distant part of your brain hope that at any moment Zippo might appear from behind a stack of sandbags and save your wounded buddy from spilling his guts out all over the battlefield? *C'mon, Zippo, don't abandon me now....*

The implications of all this are almost too bizarre to fully comprehend.

If not the most well directed, if not the most innovative, if not the most entertaining of Lugosi's Monogram films of the 1940s, *The Ape Man* is almost without a doubt the weirdest of them all. And it's that High Weirdness, stemming in part from the Brechtian sense of alienation that hovers over the storyline and the performances like a quasi-surreal cloud, that—despite its many undeniable flaws—lures devotees of the *fantastique* back to this seventy-six year old Poverty Row film generation after generation.

(Endnotes)

1   Phoebe von Held, *Alienation and Theatricality* (London: Legenda, 2011), 17-18.
2   L.M. Bogad, "Alienation Effect," *Beautiful Trouble* (website accessed June 24, 2017).
3   Barbara Leaming, *Orson Welles: A Biography* (New York: Viking, 1985), 336-39.
4   "Interview with Producer and Director Roger Corman," *The Vincent Price Collection Vol. 1, The Masque of the Red Death* (Blu-ray, Scream Factory, 2014).
5   Mark A. Miller, "The Ape Man," in Gary and Susan Svehla (eds.), *Bela Lugosi* (Baltimore: Midnight Marquee, 2007), 170.
6   Gregory Mank, "Poverty Row," *Terror in the Tropics* (DVD, Alpha New Cinema, 2006).

Ghosts on the Loose **belongs to the category of unloved Lugosi movies even more than to the Monogram Nine.** *(Photo courtesy John Antosiewicz)*

Chapter 8

Ghosts on the Loose ... Or Not.

by Gary D. Rhodes

G hosts on the loose. Ghosts... *on the loose!* Unchained. Running wild, amok even, with reckless abandon... and with Bela Lugosi leading the charge. What an absolutely wonderful film title, and what wonderful images it conjures, expectations heightened by the film's opening artwork of a vaporous, knife-wielding phantasm. And then, well, then the disappointment begins, certainly for most viewers.

Far more than *Spooks Run Wild* (1941), *Ghosts on the Loose* (1943) inhabits a zone populated not as much by the Monogram Nine, but instead by *Murder by Television* (1935), *Genius at Work* (1946), and *Bela Lugosi Meets a Brooklyn Gorilla* (1952): the unloved Bela Lugosi films, regularly shunned because they are perceived to be bad, but not bad in such a way as to be intriguing or as to inspire adoration. No, these films seem bad because they commit the ultimate sin, one rarely associated with Lugosi: they're boring.

It is not an easy task to herald *Ghosts on the Loose*, the seventh of the Monogram Nine. As Tom Weaver once wrote, "It's the sort of film that makes other East Side Kids pictures, *Spooks Run Wild*, for instance, look awfully good by comparison." For him, there isn't "an ounce of horror" in the film, or "an ounce of comedy."[1] It is difficult to disagree.

Ghosts on the Loose situates Lugosi in a haunted house intended to

Once again the East Side Kids find themselves in a haunted house that isn't really haunted. *(Photo courtesy John Antosiewicz)*

cause laughter, a type of storyline that had long since become clichéd. After all, when *Film Daily* reviewed the comedy short subject *The House of a Thousand Trembles* in 1922, the magazine's critic declared, "It will entertain an audience that is not overly particular and likes to laugh at the same old jokes."[2] Over two decades later, *Variety* said of *Ghosts on the Loose*, "Loosely constructed comedy thriller contains plenty of laughs despite the long procession of venerable gags."[3] These included the regrettable use of the stereotypical frightened African-American, a character that dates to such nineteenth-century literature as Poe's *The Gold-Bug* (1843).

As *Film Daily* wrote of *The House of a Thousand Trembles*, "Most of the laughs will come from the fear that the colored man has for the ghosts." Eight years later, *Film Daily* said of the short subject *One Nutty Night* (1930), "There is also the old standby of the [African-American] servant scared stiff by the mysterious happenings."[4] For *Ghosts on the Loose*, actor Ernest "Sunshine Sammy" Morrison assumed that role, shivering in a haunted house, just as he had in two prior East Side Kids film, *Spooks Run Wild* and *Boys of the City* (1940). These repetitions add further dimension to his dialogue in *Ghosts on the Loose*, "Here we go again!"

No, to reclaim *Ghosts on the Loose* as an important film, or even an important Lugosi B-movie, is not possible. Nor is it credible to commend the film in any major respect. What constitutes a "good" film is certainly up for debate, as is the very use of moral terminology like "good" to describe any work of art. But arguing those larger issues would still not lead most viewers to shower *Ghosts on the Loose* with praise. The film is the least beloved of the Monogram Nine, and it deserves that status, not only because of Lugosi's limited screen time, but also because it creates a generally dull and listless experience.

And yet these widely agreed-upon reactions are not the only appropriate way to understand *Ghosts on the Loose*, or any film, for that matter. Consider *Variety*'s review of the Andy Clyde short subject *Ghost Parade* (1931):

> [The 'familiar haunted house' story] has been played to death in shorts, but evidently the producers get action on those shorts, for the film audience doesn't appear to tire of them. Doesn't take too much ingenuity to contrive the plot for one of these subjects. All the ingenuity it takes is to figure out a new style of spooks.

A new style of spooks: at first such language would seem ill-suited to *Ghosts on the Loose*, as it was the third time that the East Side Kids found themselves inside a haunted house.

However, that is *exactly* what occurs in the film, far more so than in *Spooks Run Wild* or *Boys of the City*. Director William Beaudine created a lackluster movie with *Ghosts on the Loose*, a fact that has tended to obscure his singular achievement with it, a surprising ability to activate longstanding horror tropes – including the haunted house that isn't actually haunted – and to redeploy the same with noticeable variations, even to the extent of updating them for World War II. Does this make *Ghosts on the Loose* worth viewing? Perhaps not, and certainly not repeatedly. Nevertheless, Beaudine's alterations and additions to the longstanding conventions make the film worthy of discussion. Here we go again, in other words, but for the first time in this particular direction.

Not-So-Haunted Houses

In *Ghosts on the Loose*, Glimpy's (Huntz Hall's) sister Betty (Ava Gardner) marries Jack (Rick Vallin), with Mugs (Leo Gorcey), Danny (Bobby Jordan), and the other East Side Kids helping to decorate for and even sing at the wedding.[5] The shadow of horror looms even over their prepara-

Scruno (Ernie "Sunshine Sammy" Morrison) meets the living portrait of Emil (Bela Lugosi). *(Photo courtesy John Antosiewicz)*

tions. Glimpy's tuxedo is borrowed from a mortuary, and a stolen wreath sports the banner "Rest in Peace." But the key trouble comes from the home that Jack purchases for his bride. The price is cheap, because the elderly sellers believe the "big estate" next door is haunted. As they explain to the police, its "mysterious goings-on" include strange noises and screams. As was so often the case in the history of American reportage and fictional entertainment, no ghosts appear. None whatsoever. The "strange house" *seems* to be haunted, including to the East Side Kids, who try to clean it for Jack and Betty ("We'll make that place look like a million bucks"). But it isn't. No ghosts are present, on the loose or under restraint.

American newspapers had long written about similar homes, which were capable of scaring neighbors, but which under investigation had no supernatural inhabitants. In 1860, for example, the "ghost" in a house under construction was exposed as the drunken city porter.[6] A spirit hidden in the garret of another old home turned out to be a fugitive slave.[7] These revelations tended to please some readers and disappoint others. After uncovering the natural source of an eerie noise at his home in 1872, one man admitted that it was "almost a pity," given that "so capital a ghost story [had been] spoiled."[8]

In 1869, the *Charleston Daily News* reported on another fake haunted house, at which occupants heard the "clanking of chains" and witnessed "manifestations," frightening them into leaving "without giving even a day's notice." An investigation caught unscrupulous neighbors, who concocted the ruse to keep the house vacant; they used water from the well on its lot. Their "ghost method," was successful until a man "who had common sense" agreed to live there.[9]

Much more frequent were press accounts of houses made to seem haunted in order to decrease property values. In 1843, the New Orleans *Times-Picayune* described one homeowner selling at half of his original price because "strange sounds could be distinctly heard." Pipes hidden in the chimney by a bad neighbor were to blame. When the wind blew, the pipes "gave forth sounds closely resembling the whoop or moaning cry of the owl." The journalist concluded, "The story of this haunted house is but that of thousands of others."[10] His number was an overestimate, to be sure, but newspapers published comparable accounts repeatedly in the nineteenth century.[11]

These stories also provided the plots for early films. In Imp's *The Haunted House* (1911), characters masqueraded as ghosts in old houses in order to decrease their property value.[12] In Rex's *The Ghost of a Bargain* (1912), a "would be renter" pretends to be a "spook in order to diminish the apparent value of the house."[13] Lubin's *A Deal in Real Estate* (1914) features a home-buyer who disguises himself as a ghost inside an empty house in order to get a better price.[14] Then, in 1915, Lubin's three-reel *The Gray Horror* depicts a crook hired to "haunt" an estate and thus encourage its owners to sell.[15]

Writers recycled this plot on a number of occasions during the twenties. In 1921, Harold Lloyd starred in *Haunted Spooks*, a short film in which a dastardly uncle tries to scare his niece out of her newly inherited home. *The Ghost of Folly* (1926) and *A Haunted Heiress* (1926) are similar examples, whereas the short subject *For Rent–Haunted* (1922) inverted the old plot, with some kids creating "spooks" so as to best a "shrewd and unrelenting real estate operator who has driven a widow from her home."[16] For once, heroes were behind the ghostly shenanigans.

Ghosts on the Loose locates its fake haunted house not in the city, as in these prior examples, but rather in the nascent suburbs, that place where, as Mugs explains, "you got no running water, you got no trolley cars, you got nothing." Jack has managed to get a cheap price on his

It can happen here! Nazi Fifth Columnists living amongst us. *(Photo courtesy of Bill Chase)*

cozy and furnished matrimonial home, not because of its ghosts, but because – in another minor variation – "the house next door is haunted."

Thieves in the Night

Some haunted houses in America gained their reputation because criminals hiding inside them wanted to be left alone. In 1910, for example, the *Washington Post* wrote about a 15-year-old boy who bravely entered a deserted home. During its vacancy, passersby claimed to have seen "dim lights floating through the upper stories" and to have heard "sobbing voices begging pathetically not to be murdered."[17] The previous owners had left the home, with "popular rumor" contending that they had been scared away. The boy described his adventure as follows:

> Sure, I went in. I climbed through the back window, while the fellers waited outside for me. We arranged it so that if I went into the back and knocked on the parlor windows three times I was to win. I went in all right. When I got in the dining room, I saw a feller swiping electric globes. He had two of them down when I yelled at him. He was worse scared than I was – thought I was the ghost,

I guess. Well, I chased him out and knocked on the front window three times. The fellers all ran when they heard it.[18]

The newspaper added, "Again young America has succeeded in smashing a decaying and time-honored tradition," implying that the new generation was more enlightened than its forebears. The issue of age also surfaced in *Ghosts on the Loose*. The real estate agent tells Jack, "You know how old people are, always imagining things."

Criminals relying on rumors of the supernatural or encouraging belief in the same were popular with screenwriters for three decades prior to *Ghosts on the Loose*. Biograph's comedy *The Ghost* (1911), which starred its director, Mack Sennett, featured three unrelated thieves pretending to be ghosts at the same old home and scaring each other off as a result.[19] *The Haunted House* (American, 1913) has a man uncovering a band of opium smugglers using a deserted home as their hideout.[20] That same year, *Moving Picture World* described Victor's *The Ghost* (1913) as follows: "The old, familiar 'haunted house' story," in which the lover "makes a bet that he is not afraid to stay in the haunted dwelling over night. Of course, he discovers a den of thieves infesting the place, and there follows an exciting capture of the gang."[21]

In *The Ghost House* (1917), an old home is "said to be haunted"; its gardener is head of a "gang of thieves" and "does his best to keep the superstition alive."[22] Subsequent examples include *The Ghost in the Garret* (1921), with Dorothy Gish portraying an amateur sleuth who encounters thieves inside an old house, and *The Dollar-a-Year Man* (1921), in which Roscoe "Fatty" Arbuckle takes on kidnappers in yet another not-so-haunted house.[23]

Along with using these homes as hideouts, criminals sometimes relied on them as locations to conduct illegal activity. For example, Edison's *The House on the Hill* (1910) has a "notorious gang" of counterfeiters printing money in an old home.[24] Then, in 1913, Warner's Features released *Trapped in the Castle of Mystery*; its counterfeiters hide out in an old castle and dress as ghosts to keep their activities secret.[25] Over seven years later, *The Haunted House* (1921) repurposed the same story, with star Buster Keaton busting a gang of counterfeiters.

Ghosts on the Loose successfully merged the real estate plotline (Jack buying his marital home cheaply) with the story of criminals undertaking illegal activities in a house that only seems to be haunted, thanks to spooky voices, a secret passageway, and a reliance on eerie portraiture.

The Face of Horror

For centuries, artists have painted horrifying images. In addition to depictions of Satan and Hell, there have been such works as Henry Fuseli's *The Nightmare* (1781); in 1835, *The North American Quarterly* wrote that it had "elicited universal applause."[26] Francisco de Goya's *The Sleep of Reason Produces Monsters/El sueño de la razón produce monstruos* (1797-1799), *Witches' Flight/Vuelo de brujas* (1797-1798), and *Saturn Devouring His Children/Saturno devorando a un hijo* (1819-1832, aka *Saturn Devouring His Son*) are other key examples, as is Edvard Munch's *The Scream/Schrei der Natur* (1893-1910, aka *The Scream of Nature*).[27]

American-born artists like Washington Allston were also drawn to potentially horrifying themes. Among Allston's best-known paintings were *Dead Man Restored to Life by Touching the Bones of the Prophet Elisha* (1811-1813) and *Saul and the Witch of Endor* (1820-1821).[28] Also fascinating is his *Spalatro's Vision of the Bloody Hand* (1831), which depicts a scene from Ann Radcliffe's novel *The Italian* (1797). Allston wrote Gothic fiction as well, including a *Monaldi: A Tale* (1841). In it, the title character mistakenly believes that his lover has returned from beyond the grave to haunt him. His delusion leads him to paint a likeness of Satan "enthroned in the majesty of hell." It becomes his masterpiece. "Though only a picture," Monaldi declares, "*I* have known the original. What is there, I have *seen.*"

Portraiture appears prominently in many other horrifying tales, ranging from Matthew Lewis's *The Monk* (1796) to Edgar Allan Poe's *The Fall of the House of Usher* (1839). As Poe's narrator explains:

If ever mortal painted an idea, that mortal was Roderick Usher. For me at least – in the circumstances then surrounding me – there arose out of the pure abstractions which the hypochondriac contrived to throw upon his canvas, an intensity of intolerable awe, no shadow of which felt I ever yet in the contemplation of the certainly glowing yet too concrete reveries of Fuseli.

Poe returned to the subject in his short story *The Oval Portrait* (1842), with its artist more interested in capturing the appearance of his wife on a canvas than he is in her failing health. "This is indeed Life itself!" he declares of the painting, turning to find his beloved dead.

Nowhere are portraits more important than in Horace Walpole's *The Castle of Otranto* (1764), usually considered to be the first Gothic novel. In it, a painting literally comes to life when Manfred advances menacingly on Isabella and says, "Heaven nor Hell shall impede my designs." Walpole adds, "At that instant the portrait of his grandfather, which hung over the bench where they had been sitting, uttered a deep sigh, and heaved its breast." The story continues:

> Manfred, distracted between the flight of Isabella, who had now reached the stairs, and yet unable to keep his eyes from the picture, which began to move, had, however, advanced some steps after her, still looking backwards on the portrait, when he saw it quit its panel, and descend on the floor with a grave and melancholy air.

The painting audibly sighs once more, and makes a "sign to Manfred to follow him."

Well over a century later, in 1890, Oscar Wilde published the first version of *The Portrait of Dorian Gray*, its title character wealthy and attractive. Wishing to remain forever young, Gray utters a "mad wish" that a painting of him grow old, tarnished by age and sin, rather than the same happening to his own body. Wilde writes, "There were no signs of any change when he looked into the actual painting, and yet there was no doubt that the whole expression had altered. It was not a mere fancy of his own. The thing was horribly apparent." The portrait becomes the "most magical of mirrors," one "whose changing features showed [Gray] the real degradation of his life."

The major appearance of horrifying portraiture in early twentieth-century literature came in H. P. Lovecraft's short story *Pickman's Model* (1927). "Any magazine-cover hack can splash paint around wildly and call it a nightmare or a Witches' Sabbath or a portrait of the devil," he writes, "but only a great painter can make such a thing really scare or ring true." And the fictional character Pickman surpasses Doré, Goya, and Fuseli. As the tale's narrator explains, "It was the *faces*, Eliot, those accursed *faces*, that leered and slavered out of the canvas with the very breath of life! By God, man, I verily believe they *were* alive! That nauseous wizard had waked the fires of hell in pigment, and his brush had been a nightmare-spawning wand."

Supernatural paintings appeared in early cinema as well, notably in Georges Méliès' *The Inn Where No Man Rests/L'auberge du bon repos* (1903, distributed by Lubin as *He Couldn't Sleep in that Inn*). Thanks to a trick edit, a portrait briefly comes to life. Then the painting's face transforms into larger, more comical artwork, its mouth opening and

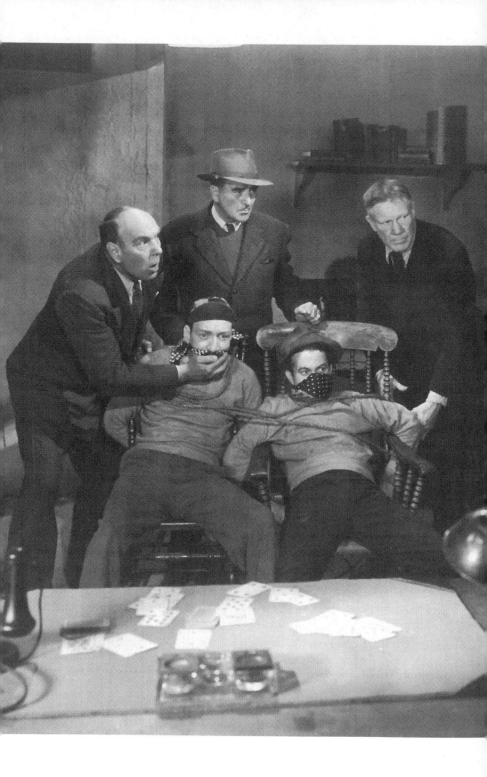

SK 211-6

closing, allowing it to devour a man's nightshirt. Over a decade later, in 1914, Great Northern released a Danish-made comedy entitled *The White Ghost*, in which a painting of the White Lady "steps down from her frame" in order to convince a man to give his consent to a marriage.[29] These were in addition to Thanhouser's two-reel adaptation of *The Picture of Dorian Gray* in 1915.

In American literature, however, the living portrait usually just *seemed* to come to life, in haunted houses that were not actually haunted. Washington Irving first explored this possibility in *The Adventure of My Aunt* (1824). He writes, "A heavy groan, and a sound like the chattering of teeth, was heard from the portrait." But there is no spirit to distress the characters, as Irving makes clear. Instead, the "picture was pulled down, and from a recess behind it, in which had formerly stood a clock, they hauled forth a round-shouldered, black-bearded varlet, with a knife as long as my arm, but trembling all over like an aspen leaf." The portrait concealed a "hiding-place" that a crook contrived "for his nefarious purpose," to the extent that he "borrowed an eye from the portrait by way of a reconnoitering hole."

To hide behind a portrait and peer through holes in its eyes became one of the most notable clichés of American haunted houses. The earliest known cinematic example came in *The Mysterious*

It's not in the cards: this publicity still depicts a scene that isn't in the film.
(Photo courtesy John Antosiewicz)

Eyes (1913). *Moving Picture World* observed, "The girl at the inn with her father discovers the innkeeper looking through the eyes of a painting on the wall at them. ... The situation is an eerie one and might have been handled in a little more probable way."[30] The following year, a variation appeared in the German-made *The Hound of the Baskervilles/Der Hund von Baskerville* (1914), which Pathé released in America in 1915.[31] In it, a character peers through the eyes in a bust of Napoleon that is flush against the wall.

Ghosts on the Loose importantly draws upon the tradition of horrifying portraiture, so much so that the film sets up the role they will play in advance. In a scene at the chapel where the wedding will be held, Glimpy suggests the place would look better if it was adorned with "paintings" or "morales." An embarrassed Mugs corrects him, saying he should have said "morals." At that point, Jack interjects with the polite question, "Do you guys mean murals?"

Later, when the East Side Kids are in the basement of the old estate, the villains, including Emil (Bela Lugosi), stare through the eyes of a painting hanging on the wall. By this time, the device was well known to film audiences, having been seen not only in silent cinema, but also in such talkies as George Crone's *Get that Girl* (1932), Frank Strayer's *The Ghost Walks* (1934) and Elliott Nugent's *The Cat and the Canary* (1939). Nevertheless, it remained effective, just as it would in the decades to come. The resulting image becomes uncanny, with eyes that are real and three-dimensional, as opposed to the two-dimensionality of the rest of the painting. The portrait is simultaneously alive and dead, animate and inanimate. Its eyes are disembodied from the owner and embodied anew in the portrait. An image meant to be looked at now looks at us.

Ghosts on the Loose hardly presents anything original in this instance, and it sadly misses an opportunity to show a frontal view of the painting with Lugosi's eyes bulging through it. By contrast, the film does experiment at length with two other paintings, both of which hang in the living room of the old house. One is an oval portrait of a lady, which opens inwardly like a door, allowing Monk (Frank Moran) and then Emil to take its place. Here is a unique approach to the plot device, one in which the villain's entire face and chest are visible, rather than obscured behind a painting. It has a forebear in *The Inn Where No Man Rests*, but in this instance represents a non-supernatural image.

It is here that Beaudine creates the film's most memorable scene, one in which Scruno dusts the mantle underneath the "painting" and causes Emil to sneeze. The picture is fully alive, as Scruno learns when Emil proceeds to growl at him. Rather than borrowing from Irving, this approach draws upon Walpole, creating a non-supernatural variation on the painting-come-to-life. As Lovecraft had written in *Pickman's Model*, "As I am a living being, I never elsewhere saw the actual breath of life so fused into a canvas." The frightened Scruno falls backwards onto a sofa. Given that Emil replaces the portrait of a woman, Scruno struggles to explain the surprising gender transformation he has witnessed, which creates another layer of originality: "Her was a him a minute ago!"

Even more unique is a painting of Napoleon that hangs in the living room. Kamilla Elliott has written on the subject of portraiture in British Gothic fiction, determining that picture identification is invariably tied to class structure. Unlike the lower classes, members of the aristocracy, the upper class, and the ascendant middle class could afford paintings. She demonstrates how "Gothic fiction assaults, co-opts and reworks aristocratic ideology's divinized chains of immanent, inherent imaged identities," and how the "aristocratic *imago dei* is brought down and ordinary middle-class identities are raised up through mimetic aesthetics in both portraiture and politics."[32] Here we return to Napoleon. And also to the mimetic Glimpy.

Napoleon's stance, his hand inside his coat, is familiar, so much so that Glimpy imitates the pose, pretending to be the portrait, a member of the lower class humorously imitating, even mocking, the aristocratic. But the painting soon turns around, as if it is a revolving door, to reveal a different portrait of Napoleon. His stance is the same, but now he wears no coat. Glimpy and Scruno become even more scared when the painting changes again, showing Napoleon standing in long underwear. The disrobed image now mocks its imitator, appropriating as it does his lowbrow sense of humor before the painting flips back to its original image. Mugs doesn't witness the changes and is left to chide his two friends. "You're imagining things," he says before invoking another form of gender inversion. "Stop acting like a couple of hysterical dames!"

The shift in the Napoleonic portraits is the film at its most uncanny, not only because they are humorous rather than horrifying, but also because the trio of images do not logically comport with the revolving portrait, which is flat and two-dimensional. Turning it from one side to the other should mean that only two images are available for display, and yet there are in fact *three*. Napoleon has literally and figuratively become a moving picture, one that in quick succession can be clowned, but also feared, a symbiotic dichotomy at the very heart of the fake haunted house in American cinema. As is so often the case in *Ghosts on the Loose*, things aren't what they seem to be.

Fifth Columnists

As early as 1934, the Congressional Committee on Un-American Activities (as it was then named) listened to surprising testimony about a "Nazi spy system" that existed in America, one that "punished persons living in Germany for the hostile utterances of their relatives" in the United States.[33] By 1937, U.S. Representative Samuel Dickstein called for an investigation into "alleged Nazi activities" in America, which were apparently supported with $20,000,000.[34] The German government vehemently denied conducting "spy ring activity," maintaining that, "espionage plots" were simply "out of the question."[35]

But of course they were lying. In 1939, President Roosevelt ordered coordination of the intelligence drive against Nazi infiltration.[36] J. Edgar Hoover's FBI increasingly focused on the problem.[37] And the "primary purpose" of the Congressional Committee on Un-American Activities became the prevention of sabotage and with it the exposure of foreign spies.[38] The Nazi "Fifth Column" was secretly operating in many countries around the world, the press revealed.[39] And yet, the *Los Angeles Times* worryingly reported that, "the nature and extent of the espionage problem [were] not realized by many Americans."[40]

To make known the dangers, Warner Bros. began producing films about Nazis in America. According to Michael E. Birdwell, the "studio exhibited the most consistent assault on Hitler's Germany and fascism in general to come out of Hollywood before 1942." He adds, "Through a score of films produced during the 1930s and early 1940s, the Warner Bros. studio marshaled its forces to mobilize a nation divided over the intervention issue...."[41] However, "restrictions imposed by the MPPDA, the PCA and the state department made it difficult to produce anti-Nazi films before 1939."[42]

One of the first was Anatole Litvak's film *Confessions of a Nazi Spy* (1939), which was based on data gathered and published by Leon G. Turrou, the real-life G-man who had smashed a Nazi spy ring. The *Washington Post* told readers, "the Warner Brothers have had the courage to make no bones about Hitler," their film being "unequivocally and provably factual."[43] Gossip columnist Hedda Hopper wrote, "Writers never had nightmares thinking up gruesome episodes. But they got headaches reading about the real ones."[44] Adding to the film's verisimilitude was documentary-style voiceover and authentic Nazi footage.

Though the East Side Kids save the day, their heroism doesn't lead to heraldry. *(Photo courtesy of Bill Chase)*

Warner Bros. then produced *All Through the Night* (1942) with Humphrey Bogart, previewing the film only days before Pearl Harbor was bombed on December 7, 1941.[45] In it, a covert Nazi group in New York tries to sink a new American battleship. "I can't be bothered," Bogart's character "Gloves" Donahue initially says. "That's Washington's racket." But stumbling upon the spy ring's insidious plan changes his mind, so much so that he makes peace with rival racketeers in order to fight the Nazis. "These babies are strictly no good from way down deep," Donahue learns. And his paramour Leeda Hamilton (Kaaren Verne) adds, "There are hundreds of them in New York, and every city of the country."

After the United States declared war on Germany in December 1941, the capture, trial, and execution of Nazi spies increased, as did newspaper accounts of the same.[46] As a result, Hollywood continued to depict the problem onscreen, most famously in Alfred Hitchcock's *Saboteur*, released in April 1942. In it, Robert Cummings plays Barry Kane, a man wrongly accused of starting a fire at an aircraft plant. The real culprits are a group of Nazi fifth columnists led by Tobin (Otto Kruger), a wealthy and friendly American who dotes on his granddaughter. His lieutenants include Fry (Norman Lloyd), who falls to his death from atop the Statue of Liberty. In this film, Hitchcock made a notable departure from the likes of *All Through the Night*, in which the chief spies were foreigners on American soil, played by the likes of Conrad Veidt and Peter Lorre, actors well known for villainous and horrifying roles.[47] "This whole house is a hotbed of spies and saboteurs," Barry Kane announces in *Saboteur*, and yet most of them eerily look and sound like all other Americans.

At the beginning of February 1943, producer Sam Katzman announced the production of *Ghosts on the Loose* under its original title *Ghosts in the Night*.[48] In early April 1943, Rear Admiral Harold C. Train spoke on CBS radio, advising listeners that Axis spies were "still operating in this country."[49] By the middle of that same month, Katzman had rechristened his film *Ghosts on the Loose*.[50] On May 17, 1943, J. Edgar Hoover warned that Germany was about to "unleash" more spies into America, with each American, whether in a small town or major city, needing to consider him or herself a "listening post" for the FBI.[51] Then, in mid-June 1943, Monogram released *Ghosts on the Loose*. *Film Daily* believed its Nazis were "properly menacing – and timely."[52]

It was hardly the first time the East Side Kids encountered the Axis powers. The title of *Bowery Blitzkrieg* (1940) alludes to the German bombing campaigns, even though its story is about boxing. Dialogue in *Spooks Run Wild* refers to the draft, as well as to the German Messerschmitt aircraft. Characters in both *Mr. Wise Guy* (1942) and *'Neath Brooklyn Bridge* (1942) serve in the U.S. military. By contrast, *Let's Get Tough!* (1942) leaves the Kids unsuccessful in their own effort to enlist. Stuck on the home front, they stumble across a Black Dragons Society. "It's open season on Japs," Muggs (Leo Gorcey) declares.

And then came *Ghosts on the Loose*. Bela Lugosi's Emil is a Nazi character who follows in the tradition of *All Through the Night* rather than *Saboteur*. He is a foreigner on American soil, which smacked similar to some newspaper reportage. For example, a "treason trial" in November 6, 1942, disclosed that the "eight German saboteurs who came to this country in U-boats last June were given $170,000 to be paid out as bribes."[53] Emil's gang of thugs includes German spies like Hilda (Minerva Urecal), as well as some American traitors, like Tony (Wheeler Oakman), who seems to have been acquainted with Jack, the male lead, for some time.

Unlike the villains in *All Through the Night* and *Saboteur*, Emil has no plans for blowing up battleships or bombing American defense plants. He is more Goebbels than Goering. For at least six months, his gang has used a printing press in the basement of the "haunted" house in order to publish subversive brochures like *How to Destroy the Allies* and *What the New Order Means to You!* The problem of Nazi literature in America predated the war. In May 1940, for example, an "angry crowd of 400 persons, headed by former service men" escorted three Nazi pamphleteers to the city limits of their Texas town, warning them not to return.[54] In January 1941, a congressional report estimated that forty tons of German propaganda entered America each year through the mail.[55] In September of that year, an Ohio man was accused of being a "secret propaganda agent of the German government."[56] Then, in March 1942, the FBI arrested nine "enemy aliens," finding guns, and radios, as well as a "quantity of Axis literature."[57] The Nazi pen was not as mighty as the sword, but it held the power to be disruptive all the same.

Authorities eventually apprehend Emil and his colleagues, thanks of course to Mugs, Glimpy, Danny, and their friends. It is, at least temporarily, V-A Day, Victory in America. But the success has been achieved not by the ingenuity of a Gloves Donahue or a Barry Kane, or even the superpowers of Captain America and Superman, who busted fifth columnists in comic books of the same era, but instead by the broom and mop-wielding East Side Kids. Unwittingly, the ill-educated and lower class characters became exactly what J. Edgar Hoover had advised: "listening posts" for the U.S. government.

Their reward? Heroism does not lead to heraldry. No one paints portraits of the East Side Kids. No *imago dei* is brought down, no *imago clipeata* is put up. No newspapers print their pictures. Instead, they are (humorously) scarred by their encounter with Nazis. As Napoleon once said, "When small men attempt great enterprises, they always end by reducing them[selves] to the level of their mediocrity."

At the conclusion of *Ghosts on the Loose*, Glimpy catches German measles, and so the entire group must be quarantined, all in the same room. Artwork hanging on the wall depicts not champions or conquerors, but instead the outside world, from which they are prohibited for seven days.

Conclusion

For many film historians, *Ghosts on the Loose* is of interest largely because of Ava Gardner's portrayal of Betty. It was not her movie, but it was the first feature in which she played a major role. Like Lugosi, she has little to do, her talents largely wasted. Nevertheless, their joint appearances do go far in illustrating the gravity of the Hollywood star. Lugosi's career was on the decline; Gardner's was in its infancy. Their paths intersected in the world of poverty row filmmaking, which so often latched onto the stars of yesterday, whose names retained some value, but whose salaries were declining, and onto the stars of tomorrow, talented and also cheap to hire. Both types of actor were usually all-too-eager for work.

As for the East Side Kids, *Ghosts on the Loose* crosses the line into the land of the inappropriate, perhaps more than any of their other films. There are jokes about the abbreviation "m.f." on sheet music. A real estate agent tells Jack, "May the house soon be filled with many pleasant memories," a reference not just to babies, but also to sex. At one point, Glimpy tells Stash (Stanley Clements) to "shut [his] big mouth," but Huntz Hall's delivery sounds distinctly like "shit up." And most surprising of all, Lugosi's sneeze is definitely not an "ahchoo." Instead, he seems to bellow out "Aww, shit." Double entendres were not uncommon for the East Side Kids; "You scared the health out of me," Glimpy complains in *Spooks Run Wild*, for example. But *Ghosts on the Loose* goes further than its predecessors, including in its ability to incorporate verboten language.

None of these facts are evidence for the movie to be heralded, of course. *Ghosts on the Loose* deserves its reputation as an undistinguished entry in the careers of all of its onscreen talent. If there is any achievement here, it belongs to director William Beaudine. Yes, the film has a great many deficits, and yes, the film recycles many longstanding horror clichés. But more than any other haunted house film of World War II, *Ghosts on the Loose* reworks those clichés with creative and contemporaneous variations that may not inspire terror or laughter, but that do deserve minimal recognition, at least before we anchor these unloosed ghosts to chains forevermore.

(Endnotes)

1   Tom Weaver, *Poverty Row Horrors! Monogram, PRC, and Republic Horror Films of the Forties* (Jefferson, North Carolina: McFarland and Company, 1993),

2   *"The House of a Thousand Trembles,"* Film Daily, August 20, 1922.

3   *"Ghosts on the Loose,"* Variety, July 7, 1943, 8.

4   *"One Nutty Night,"* Film Daily, November 23, 1930.

5   Credits for *Ghosts on the Loose* spell the character name "Mugs," as opposed to "Muggs," as in the case of the credits for *Spooks Run Wild*.

6   "Supposed Haunted House – An Officer Arrests a Ghost," *Providence Evening Press*

(Providence, Rhode Island), July 27, 1860, 2

7   "Catching a Ghost," *Nashville Union and American*, August 2, 1871.

8   *"The Haunted Closet," The Bloomfield Times* (New Bloomfield, Pennsylvania), November 19, 1872, 1.

9   "A Haunted House," *Charleston Daily News* (Charleston, South Carolina), September 16, 1869.

10 "A Haunted House," *The Times-Picayune* (New Orleans, Louisiana), February 21, 1843, 2.

11 See, for example: "Curious Trial," *The Columbian* (New York, New York), August 26, 1813, 3; "Haunted House," *The National Aegis* (Worcester, Massachusetts), June 24, 1857, 1; "Catching a Ghost Alive," *Salt Lake Tribune* (Salt Lake City, Utah), April 21, 1877.

12 *"The Haunted House (Imp)," Moving Picture World*, August 26, 1911, 548.

13 *"The Ghost of a Bargain," Moving Picture World*, September 21, 1912, 1178.

14 *"A Deal in Real Estate," Moving Picture World*, March 28, 1914, 1695.

15 *"The Gray Horror," Motography*, May 15, 1915, 801.

16 *"For Rented–Haunted," Film Daily*, October 8, 1922.

17 "Scares 'Ghost' Away," *Washington Post*, October 25, 1910, 3.

18 Ibid, 3.

19 *"The Ghost," Moving Picture World*, August 5, 1911, 292.

20 "American: *The Haunted House," Reel Life*, October 25, 1913, 15.

21 *"The Ghost," Moving Picture World*, August 23, 1913, 845.

22 *"The Ghost House," Variety*, October 12, 1917, 39.

23 "They Don't Make 'Fatty' Work Hard Enough in This," *Wid's Daily*, March 27, 1921, 17.

24 *"The House on the Hill," Edison Kinetogram*, July 1, 1910, 7-8.

25 *"Trapped in the Castle of Mystery," Moving Picture World*, December 13, 1913, 1340.

26 "Biographies of Artists," *The North American Quarterly Magazine* (October 1835), 335.

27 See, for example: Will H. Low, "A Century of Painting," *McClure's Magazine* (March 1896), 337; James Huneker, "Masters of Hallucination – Kubin, Munch, and Gauguin," *Boston Herald*, May 11, 1913, 33.

28 "The Fine Arts," *Boston Intelligencer*, May 20, 1820; "Our Artists–No. IV," *Godey's Magazine and Lady's Book* (November 1846), 211; Margaret Fuller Ossoli, "A Record of Impressions: Produced by the Exhibition of Mr. Allston's Pictures in the Summer of 1839," in Margaret Fuller Ossoli, *Art, Literature, and the Drama*, edited by Arthur B. Fuller (Boston: Roberts Brothers, 1889).

29 "A Feature that Charms," *Moving Picture World*, January 17, 1914, 263.

30 *"The Mysterious Eyes," Moving Picture World*, September 6, 1913, 1070.

31 *The Hound of the Baskervilles/Der Hund von Baskerville* has been restored using material from various archives by the Filmmuseum München.

32 Kamilla Elliott, *Portraiture and British Gothic Fiction: The Rise of Picture Identification, 1764-1835* (Baltimore: Johns Hopkins University Press, 2012), 292.

33 "Nazi Spy System Is Reported Here," *New York Times*, October 17, 1934, 1.

34 "Dickstein Charges Fascist Spy Plot," *New York Times*, March 12, 1937, 15; "Dickstein Lists 46 as Nazi Agitators," *New York Times*, July 28, 1937, 4.

35 "Berlin Denies Officers Members of Spy Ring," *Los Angeles Times*, June 22, 1938, 3.

36 "5 Officials to Meet to Co-ordinate U. S. Spy-Chasing," *Washington Post*, March 7, 1939, 2.

37 See, for example: "Seven of Spy Ring Plead Guilty Here; Three More Seized," *New York Times*, July 1, 1941, 1.

38 "Spies Stole U. S. Secrets, Dies Charges," *Washington Post*, November 21, 1939, 4.

39 See, for example: Donald C. Bingham, "The Fifth Column," *Washington Post*, April 28, 1940, B10; Lloyd Went, "We Spy! Apostles of Treachery – the German Fifth Columns," *Chicago Tribune*, July 7, 1940, D3.

40 "The Spy Problem," *Los Angeles Times*, November 12, 1939, A4.

41 Michael E. Birdwell, *Celluloid Soldiers: The Warner Bros. Campaign against Nazism* (New York: New York University Press, 1999), 2.

42 Ibid, 34.

43 Nelson B. Bell, *"Confessions of Nazi Spy* Glorifies Americanism," *Washington Post*, May 23, 1939, 16.

44   "Dramatic Story Behind Spy Film," *Los Angeles Times*, April 23, 1939, C3.

45   "All Through the Night," *Daily Variety*, October 19, 1942,

46   See, for example: Seth Moseley, "7 Nazi Spies Are Sentenced to Terms Totaling 117 Years," *Washington Post*, March 14, 1942, 5; "6 Nazi Spies Guilty in First War Trial; All Face 20 Years," *New York Times*, March 7, 1942, 1; "How Spies Were Recruited," *New York Times*, June 28, 1942, 30; "4 Spy Charges Filed Against 8 Captured Nazis," *Chicago Tribune*, July 4, 1942, 7; "Spies Tools Shown at Trial," *Los Angeles Times*, July 15, 1942, 2; "Brief Sketches of Nazis Convicted in Spy Plot," *Los Angeles Times*, August 9, 1942, 13; "Nazi Spy Tells Way Saboteurs Studied," *New York Times*, October 28, 1942, 1; "Six Nazi Spies Buried by U. S. in Potter's Field," *Chicago Tribune*, October 14, 1942, 19.

47   Conrad Veidt also played the title character in *Nazi Agent* (1942).

48   "Mono Rolls 5 Pix on February Schedule," *Daily Variety*, February 4, 1943, 8.

49   "Axis Renewing Spy Activities, Admiral Warns," *Chicago Tribune*, April 2, 1943, 10.

50   "Hollywood Making More Horror Pictures," *Film Daily*, April 15, 1943, 9.

51   "More Spies Head for U. S., Says Hoover," *Washington Post*, May 17, 1943, 1.

52   *"Ghosts on the Loose," Film Daily*, June 14, 1942, 7.

53   Charles Leavelle, "Nazi Spies Given $170,000 Bribe Fund," *Chicago Tribune*, November 6, 1942, 10.

54   "Texas Crowd Expels Nazi Pamphleteers," *New York Times*, May 23, 1940, 14.

55   Harold B. Hinton, "Raise Postage on Alien Mail, Dies Advises," *Washington Post*, January 5, 1941, 5.

56   "District Jury Indicts Ohioan as Nazi Agent," *Washington Post*, September 24, 1941, 1.

57   "FBI Traps 71 in Dawn Raid on Suspected Nazi Spy Ring," *New York Times*, March 29, 1942, 1.

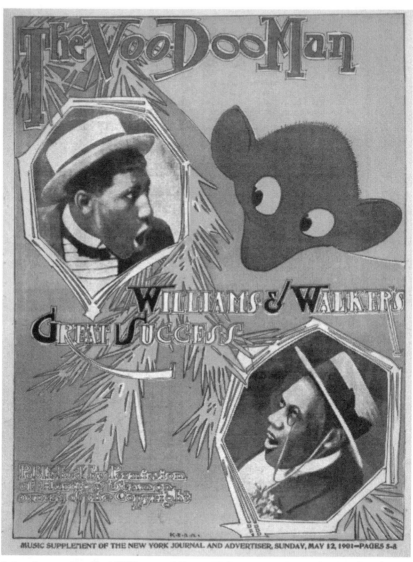

Artwork promoting Bert Williams and George Walker's song *The Voodoo Man* (1901).

Chapter 9

Voodoo Man and the Syncretic Cinema of Conjuration

by Gary D. Rhodes

I n the year 1900, Harry B. Smith's book *Stage Lyrics* appeared in print. Among its verses was a racist song entitled *De Voodoo Man*, which claimed the following of its eponymous charlatan:

> He talks to all de critters,
> Knows ev'ry bird dat twitters;
> He'll fool yo' chillen if he can.
> Look out for him! He's witchin' you – fo' money!
> He's weavin' dem Voodoo spells;
> Else de chillen wouldn't listen
> Wid dere shiney eyes a-glisten
> To de yahns Uncle Remus tells.[1]

Not to be outdone, the *Music Supplement of the New York Journal and Advertiser* published Bert Williams and George Walker's *The Voodoo Man* in 1901. Its chorus warns: "The Voodoo Man will catch yo' sure/Confess yo' sins, get gospel cure/Now let us sing, all those who can/For that's the Voodoo Man."[2] Longstanding fears of the bogeyman (and all of its variant spellings and synonyms) merged with voodoo, all for the sake of the American popular song.

Use of the term "Voodoo Man" had already appeared in the nonfiction press during the late nineteenth century. In 1888, for example, a newspaper in Arkansas reported on the death of a "Voodoo Man,"

A panel from *Weird Comics* 7 (1940).

an African-American conjuror who attempted to use "voodoo roots" to harm another man.[3] But the aforementioned songs mark the earliest occasions in which the phrase entered popular fiction.

Four decades later, the peripatetic character returned again.[4] Published by Fox Feature Syndicate from 1940 to 1942, *Weird Comics* featured "The Voodoo Man" in one of its many ongoing storylines. This new villain was neither charlatan nor bogeyman. He was instead the "Grim Master of Black Magic and the Strange Cults of Haiti," one who practiced "the rites of Lucifer."[5] He also grasped the "secret of zombies … dead men made into slaves."[6] This Voodoo Man wore various native headdresses and spoke in broken English. Pursued by a white hero, the black villain appeared in typically racist storylines, issue after issue. His very first appearance found him placing a white woman in a "horrible trance," thus implying the threat of physical violation and degradation, as well as of miscegeny, all unthinkable crimes, too horrible to consider.[7]

The comic book villain might well have inspired the title for William Beaudine's *Voodoo Man* (1944), the eighth entry in Lugosi's Monogram Nine. But the film's title may also have stemmed from a larger pattern in popular culture, one in which fictional characters were designated by the combination of gender identification and a word that distilled their existence into a single trait. Here again was the world of comic books, including nascent superheroes like Superman, Batman, Aquaman, Hawkman, Plastic Man, all created before Beaudine's film. Here was also a contemporaneous trend in horror cinema, as evidenced by *The Wolf Man* (1941), *The Leopard Man* (1943), and *The Ape Man* (1943). Indeed, the basis of Monogram's *Voodoo Man* came from an Andrew Colvin short story called *The Tiger Man*.[8]

As a film, *Voodoo Man* features a number of distinctive qualities, ranging from evocative lighting to a memorable whole-tone melody played by English horn and alto flute that moves the background music outside the major-minor tonal system. And then of course there is the cast, which brought together Bela Lugosi, John Carradine, and George Zucco for the first and only occasion.[9] Not surprisingly, Lugosi assumed the lead role of Dr. Marlowe. The Voodoo Man of the title, Marlowe relies on the religion to bring his dead wife back to life.

Voodoo is a syncretic religion, meaning an amalgamation of different belief systems, notably from West Africa and, certainly to a much lesser extent, from Roman Catholicism. It constitutes a set of spiritual folkways that flourished in Haiti, Jamaica, and elsewhere in the Caribbean. It evolved further in the United States, thanks to Francophone culture in Louisiana and, more broadly, to African American traditions of "Hoodoo," folk magic which relies on "conjuration" and "root doctoring." Discrete traditions thus merged into one: voodoo.

Syncretic may well be the best description for *Voodoo Man*. More than any other film in the Monogram Nine, it fused a number of discrete sources into a singular narrative. The traditions of voodoo cinema and literature commingled with the history of mesmerism and hypnotism, as well as elements appropriated from earlier Bela Lugosi movies, most notably *The Corpse Vanishes* (1942). Surprisingly, *Voodoo Man* is not a poverty-row patchwork, not a Monogram mélange, but instead a cinematic composite: admixture, intermixture, and commixture. The result is greater than the sum of its parts, in other words, so much so that I believe *Voodoo Man* to be the most rewardingly dense film in the Monogram Nine.

Voodoo Men

In a chapter titled "Vaudoux Worship and Cannibalism," Spenser St. John's 1884 book *Hayti, or the Black Republic* implied that most Haitians were involved in the religion.[10] Hesketh Prichard's book *Where Black Rules White: A Journey across and about Hayti* (1900) claimed "Vaudoux Worship and Sacrifice" was "widespread" in the country[11] He added, "Among the American negroes the rites of Voodoo, Voudoo, Vaudoo, Vaudoux – you can spell it as you like – are carried on in secrecy, and sedulously screened from the light of day."[12]

"The real or inner nature of *Voodooism* is as yet almost unknown, even to the learned," wrote Charles Godfrey Leland in 1893.[13] According to some press accounts, "African superstitions in America" represented a real danger.[14] As the *Boston Post* warned in 1899, voodoo worship was as "dark and as horrid as bestial savagery could make it."[15] An observer at a voodoo ceremony in South Carolina in 1890 described its participants as "weird and phantom-like, as though a hundred disembodied Druids had returned to mother earth."[16] But voodoo was hardly limited to a single American state: the same article also mentioned Louisiana, Mississippi, and Tennessee.

American voodoo not only became a subject pursued by researchers, most notably Mary A. Owen in her book *Voodoo Tales as Told among the Negroes of the Southwest* (1893), but also by writers of fiction. In the 1910 short story *The Bradys and the Voodoo Queen*, for example, detectives search for voodoo worshippers in New York, but are well aware of the connections they likely have to Haiti.[17] The foreign presence was very much present.

Early filmmakers also dealt with the topic on a number of occasions. *Voodoo Vengeance* (1913) was the first. Starring animal trainer Captain Jack Bonavita as a pagan priest, the three-reel moving picture offered the story of:

> ... a religious sect of African fanatics described as Voodoos, whose practices the British government finally stopped. The opening is where a man and woman on the way to the gold district are set upon by savages and killed. Their little girl is taken captive and raised by the tribe....[18]

Two decades later, the girl, now a beautiful woman, lures the son of a British commissioner into the jungle so that he will be able to "serve as a sacrifice to the moon god."

As the early cinema period came to a close, another American film about voodoo appeared at theatres. In 1915, Sidney Olcott directed *The Ghost of the Twisted Oaks*. Three reels in length, the movie told the story of Mary Randall (Valentine Grant), who inherits a plantation in Florida. Learning that a voodoo priest holds sway over the African-American workers, Mary has him removed from her property. One plot synopsis explained:

> After the action shifts back to the present, Mary stumbles upon

Though *Voodoo Man* borrowed heavily from earlier voodoo films and literature, its depiction of the religion being used solely by white characters is a departure from the past. *(Photo courtesy of Kristin Dewey)*

the Voodoos at worship and the priest determines to use her as a blood sacrifice, but the ghost again appears to Jack and leads him to the rescue.[19]

Unfortunately, only the third reel of the film survives. It displays some of the most impressive images of horror created during the early cinema period, particularly during the "fanatical dance of the 'Voodoos.'"[20]

Voodoo held as much potential for eerie sounds as it did for images. In 1900, Prichard claimed to have heard the "muffled reverberation of a drum beating" during a midnight ritual in Haiti.[21] And the aforementioned *Boston Post* article of 1899 described the "rhythm" at another ceremony:

Grouped around the sides of the amphitheatre were the musicians with tomtoms and gumgums, which were their only instruments.

Dr. Marlowe (Lugosi) is a hypnotist, but one who at times must rely on the voodoo god Ramboona. (*Photo courtesy of Kristin Dewey*)

Gumgums are one-stringed banjos with the skin stretched over the head of a gourd. Tomtoms are rude drums, made in much the same way, but lacking the string. One instrument is beaten with the hand and the other strummed on its single string.[22]

Drums came to be the sound most associated with the religion. Annie Calland's 1926 poem *Voodoo* included such verses as: "The big drums boon, the conch shells blare/The signal fires flame and flare."[23] Three years later, William B. Seabrook's book *The Magic Island* (1929) explained how the drums were made, named, and "baptized," and how their "throbbing" rhythms were achieved.[24]

Not unexpectedly, then, voodoo drums became important in such sound films as *White Zombie* (1932), *Voodoo* (1933), *Chloe* (1933, aka *Chloe: Love Is Calling You*), *Drums o' Voodoo* (1934), *Black Moon* (1934), and *The Devil's Daughter* (1939). A character in *Ouanga* (1935) discusses the "throbbing, pulsating beat" of voodoo drums; a character in *I Walked with a Zombie* (1943) describes their rhythms as "mysterious" and "eerie." Following in this tradition is *Voodoo Man*. Toby (John Carradine) and Grego (Pat McKee) beat drums during the pagan ceremonies conducted by Nicholas (George Zucco).

Writers of fiction also described the chants heard at voodoo ceremonies. Henry Francis Dowling's play *Voodoo*, published in London in 1914, features "Voodoo Hags" who "weirdly" spout such "sing-song" phrases as "Boonee, boonee, boo-oo-oo!/Soonee, soonee, soo-oo-oo!"[25] And David W. Guion's 1929 tune *Voodoo* described its wordless vocal chant "*m-m-m*" as "sort of a weird humming sound."[26] Numerous films featured voodoo chants, among them *White Zombie, Black Moon, King of the Zombies* (Monogram, 1941), and *I Walked with a Zombie*. And a character in *Ouanga* refers to "shuddering incantations."

For *Voodoo Man*, Nicholas offers a unique, even if nonsensical, variation on these chants, uttering gibberish in the form of a solo voice. Before him are two skulls, reflecting perhaps the influence of a chapter in Seabrook's *The Magic Island* entitled "The Altar of Skulls." Nicholas also relies on two pieces of rope that magically tie themselves together into a knot, as if his world is making a connection to another. And at least one of his ceremonies takes place just after midnight.

Nicholas' purpose is to invoke the presence and power of a voodoo god. George W. Cable's 1889 essay on Louisiana voodoo chronicled such gods as "Obi" and "Zombi."[27] Natalie Vivian Scott's play *Zombi* (1929) also intended the term in its title to be understood as the name of a voodoo god.[28] Seabrook compiled the names of the religion's deities and other related terms in *The Magic Island*, but Zora Neale Hurston's *Tell My Horse: Voodoo and Life in Haiti and Jamaica* (1938) became the most exhaustive and reliable source of the period.

Horror movies of the thirties and forties readily appropriated language from these books. "Obeah," a voodoo term that signifies the belief in sorcery, is explicitly mentioned in *The Devil's Daughter* and *I Walked with a Zombie*. The title of *Ouanga* is a reference to a voodoo charm. And the name of the voodoo god "Damballa" (sometimes spelled "Damballah") is spoken in *I Walked with a Zombie*. It had already featured in the title of Hans Mahner-Mons' novel *Damballa Calls: A Love Story of Haiti* (1936).

Enter Ramboona, the supernatural being in *Voodoo Man*. Nicholas advises Dr. Marlowe that Ramboona is "all powerful." But who is Ramboona? The film never tells us, other than implying he is a deity. His name is at once similar to voodoo gods named in earlier films and books, and also different, given that unlike its predecessors, which usually attempted to draw directly upon nonfiction, Ramboona is a confection, a nonsense invented for the sake of *Voodoo Man*. Nevertheless, Nicholas confidently proclaims, "Ramboona Never Fails."

Whatever his success rate, Ramboona requires "zombies" at the ceremonies, meaning in this case the living dead. Fictional accounts of voodoo causing the dead to return to life first appeared in Captain Mayne Reid's dime novel, *The Maroon: A Tale of Voodoo and Obeah* (1883).[29] That said, Reid did not actually use the word "zombie." By contrast, Seabrook did in *The Magic Island*, particularly in his chapter entitled "...Dead Men Working in the Cane Fields." Only two years later, Walter Futter created the first two zombie films in 1931, both for his short subject series *Curiosities*. One of them depicted "corpses being taken from the graves and prodded into life."[30] Zombies then appeared onscreen in a number of features, including *White Zombie, Ouanga, Revolt of the Zombies* (1936), *King of the Zombies, Revenge of the Zombies* (1943), and *I Walked with a Zombie*. Zora Neale Hurston's *Tell My Horse* even published a photograph of an allegedly authentic zombie. "That blank face with the dead eyes," Hurston described it with alarm.[31]

Dr. Marlowe enslaves a trio of female "zombies," all of them being recently kidnapped "motorists." He seems to be a new arrival in the area of Twin Falls, having taken possession of the "old Johnson home." The film does not indicate whether or not Marlowe has undertaken similar kidnappings in prior towns or cities. At any rate, the zombies don't possess the "perfect affinity" with his "dead" wife Evelyn (Ellen Hall) to restore her to "complete life," but their presence at ceremonies can apparently be helpful in that regard, or at least pleasing to Ramboona. All of them wear funereal gowns, appearing similar to Madeline (Madge Bellamy) in *White Zombie* and Jessica (Christine Gordon) in *I Walked with a Zombie*.

Though *Voodoo Man* borrowed heavily from earlier voodoo films and literature, it remains distinct in its avoidance of stereotypical settings, meaning Africa, the West Indies, or the American South, the latter being the locale used in *Drums o' Voodoo* and *Chloe*. To be sure, the specific state in which *Voodoo Man* takes place is never mentioned. It seems to be a reasonable driving distance from Hollywood. Certainly nothing in the film's dialogue or mise-en-scène implies that it is set in Louisiana or the American South. In other words, "Twin Falls" is more vague than it is specific.

Much more surprising is the extent to which *Voodoo Man* appropri-

Stella (Louise Currie, standing) and Dr. Marlowe (Lugosi). Their initial exchange becomes perhaps the most effective scene in the entire Monogram Nine. *(Photo courtesy of Bill Chase)*

ates a religion associated with blacks without including any black characters, as every prior voodoo film had done. Indeed, African-American actress Nellie Wan, credited onscreen as Madame Sul-Te-Wan, had become particularly associated with portraying voodoo-inspired characters in the years before *Voodoo Man*, including "Black Cindy" in *Hoodoo Ann* (1916), "Voodoo Sue" in *Heaven on Earth* (1931), "Ruva" in *Black Moon*, "Tahama" in *King of the Zombies*, and "Mammy Beulah" in *Revenge of the Zombies*.

Previous movies had shown white characters taking part in voodoo practices, or even in charge of them, notably Murder Legendre (Bela Lugosi) in *White Zombie* and Juanita Lane (Dorothy Burgess) in *Black Moon*, who refers to the voodoo faithful as "my people." Other characters in these films could be white as well, whether Madeline as the title character of *White Zombie* (the word "white" in that case referring not only to her skin color, but also to her virginal status) or the title character in *Chloe*, who is revealed to be white in a twist ending. All that said, most

In some respects, *Voodoo Man* represents a remake of *The Corpse Vanishes* (1942).
(Photo courtesy of Bill Chase)

of the characters involved in voodoo rites in those films are black.

At the ceremonies in *Voodoo Man* (a film in which the word "voodoo" is never uttered), Nicholas and Marlowe dress in black robes, but they appear closer to those that wizards might wear, adorned as they are with symbols like X's, 7's, and stars. Nicholas does appear in a headdress akin to what fictional witch doctors sometimes wore (including the "Voodoo Man" of *Weird Comics*), and he does wear some type of tribal paint on his face. But he is certainly not in blackface. Nor are Dr. Marlowe, Toby, or Grego.

The fact that *Voodoo Man* depicts the religion as being used exclusively by white characters was a clear departure from prior films and literature, the apparent result of its own syncretic blend of inspirations.

Hypnotism

In 1900, Prichard wrote, "The [voodoo] priests are no doubt to a certain extent hypnotists. They achieve the unexplainable."[32] In *The Devil's*

Daughter, "hypnotic powers" are explicitly ascribed to one character, but nowhere in voodoo cinema are they more apparent than in *White Zombie.* In it, Murder Legendre's eyes fill the screen in extreme close-ups, staring directly into the camera. At times, Dr. Marlowe also looks directly into the camera as he attempts to transfer the "will to live" from Stella and, later, from Betty Benton (Wanda McKay) into Evelyn. While Nicholas chants gibberish, Marlowe spouts the following:

> Mind to mind... mind to mind... Soul, from body to body... Soul, from body to body... Emotion to emotion... Emotion to emotion... Life to death... Life to death... Life to death.

These efforts – which are not dissimilar to the "transmigrations" depicted in *King of the Zombies* – result in minor successes. Evelyn has two brief moments in which she returns to consciousness.

But Marlowe's abilities sometimes draw more on the histories of mesmerism and hypnotism than they do on voodoo. Both subjects had gained currency in the nineteenth century, not only in scientific circles, but also in popular culture. As Daniel Pick explains:

> The puzzle of hypnotism stimulated long-standing debate amongst Victorian scientists and doctors; it inspired and troubled novelists; it aroused popular wonderment, even childlike devotion, as well as much alarm from social commentators. It disturbed the boundaries between high and low culture, education and entertainment, fact and fiction, medicine and quackery, waking states, sleep and dreams; it seemed to return its subjects to some long-lost state of being, an irresponsible world, free of the conventions of grown-up 'self-mastery.'[33]

As a result, hypnotism commanded "both awed and squeamish public attention."[34]

Hypnotism also inspired a range of fictional literature, from Guy de Maupassant's short story *The Horla/Le horla* (1887) to F. Marion Crawford's novel *The Witch of Prague* (1891).[35] However, its most notable literary expression came in George Du Maurier's *Trilby* (1894). In the novel, the Laird tells Trilby:

> He's a bad fellow, Svengali – I'm sure of it! He mesmerized you; that's what it is – mesmerism! I've often heard of it, but never seen

it done before. They get you into their power, and just make you do any blessed thing they please – lie, murder, steal – anything! [A]nd kill yourself into the bargain when they've done with you! It's just too terrible to think of![36]

The extremely popular novel became an equally popular stage production. Paul M. Potter's four-act adaptation of *Trilby* debuted in America in 1895, with Wilton Lackaye portraying Svengali. A kind of "Trilbymania" resulted, parodied in an 1897 vaudeville sketch entitled *Too Much Trilby*.[37] As one magazine wrote in 1896, "It is a moot point whether *Trilby* the play made *Trilby* the book or *vice versa*; there are those, and many, who consider the play by far to be the better of the two...."[38]

The stage play became so popular that numerous touring companies were formed, including a condensed vaudeville version in 1901.[39] However, Wilton Lackaye remained the most famous actor associated with Svengali. *The Critic* called his performance, "overwrought but indisputably strong."[40] The *Washington Post* was more enthusiastic, telling readers:

Mr. Lackaye's Svengali is an artistic triumph that will live in the history of the stage. His characterization paints vividly the curious blend of cringing cowardice, inordinate vanity, and terrible mesmeric power that can mold an independent mind into a vehicle for the materialization of his dominating will. He fills the picture of ghastly grotesqueness that Trilby names 'a great black spider.' ... And he does not depend on make-up and spotlight to secure that indefinable influence that gives the stage story its atmosphere....[41]

Lackeye appeared in numerous revivals of the play, including in 1898, 1905, 1907, and in 1915.[42] As one journalist bemoaned, "It is a pity that ... Du Maurier's Svengali will endure by virtue of printer's ink [, but] Lackaye's Svengali ... must die with each drop of the curtain."[43] The comment was true with regard to the theatre, though Lackeye did star in a film version of *Trilby* in 1915.

By that time, hypnotism had already provided the impetus for a large number of films. In *What Hypnotism Can Do* (American Mutoscope and Biograph, 1899), a hypnotist proves his powers to a "doubting client" by making a ballet girl materialize from nothingness, "poised in the air," before he makes her disappear.[44] That same year, Edison sold the Vitagraph-produced film [*The*] *Mesmerist and Country Couple*. In it, "Mr. and Mrs. Hayseed" visit a "wonderful Professor" who hypnotizes them.

Similar to Dr. Lorenz in *The Corpse Vanishes*, Dr. Marlowe heads a bizarre family in *Voodoo Man*. *(Photo courtesy John Antosiewicz)*

Mr. Hayseed stands on his head, while his wife "begins to disrobe, but she goes behind a screen." Her "bare arm appears over the top, and she drops her clothes on the floor." An Edison catalogue description promised "mystical appearances managed with wonderful cleverness."[45] Hypnotism onscreen had quickly become associated with magic, as it long had been in popular culture.

Following from Svengali, most cinematic hypnotists were villains. The earliest film adaptations of Du Maurier's story came in Edison's *Trilby Hypnotic Scene* (1895), which was advertised as a "burlesque," and Edison's *Trilby Death Scene* (1895, aka *Death Scene*), a "comic" film that attempted to "imitate" the illustrations in Du Maurier's book.[46] Other hypnotists focused on controlling women for sinister purposes, as in such dramatic films as *Hypnotized* (1910), *An Evil Power* (1911), *The Evil Power* (1913), *The Spell* (1913), *The Blood Brotherhood* (1913), *Forces of Evil, or The Dominant Will* (1914), and *The Return of Richard Neal* (1915).[47]

Post-nickelodeon movies like Universal's *The Silent Command* (1915)

Voodoo Man's Grego (Pat McKee, left) and Toby (John Carradine) echo Angel (Angelo Rossitto) and Toby (Pat McKee) in *The Corpse Vanishes*. *(Photo courtesy of Bill Chase)*

used cinematography to accentuate the villain's power. According to *Universal Weekly*, the hypnotist Dr. Sevani (Harry Carter) has eyes that are too strong to refuse. *Moving Picture World* remarked, "From the moment [a victim] gazes upon the eyes of evil ... as pictured in the close-ups, the feeling grows in the observer that something of an almost uncanny psychological nature is going to occur."[48]

Most of these screen hypnotists – and there were a large number in the decades before *Voodoo Man* – usually wore beards or goatees, their appearance similar not only to the illustrations in Du Maurier's novel, but also to Wilton Lackeye's stage makeup. To an extent, Dr. Marlowe's appearance resembles Murder Legendre in *White Zombie*, but he also resembles these earlier, bearded hypnotists, who had long exerted their powers with their eyes and hands.

Voodoo Man's opening credits show two enormous hands exerting hypnotic power over an entranced woman's body. Lightning bolts extend from the evil fingers onto her reclined body, an effect that had deep roots in fictional accounts of hypnotism. The illustrated song slide *Oh, You Spearmint Kiddo with the Wrigley Eyes* (1910), which would have been projected at nickelodeon theatres, featured the lyric "Gee! But you look wise/You mesmerize me, hypnotize me." In this case, the hypnotist is a woman. Slide 14 depicts her in a long shot, hypnotizing her lover. Lightning bolts shoot out of her hands, the image being an amalgam of artwork and photography.

Dr. Marlowe refers to his victims as "zombies," but they appear similar to those in the thrall of hypnotists, a point that some characters imply. "Your eyes look so funny," Toby tells the entranced Stella (Louise Currie). Seeing her in the same state, Ralph says, "She looks like a person in a trance." Betty (Wanda McKay) adds, "Look at her eyes. She's just staring." Later, a character says of the entranced Betty, "I thought she was in a daze or something."

Marlowe's use of hypnotism provides the culmination of *Voodoo Man*'s most disturbing scene, the one in which he first meets Stella. Tense and sexually charged, the encounter features extreme closeups of the actors' faces. With moody, low-key lighting, Marlowe explains matters to his reluctant "guest":

Stella. "Let me out of here."
Marlowe: "I'm afraid that is quite impossible."
[pause]
"I need you."
Stella: "You need me."
Marlowe: "Yes."
Stella: "What for?"
Marlowe: "Come. I'll show you. Don't be afraid. Just follow me."

One of the most effective in the Monogram Nine, this brief scene could easily have appeared in a German Expressionist film of the early twenties, or, for that matter, Browning's *Dracula*.

In the film *Svengali* (1931), the lead character is able to exert hypnotic control over Trilby even when she is at great remove from his house, giving her commands telepathically. Murder Legendre is capable of the same in *White Zombie*. Fredrik Björnström's 1889 book *Hypnotism: Its History and Present Development* spoke about this possibility:

...we refer to the effects of the so-called *mental suggestion*, which might be defined as *transmission of thought*, and which from a certain point of view, also embraces *mind-reading*. For, by 'suggestion mentale,' the French mean the operation by which sensation, will, or any psychical force affects the brain of another directly, in what may be called immaterial matter, without manifesting itself by anything perceptible to the external senses....[49]

Dr. Marlowe successfully employs the same process, though unlike his predecessors, he requires assistance.

Nicholas must help him control Stella and Betty from afar. Similar to Murder Legendre's use of Madeline's scarf in *White Zombie*, they must

also use purloined articles of clothing that belong to the two women, meaning an earring and a glove. It seems as if their ability to control Stella from a distance has begun with Marlowe's original hypnotism of her: once entranced by him, she stays that way. And as she approaches the house, Marlowe mentally knows that she is "almost" there. By contrast, Marlowe never hypnotizes Betty, but Nicholas' chants and possession of her glove still allow them to command her from afar.

Despite his need for help, though, Marlowe is ultimately in control of the two women. It is his death that releases them from their entranced state, much the same as Murder Legendre's death frees Madeline, and, more famously, Svengali's death frees Trilby. Their freedom is founded on the repetition of a narrative antecedent.

Remakes

Genres operate based upon repeated codes and conventions, which thus becomes the stuff of audience expectations. What will happen at the end of a western movie, we might ask, without even mentioning a specific title, and the response would invariably be a shootout between the good guy and bad guy. What will happen in a slasher movie when a female is running from a masked killer? The answer is trip and fall, of course, so the villain can get ever near her. These answers do

Being a syncretic film, *Voodoo Man* has commonalities with more entries in the Monogram Nine than just *The Corpse Vanishes*. (Photo courtesy of Kristin Dewey)

not always prove true, but the generic tropes are still activated: subverting our expectations still engages a dialogue with them.

Anat Zanger's discussion of film remakes describes them as a form of both ritual and disguise:

> Cinema as a social institution knows what Scherherazade seems to have known all along: to narrate is to triumph over death. Hence, in an ongoing ceremony that occurs in the darkness of the movie theater (and lasts, ultimately, more than 1001 nights), society constantly delivers its encoded messages. The constant repetition of the same tale keeps it alive in social memory, continually transmitting its meaning and relevance.[50]

And yet, repetitions in genre still allow for different film narratives, plotted and executed with much variance.

Harvey Roy Greenberg has importantly identified three different types of remakes.[51] One is the acknowledged, close remake, in which a new film reproduces an earlier film with few changes, particularly to the narrative. A second is the acknowledged, transformed remake, in which major changes to the earlier work are undertaken. Film history is rife with examples of both categories.[52]

Studios in the classical Hollywood era relied on these kinds of remakes with some regularity, particularly after the talking picture became popular. In early 1931, *Variety* calculated that 120 silent films had been remade with sound since 1928. The trade added that the "best time" for this to occur was after a "7 years' lapse" since the original was released, whereas "under 4 Years" could prove box-office "poison."[53] Studios did not necessarily heed this advice. Universal released Paul Leni's silent film *The Cat and the Canary* in 1927; it remade the film as the talkie *The Cat Creeps* in 1930.[54]

In any event, Rüdiger Heinze and Lucia Krämer remind us "remaking is always more or less transformative."[55] Variations mark any examples of remakes one might give. The difference between Greenberg's aforementioned two categories is one of degree rather than kind, a point that allows for the introduction of his third category, the unacknowledged, disguised remake. Whatever the extent of changes, major or minor, the remake does not admit its relationship to the original, repurposing earlier narratives without attribution.

In terms of the horror movie, *The Hidden Hand* (1942) clearly but quietly borrows from *Night of Terror* (1933), just as *The Man They Could Not*

Hang (1939) is reminiscent of *The Ninth Guest* (1934). *Whispering Ghosts* (1942) repeats much from *The Ghost Breakers* (1940), to the extent that actor Willie Best plays basically the same character in both. And *The Pillow of Death* (1945) features Lon Chaney as a character who goes into a trance and murders various people when he thinks he hears his dead wife's voice. The similarities to Monogram's *Invisible Ghost* (1941) are striking. George Bricker, *The Pillow of Death*'s screenwriter, had worked at Monogram in 1941, which might explain the parallels.

The unacknowledged, disguised remake could also occur at the very same studio. When reviewing Universal's *The Mummy* (1932), a critic for the *Oakland Tribune* wrote:

> The wheel of cinema horror that began to move with *Dracula* [Universal, 1931] completed its revolution at the Orpheum yesterday with the presentation of *The Mummy*. The two pictures have much in common, and, curiously enough, little in common with the multitude of shriek and giggle contraptions that have come in the interim.[56]

The similarities include the return of key cast members from *Dracula* (like Edward Van Sloan and David Manners), crewmembers (like Karl Freund), and even props (like a bedroom lamp), as well as an analogous supernatural storyline that features related scenes, most notably the re-working of Van Helsing's use of a mirror against Dracula into Muller's use of a photograph against the Mummy. In both films, the supernatural creatures lose their composure when confronted with these props, just as both shrink from the sight of religious objects, whether the crucifix or the image of Isis. Ideas from the past are repurposed, even if they are altered and cloaked.

Voodoo Man also functions as a disguised remake, not of an earlier voodoo film, surprisingly, but rather of one of its predecessors in the Monogram Nine, *The Corpse Vanishes* (1942).[57] Both movies represent the convergence of science and the supernatural (or at least implied supernatural). In the first film, Dr. Lorenz keeps his seemingly vampiric wife alive by injecting her with the blood of other women, but that blood must first be mixed with some unidentified chemical(s). Similarly, Dr. Marlowe keeps his wife – who has been "dead" for 22 years – in a state of suspended animation thanks to a "gradual intensity" of unnamed rays. Caution is required, though, as "sudden bright light could disintegrate her." Restoring her to "complete life" requires the power of voodoo. The two men show extreme devotion to their wives: kidnapping women and imprisoning them as slaves doesn't pose an ethical dilemma for either of them.

Dr. Marlowe and Dr. Lorenz also share the same profession, though their specific areas of medical expertise are not explained. Certainly both of them are expert hypnotists. Lorenz has various test tubes in his laboratory; Marlowe has test tubes and Tesla coils. Both men achieve remarkable success in their scientific pursuits, whether Lorenz with his ability to induce cataleptic states in kidnapped brides, or Marlowe, who invents a wireless device that can cause his victims' automobiles to stall. Using a television security system, Marlowe can also spy on others.

Importantly, Marlowe's family extends beyond his wife. Like Lorenz, he has managed to become head of a household of misfits, none of whom appear to be his blood relations. For example, housekeeper Marie (Mici Goty) provides crucial assistance to Marlowe, just as Fagah (Minerva Urecal) does in *The Corpse Vanishes*. And *Voodoo Man*'s Grego and Toby echo Angel (Angelo Rossitto) and Toby (Pat McKee) in *The Corpse Vanishes*. Like his namesake, *Voodoo Man*'s Toby seems mentally challenged and easily charmed by the beauty of kidnapped victims, so much so he caresses them. He also inadvertently allows Stella to escape, and, as a result, fears a beating from his "master."

And then there is Nicholas, an intelligent, middle-aged man, whose affiliation with Marlowe seems as inexplicable as Mike's (George Eldredge, credited onscreen as "George Eldridge") in *The Corpse Vanishes*. Perhaps Nicholas and Marlowe met through their shared interest in voodoo, but the film does not provide any answers. What is clear is that Nicholas' gas station makes him eerily prescient of Drayton Sawyer (Jim Siedow) in *The Texas Chain Saw Massacre* (1974), a member of horror cinema's most notorious family.

Conclusion

Being a syncretic film, *Voodoo Man* has commonalities with more entries in the Monogram Nine than just *The Corpse Vanishes*. There are the inexplicable plot points, which become expectations in these films; for example, Marlowe's risky attempt to recover the entranced Stella is hard to understand, since she doesn't bear the perfect affinity with his wife. There are oblique references to wartime rationing and the military draft. And authority figures are dimwitted. Though he does eventually shoot Marlowe, the Sheriff (Henry Hall) is both clueless ("Gosh all fish hooks"), inappropriate (drinking on duty), and even something of a malcontent, complaining his job has become a "pain in the neck." But as much as anything else, *Voodoo Man* is tethered to its forebears in its drive toward the self-referential.

Consider Ralph Dawson (Tod Andrews), fiancée of Betty Benton, the somewhat ineffectual male lead of *Voodoo Man*. For the bulk of the running time, he does little to affect meaningful change, let alone the happy ending. But he is a screenwriter at the "Banner Motion Picture Company." His boss is a producer known as "S.K." (John Ince); the reference is to the real-life Sam Katzman, who produced the Monogram Nine under his Banner Productions. During the film, Ralph refers to the craft of writing horror movies: "You know, this is screwier than anything I've ever written, and I've written some screwy ones, believe me." He also explains that zombies don't exist outside of the cinema: "That's only a scenario writer's nightmare."

The voracious world of *Voodoo Man* not only refers to itself, but in so doing conjures a small, but consistent trend in the horror movie genre, one apparent in five earlier entries in the Monogram Nine. "This looks like the place where the plot begins to thicken," Muggs (Leo Gorcey) announces in *Spooks Run Wild* (1941). In *Ghosts on the Loose* (1943), Glimpy (Huntz Hall) refers to the "Katzman mob," another nod to the real-life film producer. During the running time of *Bowery at Midnight* (1942), a movie poster for *The Corpse Vanishes* hangs outside of a theatre. Far more overt is the crazy character Zippo (Ralph Littlefield) in *The Ape Man* (1943) who announces at its conclusion, "I'm the author of the story. Screwy idea, wasn't it?" Then he rolls up a car window with the words "The End" written on it.

When it came to Lugosi, self-reflexivity was hardly limited to the Monogram Nine. *Dracula* originally ended with a curtain speech; two years later, at the end of *Night of Terror*, the Maniac (Edwin Maxwell) warned viewers not to reveal the killer's identity to their friends. Universal's 1941 version of *The Black Cat* paired Lugosi with Basil Rathbone; it makes reference to Sherlock Holmes, the character with whom Rathbone was famously associated. And at the conclusion of *The Return of the Vampire* (1944), Sir Frederick Fleet (Miles Mander) talks directly to the audience.

Curtain speeches also appear in such non-Lugosi horror movies as *The Bat Whispers* (1930) and *Frankenstein* (1931). Characters talk to viewers in *The Monster and the Girl* (1941) and *I Walked with a Zombie*. Comedic nods to the audience occur in various films, including *The Cat and the Canary* (1939) and *Hold That Ghost* (1941). When the door closes at the end of Monogram's *Revenge of the Zombies* (1943), the words "The End" are painted on it.

And then there is the conclusion of *Voodoo Man*. After Dr. Marlowe is killed and all apparently returns to normal, Ralph gives S.K. his latest script. "There you are, boss. There's your horror story." It is entitled *The Voodoo Man*. When asked who should star in it, Ralph suggests, "Say, why don't you try to get that actor Bela Lugosi? It's right up his alley."

It was indeed. *Voodoo Man* became the penultimate entry in the Monogram Nine, released to theatres in February of 1944. *Daily Variety* rightly described the syncretic film as a "nightmarish concoction."[58] "Now let us sing, all those who can/For that's the Voodoo Man."

(Endnotes)

1   Harry B. Smith, *Stage Lyrics* (New York: R.H. Russell, 1900), 25.

2   The sheet music for Bert Williams and George Walker's *The Voodoo Man* (aka *The Voo-Doo Man*) is archived as an electronic resource on the Library of Congress' online Performing Arts Encyclopedia. Available at: http://memory.loc.gov/diglib/ihas/loc.award.rpbaasm.1306/default.html.

3   "A Voodoo Man Killed," *Arkansas Gazette* (Little Rock, Arkansas), October 10, 1888. Other early examples include: "Detroit's Voodoo Man," *Grand Rapids Press* (Grand Rapids, Michigan), November 1, 1894.

4   Additional examples of nonfiction reportage using the term "Voodoo Man" include: "'Voodoo' Man," *Jackson Citizen* (Jackson, Michigan), February 26, 1901; "Negro 'Herb Doctor' Indicted," *Cleveland Plain Dealer* (Cleveland, Ohio), April 14, 1903; "'Voodoo Man' Only Hope," *Biloxi Daily Herald* (Biloxi, Mississippi), July 24, 1905; "Voodoo Man Hoodooed," *Fort Worth Star-Telegram* (Fort Worth, Texas), December 7, 1907; "Real Voodoo Man Found in America," *Daily Oklahoman* (Oklahoma City, Oklahoma), August 22, 1909; "Hold Voodoo Man in Woman Killing," *Cleveland Plain Dealer*, October 28, 1910; "'Voodoo Man' in Case Held," *Columbus Ledger* (Columbus, Georgia), April 5, 1912; "Negroo [sic] Voodoo Man Now Under Arrest," *Jonesboro Daily Tribune* (Jonesboro, Arkansas), October 23, 1919; "Witchcraft and Poison Kill Girl," *Cleveland Plain Dealer*, March 18, 1929, 1; "Sorcerer Tries Magic Against White Men," *Springfield Union and Republican* (Springfield, Massachusetts), August 2, 1931, 5E; "Voodoo Man Tells How He Slew Victim," *Seattle Daily Times* (Seattle, Washington), November 22, 1932, 1.

5   Allen Spectre, "*The Voodoo Man*," *Weird Comics* 6 (September 1940), 37.

6   Allen Spectre, "*The Voodoo Man*," *Weird Comics* 7 (October 1940), 46.

7   Allen Spectre, "*The Voodoo Man*," *Weird Comics* 1 (April 1940), 46.

8   "Hollywood," *Showmen's Trade Review*, April 3, 1943, 23.

9   Lugosi, Carradine, and Zucco were credited onscreen in *Return of the Ape Man* (1944), but despite the use of his name, it does not seem that Zucco actually appears in the film.

10   Spenser St. John, *Hayti, or the Black Republic* (London: Smith, Elder, and Co., 1884).

11   Hesketh Prichard, *Where Black Rules White: A Journey across and about Hayti* (New York: Charles Scribner's Sons, 1900), 75.

12   Prichard, 95.

13   Charles Godfrey Leland, "Introduction," in *Voodoo Tales as Told among the Negroes of the Southwest* by Mary A. Owen (New York: G.P. Putnam's Sons, 1893), vi. Emphasis in original.

14   "African Superstitions in America," *Daily Albany Argus* (Albany, New York), December 15, 1866, 4.

15   "Terrible Voodoo Dances of the South," *Boston Post*, July 30, 1899, 22.

16   "A Southern Voodoo Dance," *Current Literature*, February 1890, 123.

17 "The Bradys and the Voodoo Queen," Secret Service: Old and Young King Brady, Detectives, December 30, 1910.

18 "Voodoo Vengeance," Moving Picture World, June 21, 1913, 1237.

19 Edward Weitzel, "The Ghost of the Twisted Oaks," Moving Picture World, November 20, 1915, 1505.

20 A copy of reel three of The Ghost of Twisted Oaks is archived at the Library of Congress.

21 Prichard, 81.

22 "Terrible Voodoo Dances of the South," 22.

23 Annie Calland, Voodoo (New York: Harold Vinal, 1926).

24 William B. Seabrook, The Magic Island (New York: Literary Guild of America, 1929), 36, 46.

25 Henry Francis Downing, Voodoo: A Drama in Four Acts (London: Francis Griffith, 1914).

26 David W. Guion, Five Imaginary Early Louisiana Songs of Slavery (New York: G. Schirmer, 1919).

27 George W. Cable, "Creole Slave Songs," The Century Magazine (April 1886), 807-828.

28 Natalie Vivian Scott, "Zombi," Theatre Arts Monthly (January 1929).

29 Captain Mayne Reid, The Maroon: A Tale of Voodoo and Obeah (New York: M.J. Ivers, 1883).

30 A discussion of Futter's zombie short subjects appears in Gary D. Rhodes, White Zombie: Anatomy of a Horror Film (Jefferson, North Carolina: McFarland and Company, 2001), 83.

31 Zora Neale Hurston Tell My Horse: Voodoo and Life in Haiti and Jamaica (New York: HarperPerennial, 2009), 195.

32 Prichard, 98.

33 Pick, 69.

34 Ibid, 69.

35 Atia Sattar, "Certain Madness: Guy de Maupassant and Hypnotism," Configurations, Vol. 19, No. 2 (Spring 2011), 213-241.

36 George Du Maurier, Trilby (New York: Harper and Brothers, 1894), 75.

37 "Trilbymania," The Open Court, a Quarterly Magazine, April 18, 1895, 4465; "Variety and Minstrelsy," New York Clipper, August 15, 1896.

38 "Our Theatrical Playground," Outing, an Illustrated Monthly Magazine of Recreation, January 1896, xxviiic.

39 "Vaudeville and Minstrel," New York Clipper, December 7, 1901.

40 "Trilby at the Garden Theatre," The Critic: A Weekly Review of Literature on the Arts, April 20, 1895, 300.

41 "Lackaye in Trilby," Washington Post, June 4, 1907, 4

42 "Trilby at Great Northern," Chicago Tribune, March 21, 1898, 5; "Trilby Revived with the Original Players," Washington Post, May 14, 1905, T1; "Lackaye in Trilby," p. 4; Alexander Woollcott, "An All-Star Trilby," New York Times, April 4, 1915, 5.

43 "Actor-Made Svengali Is Greedier than Author's," Los Angeles Times, September 28, 1905, II1.

44 Picture Catalogue (New York: American Mutoscope and Biograph, November 1902), 67. Available in A Guide to Motion Picture Catalogs by American Producers and Distributors, 1894-1908: A Microfilm Edition, Reel 2.

45 No. 105, Edison Films, Complete Catalogue (Orange, New Jersey: Edison Manufacturing Company, July 1901), 84-85. Available in A Guide to Motion Picture Catalogs by American Producers and Distributors, 1894-1908: A Microfilm Edition, Reel 1.

46 Charles Musser, Edison Motion Pictures, 1890-1900: An Annotated Filmography (Washington, D.C.: Smithsonian Institution Press, 1997), 187.

47 "Hypnotized," Moving Picture World, December 31, 1910, 1550; "An Evil Power," Moving Picture World, December 16, 1911, 903; "The Evil Power," Moving Picture World, August 30, 1913, 994; "The Spell," Vitagraph Life Portrayals, July 1913, 48; "Black Hander Has Singular Influence Over Girl," Universal Weekly, November 8, 1913, 20; Hanford C. Judson, "Shows Power of Hypnotism," Motography, July 25, 1914, 123; "The Return of Richard Neal," Moving Picture World, May 1, 1915, 728.

48 Robert C. McElravy, "The Silent Command," Moving Picture World, May 1, 1915, 743.

49 Fredrik Björnström, Hypnotism. Its History and Present Development (New York: The Humboldt Publishing Co., 1889, 71.

50 Anat Zanger, Film Remakes as Ritual and Disguise: From Carmen to Ripley (Amsterdam:

Amsterdam University Press, 2006), 9.

51 Harvey Roy Greenberg, "Raiders of the Lost Text: Remaking as Contested Homage in *Always*," *Journal of Popular Film and Television*, Vol. 18, No. 4 (1991), 164-171.

52 For example, in the years between 1908 and 1913, American exhibitors screened approximately six versions of Robert Louis Stevenson's *Strange Case of Dr. Jekyll and Mr. Hyde* (1886): *Dr. Jekyll and Mr. Hyde* (1908), *Dr. Jekyll and Mr. Hyde; or, a Strange Case/ Den skæbnesvangre opfindelse* (1910), *Dr. Jekyll and Mr. Hyde* (1912), *Dr. Jekyll and Mr. Hyde* (Imp, 1913), and *Dr. Jekyll and Mr. Hyde* (Kinemacolor, 1913). The sixth version – though it has yet been difficult to determine whether it was screened or even completed – was Theatrephone's *Dr. Jekyll and Mr. Hyde* in 1908. Four more versions appeared in the years before *Voodoo Man*: *Dr. Jekyll and Mr. Hyde* (Paramount, 1920), *Dr. Jekyll and Mr. Hyde* (Pioneer 1920), *Dr. Jekyll and Mr. Hyde* (1931) and *Dr. Jekyll and Mr. Hyde* (1941).

53 "Studios on the Remake," *Variety*, January 21, 1931, 11.

54 Universal was hardly alone in these efforts. MGM remade *London After Midnight* (1927) as *Mark of the Vampire* (1935); Tod Browning directed both. Likewise, Roland West remade *The Bat* (1926) as *The Bat Whispers* (1930), both being distributed by United Artists. In all of these cases, the remakes were official, legally and otherwise, meaning that the producers did not conceal the source material (as in film credits and publicity), even if the remake sometimes bore a different title. To return to Greenberg, it would be worthwhile to consider which of these were close remakes (*The Bat Whispers*, arguably), and which were not (*Mark of the Vampire*, perhaps).

55 Rüdiger Heinze and Lucia Krämer, "Introduction: Remakes and Remaking – Preliminary Reflections," in *Remakes and Remaking: Concepts–Media–Practices*, edited by Rüdiger Heinze and Lucia Krämer (2015).

56 Wood Soanes, "*The Mummy* is New Type of Horror Cinema," *Oakland Tribune*, February 11, 1933, 8. Despite the article title, Soanes strongly argued that *The Mummy* and *Dracula* featured similar storylines.

57 Tom Weaver has referred to *Voodoo Man* as a "semiremake" of *The Corpse Vanishes*. See Tom Weaver, *Poverty Row Horrors! Monogram, PRC, and Republic Horror Movies of the Forties* (Jefferson, North Carolina: McFarland, 1993), 136.

58 "Film Preview," *Daily Variety*, February 10, 1944, 3.

Bela Lugosi is about to introduce prehistoric Frank Moran to the wonders of fire in this publicity still for *Return of the Ape Man*. *(Photo courtesy of Bill Chase)*

Chapter 10

"I See You and I Do Not Think Alike":
Return of the Ape Man, Stanislav Szukalski, and the Imminent Yeti Takeover of the World

by Robert Guffey

"Until my discovery of their historic veritability no archeologist had ever suspected that the Pans which so commonly occur on the Greek vases, are factual truth, not poetic invention. The Pan was anciently called 'Ban' which means 'Feared', because this was actually the species of large apes that attacked human women and raped them."
—Stanislav Szukalski, *Behold!!! the Protong*, 1982[1]

In February of 2013, the Cal State Fullerton Begovich Gallery hosted an exhibit entitled "Szukalski: Drawings," which spotlighted the mind-bending artwork of an unjustly obscure genius named Stanislav Szukalski. According to Mike McGee, the curator of the show, this was the "first extensive survey of surviving Stanislav Szukalski drawings."[2]

Though he was born in Poland in December of 1893, Szukalski lived and worked in Burbank, California for many decades until his death in May of 1987. His eccentric artwork, which include drawings as well as masterful sculptures, were eventually embraced by an eclectic mixture of notable Southern Californians such as Glenn Bray, Leonardo DiCaprio, Robert Williams and Jim Woodring (among many others). If you haven't seen a copy of Szukalski's book *Behold!!! the Protong*, available from Last

Bela Lugosi and John Carradine discuss the exciting virtues of cryogenic freezing. Appropriately, Lugosi's shadow (his overly ambitious, evil side) falls between the two scientists. *(Photo courtesy of Bill Chase)*

Gasp Publishing, you *truly* don't know what you're missing.

Szukalski's theory is a rather complicated and peculiar one, but Richard Chang of the *Orange County Register* offers a fairly accurate condensed version of it below:

> Szukalski developed the pseudoscientific-historic theory of Zermatism—the belief that after the biblical flood of Noah's time, as described in the Book of Genesis, mankind fled to two main high-ground locations—Easter Island and Zermatt, Switzerland (hence, "Zermatism").
>
> He used pictographs to illustrate how these locations provided the origins of a single, ancient language—*Protong* (his own term). He also believed that the human race had bred with a competitive race of Yeti (Abominable Snowmen or Bigfoot, for the uninitiated), and the result was a hybrid that polluted the purity of Homo sapiens. Szukalski argued further that the hybrids were responsible for many of people's problems throughout history.
>
> While his evolutionary theories are fascinating, they're bizarre

Bela Lugosi has his mind set on performing an experiment that is far more nefarious than scientific while John Carradine fruitlessly attempts to thwart the older man's perverted ambitions. *(Photo courtesy of Bill Chase)*

and highly unscientific, and through the decades, no other legitimate source has backed them up. Szukalski's drawings in the Fullerton exhibit do encompass some of his ideas, but they merely scratch the surface of what appears to be a labyrinthine Pandora's box of contorted conceptions.

A significant amount of Szukalski's work is believed to have been destroyed in Poland, particularly during World War II [in fact, an entire museum devoted to Szukalski's works was burned by the Nazis]. But some of it survived in a trunk left in California. A 1920s sketchbook in a glass case, with the title "Lest We Forget" stenciled on the cover, contains intricate and amazing sketches. A video nearby helps disclose some of these works, which were created on plebian, daily journal paper.

In Poland, Szukalski wrote and illustrated a mythological tale entitled "Rege Rege." Several illustrations from a later, longer version are in the Begovich exhibit, and they demonstrate how detailed, wild and cinematic his vision was.[3]

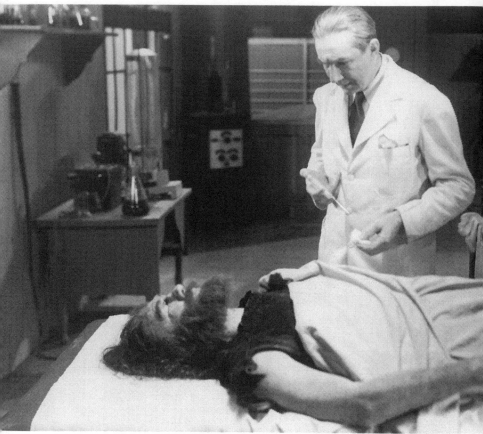

Bela Lugosi prepares to perform dangerous brain surgery on the unwitting Frank Moran. *(Photo courtesy of Bill Chase)*

A few years before the Fullerton show, on October 16th of 2009, I attended an exhibit that featured the work of Szukalski and—as an added bonus—the infamous Richard Shaver, an American painter and Hollow Earth theorist whose ideas about Earth's secret history weirdly parallel Szukalski's. I was so impressed by this show that I wrote a review of it the second I returned home. The curator later told me I was the only writer who'd actually bothered to cover the exhibit, which stunned me.

The show was entitled "Mantong and Protong: Richard Sharpe Shaver and Stanislav Szukalski." This exhibit was the brain child of curator Brian Tucker, director of the Pasadena City College Art Gallery. Despite being modest in size, limited to two rooms the length and width of an average studio apartment, the exhibit itself possessed a scope that was almost cosmic in nature.

Surrounded by Szukalski's strange works, I unexpectedly found my thoughts drifting to *Return of the Ape Man*, the last of Bela Lugosi's Monogram films of the 1940s.

"I have made the greatest discoveries that a human was ever capable of. Why was I able to discover Protong? Why did I discover the meaning of EVERY pictograph, no matter where or when it was created? Why did other, professional scientist[s] not discover these things before me? Because they were educated by those who were educated in those incubators of nonentities who can only think in formulas, repeated from one generation to the other by learned automatons. I intentionally avoided that education, so that I would save the Wisdom all humans are born with, my innate capacity to solve the dilemmas that previous scientists failed to budge. Educated men are basically cowards in their thinking. They must have authorities behind them. I dismiss all authorities. I deal with Culture, not with Civilization. I am a kite whose only connection with this prosaic earth is the frail string on which I soar way, way above the rubberstamp thinking of the well-educated bi-peds."
—Stanislav Szukalski, *Behold!!! the Protong*, 1982[4]

I often wondered if Szukalski was aware of *Return of the Ape Man* when it was released on June 24, 1944. Szukalski was already living in California in those days, and was reportedly working in Hollywood from time to time doing set designs. According to Glenn Bray, Szukalski's official archivist, Szukalski told him that during this period he had worked on *Portrait of Jennie* (1948), the classic William Dieterle fantasy film released only a few years after *Return of the Ape Man*. In an August 2016 email, Bray elaborated on this: "...towards the end [of *Portrait of Jennie*, there's a scene] with a miniature lighthouse. [Szukalski] worked on that (with no credit). Many have speculated that he also worked for countless other movies, but he never mentioned them over the course of my 13 years with him."[5]

Given Szukalski's obsessions, particularly with regard to the notion of half-man/half-apes slowly dominating the human race, it's difficult to imagine that the title *Return of the Ape Man* wouldn't catch his eye. In 1944, Szukalski was apparently living in Reseda, California. *Return of the Ape Man* played in movie theatres and drive-ins all throughout the Southland at that time. How could Szukalski resist the temptation? If he didn't resist, and actually caught the film during its first release, what was his reaction to it? Perhaps he would have concluded that Hollywood filmmakers had made discoveries that paralleled his own scientific research and were distributing these findings in the form of popular entertainment. Or perhaps he concluded that the screenwriter (Robert Charles) had unconsciously tapped into Szukalski's unparalleled brain.

I suspect Szukalski would have found much to sympathize with in not just *Return of the Ape Man*, but in many Bela Lugosi films. Szukalski, despite the fact that he began his career as a highly lauded professional artist, eventually devolved (or evolved?) into the ultimate Outsider Artist, one who creates art for no commercial gain whatsoever, and often for no audience except himself.

So many of the characters Lugosi portrayed in film had this "Outsider Artist" personality. Many of Szukalski's rants, like the one quoted above, easily could have been mouthed by one of Lugosi's numerous characters who seem to be obsessed by passions that lay far beyond the fringe. Though Lugosi's characters were often scientists, the way they behaved and spoke seemed to suggest that these driven men were closer to artists or poets than men of pure reason. All you have to do is listen to the various soliloquies delivered by Lugosi's characters to know that these are not, at their core, men driven by logic. These are men whose veins are filled with fire and concentrated strains of dark poetry. Often they are contemptuous of others and believe they themselves are the only humans on the planet who understand the Truth. They're often willing to go to great lengths to prove this insane Truth to others, whether it's Dr. Mirakle in *Murders in the Rue Morgue* (1932) mixing the blood of human females with that of apes, Dr. Richard Vollin in *The Raven* (1935) who's obsessed with recreating the works of Edgar Allan Poe in the real world to a degree that could only be described as deeply fetishistic, Dr. Paul Carruthers in *The Devil Bat* (1941) who demonstrates the efficacy of his genetically engineered giant bats in the most dramatic—and fatal— way possible, Dr. Lorenz in *The Corpse Vanishes* (1942) who's hell-bent on using his eccentric breakthroughs in botany to keep his beloved wife youthful, Professor Brenner in *Bowery at Midnight* (1942) who tests his theories regarding criminal psychology like a psychotic method actor, Dr. Zabor in *Bela Lugosi Meets a Brooklyn Gorilla* (1952) who takes Dr. Mirakle's act from twenty years earlier several steps further by transforming humans into gorillas with the injection of an experimental formula, and Dr. Eric Vornoff in *Bride of the Monster* (1955) whose mastery over atomic energy will (theoretically) result in an army of supermen who will "conquer the world." Obsessed outsiders all.

Prof. Dexter in *Return of the Ape Man* is a perfect example of this archetype that Lugosi made his own in role after role. Though Dexter's

Bela Lugosi attempts to control the primal urges of his experimental subject, with little success.... *(Photo courtesy of Bill Chase)*

colleague, Prof. John Gilmore (John Carradine), is clearly a brilliant man himself and is devoted to helping Dexter achieve his scientific goals, Gilmore's faith is not enough. Dexter holds his junior partner in contempt. In fact, he holds everybody in contempt. In one of the most memorable scenes of the film, Dexter is attending a social gathering at Gilmore's home where Dexter is the guest of honor. While broodily observing the partygoers from a corner of the room, Dexter comments to a fellow guest, "I enjoy studying people. You know, some people's brains would not be missed." Dexter, like all true Outsider Artists, exiles himself from humanity and is willing to sacrifice almost anything to see his eccentric vision through all the way to fruition.

"I see you and I do not think alike," Dexter says to Gilmore at one point. He thinks Gilmore is not as dedicated to his work as he should be. When Gilmore wants to abruptly back out of a months-long research expedition in the Arctic, citing his responsibilities back home as the main reason for his desire to leave, Dexter comments without emo-

Potential murderer Bela Lugosi (left), potential victim Tod Andrews (center), and potential savior John Carradine (right). *(Photo courtesy of Bill Chase)*

tion that a true scientist should be married to his work. Dexter claims that scientific work is all that matters to him. And yet, if one observes his actions, one must come to a somewhat different conclusion. Pure science, it seems, is a secondary goal.

Early in the film Dexter succeeds in demonstrating that his experimental technique for cryogenic suspension is a success. He does this by kidnapping a random homeless man from a park bench (oddly enough, the local newspapers actually take note of the transient's disappearance and even refer to him as a "notorious tramp") and freezing him for four months. After the man has come out of the process, with no apparent damage, Dexter rewards him with a five dollar bill and tells him to be on his way, not even letting the man know how much time has passed since his abduction. Gilmore goes along with these questionable techniques in an obvious show of loyalty to Dexter. Gilmore is impressed by what Dexter has achieved, as well he should. After all, creating a fully functioning cryogenic suspension machine in 1944 is no minor feat. One would think that Dexter would be happy with these tremendous results. But he doesn't seem happy, not at all. Instantly, like a mad artist, his mind shoots off into left field. He tells Gilmore that what he would like to do now is find a creature that has been frozen for centuries and revive it with his new process. Why? The explanation is never clear. One would think that the main benefit of Dexter's device would to help people who are living today, not beings who were once alive in the distant past. Besides, as Gilmore rightly points out to Dexter, where would one find such a frozen being? It's at this point in the narrative that Dexter drags Gilmore to the vast Arctic wasteland and within ten months succeeds in finding exactly what he's looking for: a perfectly preserved frozen creature, a missing link between human and ape, what Szukalski refers to in his book *Behold!!! the Protong* as a "Manape."

> "The history of mankind up to this moment is the enumeration of STRUG-GLES caused by the elemental foes of mankind, the results of the rapes of human women by Manapes who, having been born among us and speaking our languages, are mistakenly taken for our own countrymen. But it is these hateful, deadly and fiendishly exterminatory descendants of the Yeti that, on having been thoroughly admixed with the Humans, think up all the ideological Isms that create subversion, treason, revolutions, wars, and the eventual downfall of all Civilization and Culture."
>
> —Stanislav Szukalski, *Behold!!! the Protong*, 1982[6]

When the creature is first revived in Dexter's laboratory, at first one might assume that the beast is a Neanderthal Man, not a missing link. The Manape (played by Frank Moran) seems to be nothing more than a hairy adult male clothed in prehistoric animal skins. And yet there are several indications that this is not the case. At one point in the film, not long after Dexter has discovered the Manape, Gilmore says, "It's the greatest discovery since the Neanderthal Man." Obviously, this means that the beast Dexter and Gilmore have revived is *not* a Neanderthal Man, but instead something utterly unique. Later, as the local police are tracking the Manape through a park, two cops come across the beast's footprints. One of the cops doesn't believe that the footprints could even be real because they're too large. This seems to suggest that Robert Charles' script called for a creature quite different from what is seen on screen. When the film begins, the titles run over an illustration of a fierce looking Manape trapped behind bars. This, I suspect, is another

Bela Lugosi's illicit basement experiments once again attract the unwanted attention of the Boys in Blue.... *(Photo courtesy of Bill Chase)*

indication of what the beast was actually supposed to look like. I think it's fair to deduce that Monogram's shoestring makeup department was not able to pull off the look suggested by the screenwriter's original idea, and provided the next best thing: a hairy man in animal skins. Though Frank Moran's Ape Man does not physically resemble Szukalski's "Man-ape," there are many clues in the script that suggest that Charles, the screenwriter, may have been plugged into Szukalski's brain on some unexplainable, extrasensory level.

"This is the epoch of the total eclipse of Art. Our nations are suffering from physical and moral Decadence, from Karl Marx and Picasso to Roosevelt's Yalta Conventicle and Henry Moore's Sabretooth-Tiger-left-behind-dumplings with warm perforations. If these are acclaimed as our Art, the materialization of our innermost Aspirations, then which of the snob-specialists on Culture Is wiser than the next psychotic fool, posturing heroically and no better than the other 1200 Napoleons in the insane asylum? The more books, treatises and doctorates they write, the more ridiculous and pompous their pseudo-learned discourses sound. No writer on Art deserves to be listened to, since all their theorizing comes out of the drags of an empty bottom. There was no epoch in the history of the world as impoverished, as totally sterile, as suicidally thrashing as a fish out of water, as ours. We are the victims of 'Modernism' that was encrusted on this pooped-out, ancient volcano by total absence of Talents, the chief carriers of this plague being the 'critics of Art'. They destroy our Culture, what remains of it."

—Stanislav Szukalski, *Behold!!! the Protong*, 1982[7]

The entire theme of the film supports Szukalski's peculiar views regarding the Manapes' relationship to mankind. For example, Szukalski believed that higher culture was the direct result of the efforts of pure humans, while mere pop culture could never be anything more than the sad byproduct of ape-human hybrids. This is why, when Dexter fiendishly transplants a portion of Gilmore's brain into the skull of the Manape, we see the Manape return—as if by some subconscious pull—to Gilmore's house where he proceeds to sit down at a piano to perform Beethoven's 1801 composition, "Moonlight Sonata" (a piece we saw Gilmore playing earlier in the film during the aforementioned party thrown in honor of Dexter's scientific accomplishments). However, from Szukalski's (and/or Robert Charles' perspective), the Yeti part of the Manape's consciousness will always hold greater sway. When Gilmore's consciousness fades into the background, what Szukalski believes is the natural, primitive instinct of the Yeti comes to the fore.

"The Pans, according to legends, liked to hover near herds of grazing cattle. In a certain state of venereal infection these creatures had persistent erections, due to inflammation, so that they were seeking any kind of sexual satisfaction. Most commonly they contented themselves with sheep or goats, hence the goat-legged mutant Pans. I insist that syphilis is a purely animal disease and therefore so destructive to humans. The fact that humans have syphilis is due to rapes by these Pans, and all the wart-nosed Greek philosophers, the pot-bellied, waddling pygmoids, were actually descendants of such inter-species bastardy. On this matter I assembled a volume of 344 drawings like these, to be eventually published, because it is of the utmost importance to know that our Human Destiny is afflicted with the greatest calamities (like the two World Wars) because our HUMAN female ancestors were raped by the Apes, the Yetis, the Sasquatches, and our male forefathers copulated with female anthropoids. Please follow my line of reasoning briefed in this chapter."

—Stanislav Szukalski, *Behold!!! the Protong*, 1982[8]

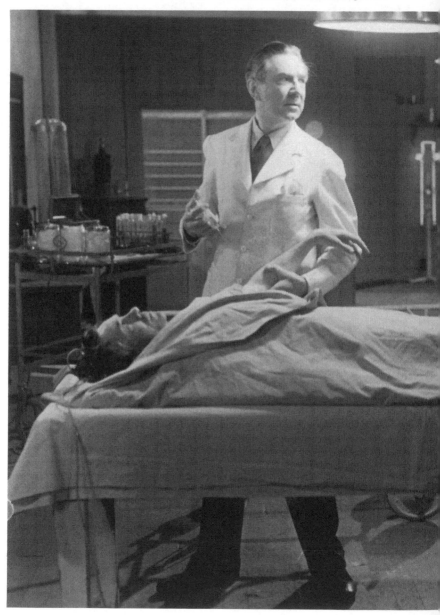

According to Szukalski, the Yeti's natural instinct is to abduct human women and rape them, thus creating further hybrids to eventually take over the human race. When Gilmore ceases playing the aforementioned classical composition, he immediately does what Gilmore may have wanted to do all along. The Manape strangles his domineering

wife, Mary (Mary Currier), then abducts his beautiful niece, Anne (Judith Gibson), with intentions that are clearly carnal in nature. As film historian Tom Weaver writes in his 1993 book *Poverty Row Horrors!*, "One interesting explanation is that the ape-half of the brain allows Carradine to do all the things he's always wanted to do, like murder his snotty wife and carry off his luscious young niece!"[9] There are suggestive indications that Weaver's speculation is accurate. During the previously mentioned party scene, for example, one of Gilmore's colleagues says to him, "It must have been terribly lonesome up there (i.e., in the Arctic) without your wife." Tellingly, Gilmore does not respond. Szukalski would no doubt agree with Weaver's suggestion. Though the purity of Carradine's humanity previously prevented this

Bela Lugosi and John Carradine debate the ethical quandaries of experimental research as a life hangs in the balance....
(Photo courtesy of Bill Chase)

Towarzysze i towarzyszki !!

One of Stanislav Szukalski's most iconic images, *Screaming Gorilla,* **in which the modern politician's civilized veneer is torn aside and the manape within is revealed for all to see....**

base behavior, it's the introduction of the Manape consciousness that leads to the attempted rape, murders, destruction of private property, and general mayhem that follow.

At one point Dexter says to Gilmore, "The Ape Man, after I'm through with him, will no longer have the instinct to kill." Based on this comment, we can conclude that one of Dexter's main purposes is to figure out how to eliminate Manape consciousness from the human race. In this way, Dexter's purpose aligns with that of Szukalski. Alas, neither men succeeded at their goals in their lifetimes. Indeed, in Dexter's case at least, such efforts completely backfire. As a direct result of Dexter's experiments, the Manape ends up killing a policeman and Gilmore's wife, nearly rapes Gilmore's niece, and destroys an entire theatre.

The latter scene, in which the Manape brings Gilmore's niece, Anne, to a theatre in order to assault her sexually, links *Return of the Ape Man* with William Beaudine's *The Ape Man* (1943), at least in terms of the latter film's Brechtian undertones (as delineated in my chapter on *The Ape*

Man). In prime Brechtian, self-referential fashion, the use of a theatre as a setting serves to highlight and expose the artificiality of popular entertainment as traditionally played out on either the stage or the screen. The fact that the filmmakers chose to have the Manape destroy the theatre is, from a Brechtian perspective, highly symbolic. Not only is this film intent on deconstructing traditional views of human evolution, but it also appears hell-bent on bringing down the very genre conventions the film was meant to satiate, symbolized (though perhaps unintentionally) by the rampant destruction of the theatre.

On one level, the message to the moviegoing audience couldn't be clearer. "Why are you putting up with this trash?" the film seems to be asking the audience in its own subtle way. I suspect the filmmak-

Another iconic Szukalski image, *Portrait of a Yeti*, based no doubt on alleged eyewitness descriptions of the cryptozoological beasts detailed in Ivan T. Sanderson's book *Abominable Snowmen: Legend Come to Life* (a volume Szukalski references in his own book, *Behold!!! the Protong*).

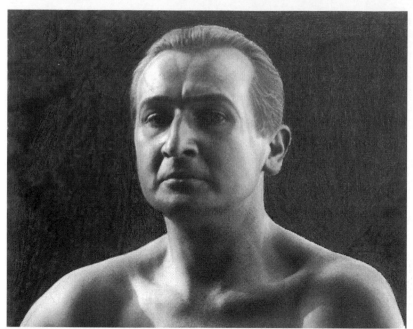

A photo portrait of Szukalski taken around 1940, only a few years before the release of *Return of the Ape Man*.

ers would not have been disappointed had the audience emulated the Manape, risen to their feet, and (symbolically, if nothing else) burned down the theatre that had decided to book *Return of the Ape Man*. But that's just wishful thinking on the part of any artist with a revolutionary spirit, whether they're Bertolt Brecht or the lowly screenwriter of *Return of the Ape Man*. Such secret messages are far too nuanced to have any immediate effect on a mass audience.

Perhaps that's why Szukalski never altered his techniques or attitudes in order to connect to such a popular audience. Szukalski was not the type of man to ever overestimate the intelligence of the average person. After all, as Szukalski himself might have said, some people's brains would not be missed.

"The above traits I pointed out, occur in every nation on earth. But it is the great prevalence of the Manape type in a nation that instigates its *predatory existence*, hence foments wars of conquests and the victimization of other nations. Look about you and observe which nations, up to recent years, were the greatest empire amassers, and you will understand why the prevalent type among their members of government was the type with the undercut nose.

"Each of [us] can feel his own Manape tail between his buttocks [...,] too delicately fragile to be exposed. One can bend it to a small extent by

A self-portrait photo of Szukalski taken circa 1920, when Szukalski was about twenty-seven years old.

pressing it farther in. Some years ago a nine-year-old German girl came to the John Hopkins Hospital in New York with her father, to have her tail amputated. It was a mobile appendage, for she could wiggle it at will. I drew this from a medical book."

—Stanislav Szukalski, *Behold!!! the Protong*, 1982[10]

From the theatre, the Manape flees back to Dexter's laboratory and inevitably ends up engulfed in flame. Meditate on the symmetry of the story arc here: the Manape emerges from ice and dies in flame—appropriate symbolism from the perspective of Szukalski, as the artist often argued that the survivors of a catastrophic worldwide Flood/Ice Age ended up emerging from the detritus of the Earth as humans and Yetis, kicking off a centuries-long battle for dominance of the Earth that will one day end in fire, i.e., Global Warming (though that term had not yet been invented when Szukalski first wrote about it), an epic battle that was somehow recapitulated in the form of a sixty-minute horror/science fiction flick in 1944 when the Nazis (the Sons of the Yeti, according to Szukalski) were busy burning all of Szukalski's artwork in his native Poland.

"Here I show you what happened in recent years in Anchorage, Alaska. Contrary to scientific claims that we are nearing another Ice Age, I insist that we are nearing the opposite to it, the Dehydration of the Globe in the oncoming Nearsolar Epoch. The ocean bottoms begin to bloat due to our nearing the Sun. The gaseous combustions intensify and the lavaic 'roof'covering the gasses, the present ocean bottoms, is being heaved upwards, incidentally tearing their rims away from the Alaskan moorings. Thus, many chunks of land suddenly lost their foundation and fell into the newly created vacuum [...] and whole city blocks dropped in the town of Turnagin. The seas will progressively rise and the Primary (Geologic) Globe will begin to submerge under the waters forced to migrate off the bloating ocean bottoms."

—Stanislav Szukalski, *Behold!!! the Protong*, 1982[11]

Szukalski always saw the fire-spewing Nazis as both the physical and spiritual (non-spiritual?) descendants of these Yeti, and no doubt often wished he could turn the Nazi's flames back on the perpetrators of so many destructive crimes against humanity. If Szukalski managed to see *Return of the Ape Man* in June of 1944, perhaps he would have projected onto the flickering silver screen his own intense yearning to get back at those who had wronged him, a wish fulfillment in which the vile Sons of the Yeti were consumed in tongues of flame rather than his own collection of precious artwork. By cremating the Ape Man, Monogram was symbolically burning down the very same creatures that were attempting to destroy all remnants of human culture on the other side of the world, a world from which Szukalski and many other visionary artists had been permanently exiled, just like the survivors of the original Deluge with which Szukalski was so fascinated.

In June of 1944 neither Szukalski nor the filmmakers had any way of knowing how the war would ultimately end. This was something they shared in common, though such commonalities no doubt terminated there. The chances are, of course, that Szukalski and the filmmakers never even met each other, had no knowledge of one another whatsoever, and did not think alike. Furthermore, the American moviegoing public were no doubt unaware of any of this strange symbolism on a conscious level.

Nonetheless, perhaps a parable as stark and absurd and out-of-left-field as *Return of the Ape Man* succeeded on multiple levels at once, beyond the mere bottom line goals of traditional Hollywood filmmaking; perhaps this weird little film helped inject a kind of psychic spell into the global unconsciousness, boosted the morale of war-fatigued moviegoers during the final months of WWII by presenting the character of the Ape

Man as a kind of voodoo stand-in for the out-of-control, primitive actions of the *real* Manapes torching Europe and all human culture at the very same moment that the film was being projected in movie houses all across America, and (perhaps most importantly) subtly helped convince Szukalski that his unique investigations into the origins of the human race, despite all evidence to the contrary, were somehow pointed in the right direction—a direction either ignored or held in contempt by all of Szukalski's contemporaries, not unlike the attitudes of so many fictional mainstream scientists who often looked down on the visionary works of mad scientists/poets/artists like Lugosi's Prof. Dexter and all his interminable, tenacious kith and kin.

"I was sent to this world to Give, to Create in many fields, but [...] everything will be destroyed. No creature on earth is free from the Curse, the Plague, the corruption by the Abominable 'Man', the species of Yetinsyn Predator that, as Kipling so observantly pointed out, 'walks like man'....

—Stanislav Szukalski, *Behold!!! the Protong*, 1982[12]

(Endnotes)

1   Stanislav Szukalski, *Behold!!! the Protong* (San Francisco: Last Gasp, 1982), 56.

2   Richard Chang, "Fullerton Exhibit Reveals Crazy World of Artist Szukalski," *The Orange County Register*, February 9, 2013 (website accessed May 31, 2013).

3   Ibid.

4   Szukalski, *Behold!!! the Protong*, 18.

5   Glenn Bray, Interview Conducted Via Email, August 11, 2016 and July 28, 2017. Bray also has this to say about Szukalski's brief run-ins with Hollywood: "Because of working on *Struggle: The Life and Lost Art of Szukalski* [Irek Dobrowolski and Stephen Cooper's Netflix documentary about Szukalski], the director and some assistants did some digging around to see about any other possible film tie-ins: They discovered that Szukalski did a portrait of the leading lady – shown in the film *The Paradine Case* and has a credit at the end [...]. But at any rate, Szukalski never 'put on his resume' any movie work. I think he got paid a few bucks and moved on. He certainly could have had more work, as [his friend, the screenwriter] Ben Hecht was ingrained in Hollywood circles and could have gotten him grunt-work. I don't believe Szukalski ever thought it was serious or needed to be talked about."

6   Szukalski, *Behold!!! the Protong*, 59.

7   Ibid. 4-5.

8   Ibid. 56.

9   Tom Weaver, *Poverty Row Horrors!: Monogram, PRC and Republic Horror Films of the Forties* (Jefferson: McFarland, 1993), 173.

10   Szukalski, *Behold!!! the Protong*, 62.

11   Ibid. 11.

12   Ibid. 6.

MONOGRAM PICTURES presents

BELA LUGOSI IN

"VOODOO MAN"

featuring

JOHN CARRADINE
GEORGE ZUCCO

Produced by SAM KATZMAN and JACK DIETZ
Associate Producer, BARNEY A. SARECKY
Directed by WILLIAM BEAUDINE
Original Story and Screenplay by ROBERT CHARLES

Acknowledgements

The authors would like to express gratitude to the following institutions that assisted in the research for this book: the Billy Rose Theatre Division of the New York Public Library, the Harry Ransom Center at the University of Texas at Austin, the Margaret Herrick Library of the Academy of Motion Picture Arts and Sciences in Beverly Hills, and the Cinematic Arts Library of the University of Southern California in Los Angeles.

The authors would also like to extend sincere thanks to the following individuals who assisted on the research and images for this book: Matthew E. Banks, Marty Baumann, Buddy Barnett, Eric Blair, the late Richard Bojarski, Catherine Bottolfson McCallum, Glenn Bray, Bob Burns, Roland Bush, Mario Chacon, Ned Comstock, Steve Cooper, Michael Copner, Bob Cremer, Richard Daub, Irek Dobrowolski, Jack Dowler, Chris Doyle, Rainer Engel, Theodore Estes, Beau Foutz, Fritz Frising, Christopher R. Gauthier, Donald F. Glut, Melissa Guffey, Olivia Guffey, Bob Gutowski, Lee Harris, Eric L. Hoffman, Roger Hurlburt, Bill Kaffenberger, the late John A. Keel, Dwight Kemper, Nancy Kersey, Dr. Robert J. Kiss, Randy Koppang, Michael Kronenberg, Bela G. Lugosi, Lugosi Enterprises, Mark Martucci, Lisa Mitchell, D'Arcy More, Constantine Nasr, Henry Nicolella, Dennis Phelps, Robert Rees, Donald Rhodes, Phyllis Rhodes, the late Gerald J. Schnitzer, Ellen Schnitzer, the late Richard Sheffield, Robert Singer, John Soister, Lynne Lugosi Sparks, Brian Taves, Brian Tucker, Mario Toland, Dale Townshend, Maria Viera, David Wentink, Leo Wiltshire, Jack Womack, Kristopher Woofter, and Ray Zepeda.

Much appreciation must also go to John Antosiewicz, Bill Chase, and Kristin Dewey for graciously providing so many illustrations, to Tom Weaver, who provided important suggestions, to John Soister, who kindly proofread the entire manuscript, and to Larry Blamire, for writing the foreword.

Author Biographies

Robert Guffey is a lecturer in the Department of English at California State University – Long Beach. His most recent book is *Until the Last Dog Dies* (Night Shade/Skyhorse, 2017), a darkly satirical novel about a young stand-up comedian who must adapt as best he can to an apocalyptic virus that destroys only the humor centers of the brain. Guffey's previous books include the journalistic memoir *Chameleo: A Strange but True Story of Invisible Spies, Heroin Addiction, and Homeland Security* (OR Books, 2015), which *Flavorwire* has called, "By many miles, the weirdest and funniest book of 2015." A graduate of the famed Clarion Writers Workshop in Seattle, he has also written a collection of novellas entitled *Spies & Saucers* (PS Publishing, 2014). His first book of nonfiction, *Cryptoscatology: Conspiracy Theory as Art Form*, was published in 2012. He's written stories and articles for numerous magazines and anthologies, among them *After Shocks, The Believer, Black Dandy, Catastrophia, The Chiron Review, The Los Angeles Review of Books, The Mailer Review, Pearl, The Pedestal, Phantom Drift, Postscripts, The Third Alternative*, and *Video Watchdog Magazine*. His next book, *Widow of the Amputation and Other Weird Crimes*, is due to be published by Eraserhead Press in 2019.

Gary D. Rhodes, Ph.D. is Postgraduate Director for Film Studies at The Queen's University of Belfast, Northern Ireland, as well as a published poet and novelist. His most recent book is *The Birth of the American Horror Film* (Edinburgh University Press, 2018). He has authored eight previous books on Bela Lugosi and his films. *Fangoria* magazine observed that Rhodes' work was largely responsible for the cult interest that surrounds Lugosi. A film historian, Rhodes has also authored such books as *Emerald Illusions: The Irish in Early American Cinema* (IAP, 2012) and *The Perils of Moviegoing in America* (Bloomsbury, 2012). He is also the writer-director of such documentary films as *Lugosi: Hollywood's Dracula* (1997) and *Banned in Oklahoma* (2004). At present, he co-edits ReFocus, a series of books from Edinburgh University Press that concentrates on neglected film directors. Rhodes is currently coauthoring a book entitled *Film Art and the American Television Commercial*, as well as writing *The Birth of the American Horror Film: Volume Two, 1916-1931*.

Made in the USA
Middletown, DE
28 December 2022

20595192R00144